THEORY IN THE PRACTICE OF
THE NICARAGUAN REVOLUTION

Statue in central Managua. *Photograph by author*

THEORY IN THE PRACTICE OF THE NICARAGUAN REVOLUTION

Bruce E. Wright

Ohio University Center for International Studies
Monographs in International Studies

Latin American Studies Number 24
Athens

The books in the Center for International Studies Monograph
Series are printed on acid-free paper ∞

This book is printed on recycled paper

Library of Congress Cataloging-in-Publication Data

Wright, Bruce E. (Bruce Ethan), 1940–
    Theory in the practice of the Nicaraguan revolution / by
Bruce E. Wright
    p. cm. – (Monographs in international studies. Latin
American series ; no. 24)
    Includes bibliographical references and index.
    ISBN : 0-89680-185-3 (alk. paper)
    1. Revolutions—Nicaragua. 2. Revolutions and
socialism—Nicaragua. 3. Nicaragua—Politics and
government—1979–1990. 4. Nicaragua—Politics and
government—1990–
I. Title II. Series.
JL1602.W75 1995
972.5505'3—dc20   95-12297
                                        CIP

02 01 00 99 98 97 96 95   5 4 3 2 1

CONTENTS

PREFACE ix

INTRODUCTION 1

PART I
Theory in the Sandinista Revolution 10

1 THE NICARAGUAN REVOLUTION
IN PERSPECTIVE 13
The Last in a Series of Socialist Revolutions 13
The First in a New Series? 15
The Internal Basis of the Nicaraguan Revolution 19
No Counterrevolution by Election 21
The FSLN in Opposition 23
The Continued Legitimacy of the FSLN 27
The Election as a Sandinista Victory 27
Foundations of the Continuing Revolution
in Sandinismo 30
Making Sense of the Election Defeat 32
FSLN Self-Criticism and Internal Reform 33
New Revolutionary Actors: The *Revueltos* Emerge .. 38
Labor as an Independent Revolutionary Actor 44
Sandinistas in the Streets 47

2 DEVELOPMENT OF THE POLITICAL
IDEAS OF THE NICARAGUAN REVOLUTION:
FROM SANDINO AND FONSECA
TO THE TRIUMPH 49
Fonseca and Sandino 49
Lessons from Cuba 53
Politics, the Armed Struggle, and the PSN 55
Fonseca's View of Nicaraguan History 57

v

Contemporary Consequences of Fonseca's Theory   73
The Three Tendencies and Theory   74
FSLN Principles of Government   78

3 FROM CORPORATIVIST PLURALISM
  TO ELECTORAL DEMOCRACY   81
  The Vanguard and Pluralism in Marxism-Leninism   81
    The Development of the Concept of Pluralism
    in Western Liberal Thought   83
    The FSLN, Pluralism, and Hegemony   85
  Plural Actors in the Anti-Somoza Struggle   88
  Pluralism, Hegemony, and the Revolutionary State   91
    The Governing Junta of National Reconstruction . . .   93
    The Council of State: Functional Representation . . .   95
    The Mass Organizations and Pluralism   96
    The CDS   97
    The Military and Hegemony 100

PART II
  Theory and Practice in the
  Consolidation of the Revolution:
  A Critical Analysis 107

4 CONSTRUCTION OF NICARAGUAN PLURALISM
  BY THE VANGUARD: PROBLEMS OF A
  CONSCIOUS HEGEMONIC AGENT
  The Theory of Advance to Socialism:
  Pluralism and a Mixed Economy 113
  Fashioning New Rules for the New Economic Elite:
  Separating Patriotic Producers
  from Counterrevolutionaries 121
  Participation of the Masses in Pluralism 126
    Sandinista Defense Committees:
    Towards Demobilization 127
    Setting the Limits on the Role of Unions:
  The Agricultural Workers Divide 131
  Urban Unions, Incomplete Consolidation;
  Controlling the "Left" 144

5 PLURALISM AND PARTICIPATORY
   DEMOCRACY THROUGH THE
   1984 ELECTIONS 150
   Some Guidelines for Assessment 150
   Some Dangers in Success 151
   Problems of Guided Pluralism 152
   The 1984 Election Strategy:
   Success through Explanation 153
   Popular Organizations and the Vanguard 157
   Demobilization, not Dictatorship 158
   Political Pluralism, Participatory Democracy
   and Class 159
   The FSLN on the Place of Mass Organizations 161
   Critique of the FSLN Position 163

6 THE REVOLUTION IN SURVIVAL MODE:
   REWARDING ENEMIES AND LOSING FRIENDS .. 169
   Priorities Shift: City-Country,
   Social-Private Producers 169
       Facing Down the Colossus of the North 170
       The U.S. Sets the Economic Part of the Trap:
       Nicaragua Refuses to Enter 171
   The Owl of Minerva 175
       Political Successes in the 1985–1990 Period 175
       Some Paths Not Followed 177
   Pluralism and Economic Analysis 179
   Losing the Election 180
       Priority to the Country 182
           Distinguishing the Countryside from the City ... 182
           Loss of Base in the Countryside 183
           How the City Had Been the Priority 183
           Campesino Unhappiness with Losing Old
           Intermediaries 185
           New Directions for Agrarian Reform 186
           The Move Toward Individual Production 187
           The Worker-Campesino Alliance before 1985 ... 188
           Rethinking the Worker-Campesino Alliance 189
           Giving Priority to the Individual
           Campesino Producer 191
       Economic Rationality Replaces Revolutionary Logic . 199

Reaching the Bottom of the Barrel and
Costs of War 199
Economic Adjustments 1985–87 200
With the Promise of Peace Comes Economic
Austerity 201
The 1990 Election: Everything Will Be Better 207

7 CLASS, STATE AND PARTY 211
Sandinista Theory and the
Rejection of "Orthodoxy" 211
The Third Force as Social Subject of the Revolution   212
The Vanguard and Social Forces 213
The Too Orthodox Nature of FSLN Class Theory   214
Class Complexity and the Vanguard 215
The Proletariat Must Suffer,
Other Classes Get Preference 218
The Third Force Must Suffer, Too 219
The "Forces" and the Working Class 220
The Party as Intermediary 221
Sandinista Theory as Developmentalist Marxism:
State, Class, and Party 222
Agriculture as Guided Development 223
Class Division, Not Class Consolidation
in Agriculture 224
The Economics of Large Scale Agriculture 226
The Urban Dynamic 227
Marx on Class 229
The Immense Majorities as the Working
Class in Nicaragua 229
Can Grassroots Movements Replace Class? 230
The Vast Majority as the Working Class in Nicaragua   231
Reducing Differences among Workers as a Class   232
New Opportunities since the Electoral Loss 236
Conclusion 238

REFERENCES 245

INDEX 268

PREFACE

This work is an attempt to contribute to the ongoing development of revolutionary theory by critically examining the experience of the Nicaraguan revolution. My interest in Nicaragua was sparked by a desire to examine issues of political theory in the context of an actual revolutionary experience. My first experience in Nicaragua was as a member of a group of teachers from Southern California who did construction work on schoolhouses. Meeting Nicaraguans who worked with us on that project, sawing boards, pounding nails, and constructing blackboards gave me an insight into the very practical aspects of the Nicaraguan revolution and the extent to which even the most humble Nicaraguans had a thirst for political understanding at an abstract level. I later worked with the Nicaraguan Institute for Economic and Social Research (INIES for its initials in Spanish), which I served as U.S. academic representative from 1986 until 1991. I met a number of researchers and scholars from both Nicaragua and the United States through this work.

I am indebted to Bismarck Jaime for introducing me to INIES and for much else. Francisco López and Maria Aminta Díaz who served as Director and Executive Director of INIES throughout most of my connection with that institution have continued to aid me in my work even after leaving that institution and continue to be valued associates and friends. I can never fully express my appreciation for their aid and for that of all of the other researchers and librarians with whom I came in contact at INIES, especially my friend Félix Delgado. I also travelled twice to Nicaragua with the Latin American Studies Association Summer Seminar. The Nicaraguans I met through this experience, from the most humble members of cooperatives to President Ortega, contributed invaluably to my understanding of Nicaragua. I remain indebted to Thomas Walker and Harvey Williams whom I came to know well through their leadership of this group. My thanks, as well, to the members of both seminars, especially Fred Weaver, who put up with my snoring so amicably.

My most fundamental understanding of the reality of Nicaraguan life has been based on knowing several individual Nicaraguans and their families for nearly a decade. I owe a substantial debt to all of the residents of Ciudadela San Martín, two kilometers north of Tipitapa, whose hospitality made clear to me the dignity with which it is possible to face life in even the most adverse circumstances. I owe a special debt to the family of Ramona Bermudez, who put me up for several nights when I was first learning the rudiments of the Nicaraguan language. Elvira Torrez showed me how a truly strong woman can devote her life to a political cause as well as serving those in need of health care. Her compañero Enrique knows of the many travels and travails we shared. Lillian and Rosa Cabrera were helpful to me in many ways both in Managua and Los Angeles. In Estelí I am in special debt to Blanca Sevilla, to Licenicada Maria Eudocia Zeledón, Egdelina Lanuza Centeno, and Rosario Zeledón (the latter of whom so kindly introduced me to National Assembly member Orlando Piñeda). The Centro Nicaragüense de Aprendizaje Cultural and the Movimiento de Mujeres Desempleadas with which these women are connected were very helpful to my work.

I am indebted to many individual Nicaraguans who agreed to talk to me. These people range from the vice president, who talked with me at my home in Los Angeles, through members of the National Assembly, to Nicaraguans in all walks of life. Assembly members Orlando Piñeda and Carlos Zamora were both willing to meet and talk with me on extremely short notice. I am grateful for their willingess to speak frankly to me with so little knowledge of what my project entailed. I owe special gratitude to Norma Caudra, who not only took many hours of her time to explain her views and observations of events but contributed some of the fundamental theoretical insights upon which my final analysis rests. She is not, of course, responsible for any of my conclusions.

My brother Angus Wright knows in how many different ways he was helpful to me in this project as well as in many other things. His aid to me in all aspects of understanding Latin America can never be repaid. My wife, Marilee Marshall, has been, and remains, my constant political and intellectual mentor and guide, as well as my one true love. Her willingness to read sometimes uncompleted versions of the materials that make up this book was amazing. My daughters Samantha, Sara, and Athena have had to put up with a crazy father for so long that I am sure they have not noticed my failure to pay attention to them, as I preferred traveling to distant Nicaragua to visiting their homes.

An earlier version of part of what is now chapter 3 was published by *Latin American Perspectives,* Sage Publishers (Summer 1990) as "Vanguardism and Pluralism in the Nicaraguan Revolution." I am especially indebted to Professor Tim Harding of California State University, Los Angeles, for his careful and meticulous editorial work on the article as it appeared there. Some elements of the present analysis of class in relation to the Nicaraguan revolution are drawn from my article "Class and Revolutionary Actors in Latin America" (*Review of Latin American Studies* 1989), based on a paper presented to the Pacific Coast Conference on Latin American Studies. The discussion of the relationship between Fonseca and Sandino is largely drawn from my paper, "Political Theory and Political Practice in the Nicaraguan Revolution: The Relation between Sandino and Fonseca," presented to the Latin American Studies Association at Miami, Florida, December 7, 1989.

Roger N. Lancaster provided a fine and helpful review of the manuscript, which aided me immeasurably in creating the final version of the book. I am indebted to him and to Ohio University Press for aid in making the book a reality.

California State University at Fullerton provided me with a small grant and with the opportunity to work on this project during a one-semester sabbatical.

The book is dedicated to my parents, Thelma and Howard, and to my second "brother" in San Martín, Pablo Pérez who, with his family, has shown me the true commitment of those devoted to the revolutionary goals first set out by Sandino. Irayda Pérez should know that her "barbudo" will never forget her smiling face and that she and all her brothers and sisters, of the family of Pérez, of Nicaragua and of the world, are the inspiration for any bit of wisdom this work may contain.

All translations of Spanish materials are mine unless otherwise indicated. Interview material was largely drawn from two sources, informal discussions and those arranged with the Latin American Studies Association summer seminar. Citations to the latter are labelled as "LASA interview." Copies of relevant notes are available from the author.

INTRODUCTION

Marxism is in retreat. Nicaragua was caught at the end. It was the last country to complete a revolutionary triumph by a party based substantially on Marxian analysis; it was the first where the people, through a popular election, replaced that party with a government committed to neo-liberal principles. Poor Nicaragua, the victim of a failed theory and practice. Nothing is to be learned from its revolution except the futility of it all.

Or so it would seem. This work is an attempt to demonstrate the opposite. Nicaragua helps us to see, as Robert Meister put it in another context, that "the Marxian moment is now" (1990: 348). A clear understanding of the Nicaraguan revolution can show the fundamental soundness of much of Marxian theory as well as help make sense of much of what has happened to what its supporters often called "really existing socialisms" in the twentieth century; it can demonstrate that revolutionary socialism is compatible with, indeed requires, democracy; it can help us understand that a revolution is not merely the seizure and maintenance of state power by a single party. The present work is an attempt to use the Nicaraguan experience to make sense of a limited set of issues. It also considers the fundamental notion of class as it relates to this topic. A clear understanding of the nature of classes in this particular case can aid in developing better theory and more profound practice. Fundamentally, this work considers problems that arise in attempting to combine the non-Marxist concept of pluralism with the idea of participatory democracy. To consider these issues it is essential to put the Nicaraguan experience in a theoretical and practical context and to examine events in Nicaraguan history in substantial detail. All Nicaraguans, they say, are poets—few are systematic political theorists, though the poetry of their actions has much to contribute to serious political thought.

The research on which this work is based began with far different assumptions than those with which it concludes. Political

1

philosophy has as its most important function the comprehension and guidance of political practice. If Marxism is a sound theory, one should be able to examine how it works in contemporary practice. If Marxism is a revolutionary theory it would make sense to examine it as it is practiced in a contemporary revolution. Thus my research was begun with the assumption that familiarity with the theory and practice of the Sandinista National Liberation Front (FSLN) would show how Marxian political theory relates to political practice in the late twentieth century. In fact, when one looks to Marxism as the guide for the policies of the FSLN in government, it may appear that it simply was not consulted. Indeed, many liberal analysts in the U.S. have been at pains to argue that the Nicaraguan revolution is not and was not, as its detractors argued at the time, a Marxist-Leninist revolution.

Yet more substantial analysis indicates that the interrelation of Marxist theory and Nicaraguan practice is a great deal more complex than it might seem. In the first place, it may well be that Nicaragua has more to teach Marxian theory than many Nicaraguan revolutionaries learned from Marxism. Sandinista practice was not merely the application of a pre-existing theoretical framework; it is a sophisticated practice that includes creative new theoretical developments. In the second place, contemporary Nicaraguan experience may serve better as a model for attempts to salvage some elements of socialism in Eastern Europe and Asia than the systems of "really existing socialism" in those regions did for Nicaragua. The original Sandinista incorporation of pluralism into the development of socialism preceded similar attempts in long-established socialist systems. At this writing it remains to be seen whether this fact will aid Nicaragua in avoiding some of the worst consequences of the apparent turn away from socialism in the former Soviet Union and Eastern Europe.

Examination of the Nicaraguan case is illuminating in making sense of the role of class analysis in attempts to produce socialist transition in economies outside the most developed systems of capitalism. Marxist theory would seem to suggest that its function is the guidance of an international movement, based on the solidarity of the international proletariat. In fact, in the twentieth century it has had its largest role in national liberation movements, based on unifying apparently quite disparate class groups in the context of predominantly agricultural economies. Lenin's theory of

2

imperialism attempted to make sense of this fact in the context of revolutionary possibilities in the Russian empire at the time of the First World War. The Soviet Union was based on the fundamental premise that a socialist revolution was possible that could unite members of disparate national groups within a political system, the contours of which were set by a basically pre-bourgeois authoritarianism. The Chinese revolution was guided by Mao Zedong's explicit analysis of conjunctural relations among different classes. Each of these revolutions took place within the context of political and economic systems that were legally sovereign and politically independent of the more powerful states that exercised substantial economic influence on them.

Much of the remainder of the experience of revolutionary national liberation movements in the last half of the twentieth century has been in pursuit of freeing colonies from European control. In many cases, especially in Africa, the entities that freed themselves were not nations. They often contained groups from different linguistic, religious, and cultural backgrounds that were united merely because of the politics through which the colonial powers divided their possessions into administrative units. The well-known policy of British colonialism was to divide natural groups into different entities and to include groups in the same administrative units (later independent states) that were not only different from, but also hostile towards, one another.

Thus, the irony of twentieth-century Marxist political practice (outside of Western Europe, where social democracy has been the norm), is that a theory based on the notion of an international class has, in fact, served to make sense of nation-building and the attempt to hold together states as diverse as those of the Russian elites in their far-flung multinational empire and those of Western European nation-states in their colonial possessions. Some aspects of the present crisis of what was termed "really existing socialism" in Eastern Europe and Eurasia is at least partially a consequence of this fact. As the Soviet Union disintegrated, various nationalist movements asserted themselves. While the old system had depended to a substantial extent on the mobilization of Soviet citizens on a class basis, the new situation is marked by mobilizations against new hardships on the basis of other identifying elements, including nationalism (sometimes in terms of a sense of "nation" that does *not* predate the Soviet system), language, ethnicity, and religion as well

3

as region. The failure of socialism as an economic system cannot fully explain what has happened. As the Soviet Union began to relax repressive centralized political control it rapidly disintegrated into states driven by the old Wilsonian concept of national self-determination, even if some of these "nations" are really of very recent vintage.[1]

The theoretical significance of the facts addressed above is unclear. There are at least two fundamental ways to understand it: One is that Marxism as such is a fundamental theoretical and practical failure; it simply cannot account for the continued significance of nationalism because it insists on falsely emphasizing classes as the fundamental political actors. In this case there is little reason to even consider the further development of Marxian theory or practice. However, a more complex possibility is that the political failures of Marxism, especially in terms of the development of a repressive state apparatus and inflexible party structures, are a conjunctural problem which can be comprehended through a more complex understanding of the relations of classes and other social and political entities. Such an analysis might be of use in making sense of what has occurred in Europe and Asia in a manner that comprehends many of the failures of the Soviet system yet does not cast aside the possibility that Marxian analysis may remain a fruitful source of political theory and political practice. The present work is at best the beginning of such analysis. It is based on examination of a case that has many dissimilarities from developments in Europe, Asia, and Africa; the case of a single Latin American revolution in Nicaragua.

At first sight it may appear absurd to put such emphasis on a country as small and insignificant as Nicaragua. Being an extremely poor country with about three million inhabitants, it is of little economic importance. Further, its history as a country has been marked by extremely contentious and anachronistic political disputes and it has been dominated by the United States almost to the extent of being a U.S. colony. Indeed, as in the case of the Cuban revolution, the Nicaraguan revolution has been understood by many who have participated in it and by many outsiders who have

---

[1] I owe the present formulation of this, as well as many other points, to the comments of Roger Lancaster.

4

attempted to understand it as a case of a national liberation struggle. After all, the leading organization in the Nicaraguan revolution calls itself a "front" for "national liberation." In addition, the Nicaraguan revolution is widely viewed as having been defeated in an election and thus now stands as merely an historical curiosity. Even ignoring all of these factors, it may seem that Nicaragua is simply a specific case of Marxism-Leninism in practice, guided by the same basic theory as developments in the Soviet Union. Yet further analysis shows these views to be shortsighted and incomplete.

Plato suggested in *The Republic* that it might be easier to discover what justice consists of in the individual than by examining the larger case, that of the *polis* as a whole. Yet this move from the micro to the macro can be reversed. All political systems are extremely complex. To isolate any one factor or set of factors in an attempt to make sense of the world political system as a whole is more difficult than to do so in the case even of large and complex systems such as the United States or the former Soviet Union. The examination of a small and relatively simple case may allow us to understand some elements of the larger cases. Here, in relation to the experiences of a system as complex as that of the former Soviet Union, we may be able to observe dynamics that are closer to the surface in the smaller system. It sometimes makes sense to follow Aristotle's advice to break larger systems into their parts in order to understand how all of the parts go together. The very fact that what happens in Nicaragua makes little difference to the world while every event in the Soviet Union has been made to seem of some world historical significance makes the Nicaraguan case one where analysis of particular events and phenomena may provide sharper theoretical focus. Comparing Nicaragua to the Soviet Union may appear to be comparing apples to oranges. The point is to learn something about fruit. While knowing about one of these cases will not provide us with direct knowledge about the other, understanding of both is essential to making sense of Marxism in practice.

Prior to 1979 virtually every commentator on Nicaraguan affairs, even Nicaraguans, noticed the fundamentally anachronistic character of Nicaraguan politics. The Somoza dictatorship was understood as a rather simple case of despotism in an under-developed political system. Insofar as there was political activity apart from the Somozas themselves, it was characterized by the

5

continuation of nineteenth-century disputes between "Liberals" and "Conservatives," whose disagreements could be understood only as clashes of interests between the elites of one town, Granada, and another, Leon. There was hardly a better example of an "under-developed" political system than that of Nicaragua. Yet since the election of 1990, Nicaragua has a functioning democratic system, marked by multi-party elections in which a party that obtained power through armed revolutionary struggle peacefully passed the reins of governmental power over to an opposition front that received substantial aid from the United States. How did such a change take place? Viewed in this context Nicaraguan politics would seem of dramatic interest.

Although the Cuban and Nicaraguan revolutions are often seen as analogous to anti-colonial national liberation struggles, they took place in countries that were formally independent and sovereign. Yet it is odd—except in the very limited case of the Atlantic Coast of Nicaragua[2]—to think that in any sense these revolutions took place in multinational systems. Indeed, both countries had established their own sense of national identity prior to the revolutions of the mid-twentieth century. If they were national liberation movements, what were the nations being liberated from? The clear answer is that they were liberated from U.S. imperialism and from repressive dictatorships with a very narrow national base. Yet this is a far different thing from the liberation of colonial states from colonial domination. It is even further from the overthrow of the czar in a far-flung empire in

---

[2]Although developments on the Atlantic coast of Nicaragua have been quite significant, it is important to notice that the total population of this area is quite small. Although the population of the area is less than three hundred thousand (or less than 10 percent of the total population of Nicaragua), nearly two-thirds of these people are Spanish-speaking mestizos, that is, ethnically similar to other Nicaraguans. The various indigenous groups account for substantially less than 3 percent of the total population of Nicaragua (fewer than seventy-five thousand people). While this does not excuse problems that the Nicaraguan government has had with these people, it does show that it is a substantial exaggeration to think of Nicaragua as a "multinational state." To do so is to say that there are no nation-states as such. Population data for the Atlantic coast are drawn from Vilas (1989: 4).

which the Russian nation maintained an internal domination in the new state. If anything, it is more analogous to the liberation of Eastern Europe from Soviet domination—a phenomenon so new as to defy serious theoretical analysis as national liberation movements on the older models. It is also far different from the Chinese experience, in which first a nationalist revolution occurred, struggling against a system of spheres of influence dominated by multiple powers, and then a socialist revolution overthrew the nationalist state. Neither Batista nor Somoza resembled the Kuomintang or Chiang Kai-shek. Thus, if these are national liberation movements they are so distinct from other cases that they deserve separate analysis.

Further, besides Cuba and Nicaragua, there are no other cases of states that have presumably freed themselves from the complex and subtle domination of the United States through revolutionary action. Once more these two cases would seem better understood as distinct from, rather than analogous to, national liberation movements. Here we have independent sovereign states that presumably required national liberation. Yet Cuba and Nicaragua are also quite different from each other. In the first case, after over thirty years the same political organization holds exclusive power; in the second case, after little more than ten years, governmental power has changed hands through an electoral process. Why did the Nicaraguan revolution seemingly succeed for a short period in freeing itself and then hold an election in which the goal of national liberation took such a dramatic turn?

To answer that the revolution failed through election is simply to beg the question. This has happened nowhere else. What explains its appearance here? How did a revolutionary movement based on Marxism-Leninism find itself in the position of supporting an electoral option in which the opposition was allowed to take power? Surely if this is seen as the end of a failed Marxist-Leninist movement we must understand some of the problems of Marxist-Leninist theory in a fundamentally different manner than is usually proposed to explain the larger-scale events in Europe and Asia. The complex relationships between class analysis, political structures, and non-class divisions in political systems are some of the elements that must be carefully considered in all of these cases. The examination of these elements in the relatively limited Nicaraguan experience may help to make sense of the larger

7

theoretical conjuncture of such phenomena in a new and creative manner.

The final objection to taking the Nicaraguan case seriously as providing a further understanding of Marxian theory is to suggest that it is merely another case of what happens with revolutions based on the imperialist policies of the Soviet Union as manifested through the Communist International. The problem with this analysis is simply that it misunderstands the historical facts. Like the July 26 Movement in Cuba, the FSLN in Nicaragua proceeded from a rejection of the policies of the pro-Soviet party. From the rejection of Sandino by the Communist International to the development of the FSLN as an option to the Nicaraguan Socialist Party (PSN for its initials in Spanish), the Nicaraguan revolution was always distanced from Soviet analysis and Soviet policy. The fact that the Soviet Union provided substantial military and economic aid to the Sandinista government should lead us to inquire why it supported a system built on an organization outside of the official Communist movement.

The first step in examining the theory and practice of the FSLN is to lay out the basic theoretical underpinnings of its practice. Here it is essential to examine both theoretical and practical developments that made it possible for the FSLN to take leadership of an insurrection that overthrew the Somoza dictatorship and which led to the formation of the state under FSLN control. The first part of the work which follows attempts to do this, beginning with the role of Augusto C. Sandino and continuing through the basic elements of the theory that guided the FSLN in government.

The second step is to engage in a critical analysis of the actual practice followed by the FSLN government in relation to the theory that presumably guided it. There were two fundamental stages in these developments, one prior to the election of 1984 and the other extending from that date until the electoral loss of 1990. The second part of this work examines these two stages and draws some conclusions about contradictions that arose in practice as the FSLN attempted to unite pluralism and participatory democracy. It focuses on the relationship of these issues with the theory of class that is at the basis of the FSLN's practice. The conclusion suggests the importance of adopting a broader sense of class than that used by the FSLN and a heightening of awareness of the problems that arise in making sense of the relation between class, party, government, and state in revolutionary analysis.

PART I

Theory in the Sandinista Revolution

The FSLN has always been based on serious intellectual debate of a theoretical nature. While the original actions of Sandino and his army developed out of a series of events that were clearly unanticipated by Sandino himself, he developed a rather sophisticated analysis of these events as they occurred. Sandino's efforts were successful in the sense that they led to the withdrawal of U.S. military forces from Nicaragua in 1932. Yet his long-term vision was frustrated by his assassination, the destruction of the agricultural cooperatives that his disarmed men had established, and the deliberate efforts of Anastasio Somoza to defame his struggle.

There were sporadic acts of resistance to the Somoza regime and the memory of Sandino remained alive as a symbol of that resistance. Yet serious organized resistance to the regime was blocked by the fact that the Nicaraguan Socialist Party (PSN) held to the view of the Communist International that Sandino's efforts had been those of a "petty bourgeois caudillo." Armed struggle was disdained as a result of current official Marxist theory, insofar as it seriously penetrated Nicaragua at all. The development of the FSLN was a result of serious theoretical reflection by a small group of people, including Carlos Fonseca as a sort of intellectual leader. Fonseca looked to Sandino as a source for understanding Marxian theory in the Nicaraguan context. Based on his analysis, the FSLN developed a unique and powerful understanding of revolutionary practice that led to a startling and unexpected victory by the FSLN over the Somoza regime, transforming Nicaragua into a system wholly original in its theoretical self-understanding.

Theoretical analysis has always been a fundamental aspect of Sandinista practice. Even among FSLN militants at the very base it is possible to open a discussion of theoretical issues and to suddenly find oneself examining rather complex texts of political theory that have been produced from a room in a house with a dirt floor and no television set. At higher levels, one finds people with knowledge not only of all aspects of Marxian theory but of Kant, Hegel, and Mariategui.[1] It is almost incredible to discover that the basic task of one of the original four members of the governing body of the Rural Workers' Association (ATC) was to introduce books such as those written by Mariategui, Paul Sweezy, Marta Harnecker, and Antonio Gramsci into the semi-clandestine organization during the last two years of the Somoza regime (interview with the wife of the ATC leader, April 7, 1992). Reading the works of Tomás Borge written while he was minister of the interior or of Sergio Ramírez while he was vice president of the country is a task that requires understanding of philosophy, literary criticism, anthropology, and poetry. There can be no understanding of the Nicaraguan revolution without an understanding of its fundamental theoretical roots.

Those roots have sprung from the seeds laid by Sandino himself. They were nourished by Fonseca and with the revolutionary triumph the tree sprang forth and produced substantial fruits. Yet theoretical growth was not to cease as the revolution became an active force. Within the FSLN, and even between the FSLN and some of its critics, a lively theoretical debate continues. All such discussion assumes respect for the work of Sandino and Carlos Fonseca Amador.

Anyone who wants to understand the present conjuncture must see how it has arisen from the active theoretical foundations of the FSLN. Two fundamental themes must be examined to make sense of the theory of the FSLN. The first relates to the role of Carlos Fonseca in understanding the significance of Sandino and his development of basic principles of the revolutionary struggle. Fundamentally, it is essential to see how Fonseca's ideas led to the successful insurrection of 1979. The second basic theme is the development of a unique Sandinista conception of how a revolutionary vanguard can guide the development of a pluralist system

---

[1]In discussion with Orlando Piñeda, FSLN deputy to the National Assembly, all of these texts arose. When asked whether the revolutionary triumph was a result of theory he responded emphatically that it was. As an associate of Fonseca and Borge as well as other founders of the FSLN, Piñeda said that in fact the triumph unfolded precisely as they had planned it, based on theoretical discussions.

11

that is combined with participatory democracy. The unusual combination of theoretical elements that guided the FSLN requires an analysis that depends upon the explication of these ideas in the context of revolutionary practice. Assessment of the ideas requires an analysis of the practice of the revolution that takes into consideration possible contradictions that arose in the attempt to develop those ideas in practice. The following two chapters consider the theoretical underpinnings of Sandinista practice. The remainder of the book is an attempt to consider problems that were revealed in that practice, especially in relation to the concept of class.

1

THE NICARAGUAN REVOLUTION
IN PERSPECTIVE

The Last in a Series of Socialist Revolutions

The triumph of the revolution of Nicaragua led by the Sandinista
National Liberation Front (FSLN) marked the end of a long process
of socialist revolutions in the twentieth century.[1]   The first

---

[1]Some would deny that the Nicaraguan revolution is, or was, socialist.
It is clearly true that a fully socialist system was never developed in
Nicaragua and that the revolution continues with obvious representatives
of capitalist interests holding the bulk of governmental power. In this
sense, perhaps, socialism does not exist in Nicaragua. Nevertheless, it is
clear that the major actors who consciously guided the revolution thought
of themselves as working, at least in the long run, to establish socialism.
If we insist on confining the term "socialist revolution" to systems that
have actually achieved socialism, we simply put ourselves in the midst of
a theoretical quagmire in the contemporary period; after all, one could
argue that the Bolshevik revolution has led to the incipient development
of capitalism in Russia and other states that were part of the Soviet Union.
It does not therefore make sense to see it as a capitalist revolution. It
might be useful to consider the question of whether the Nicaraguan
revolution is better understood as fitting into a series of Latin American
revolutions commencing with the Mexican revolution. Yet the theoretical
discourse of the leaders of the FSLN seldom points in this direction and
here it has been preferred to follow their lead, basing their theory and
practice on some variety of theory derived from Marxism. Of course, the
alternative analysis would be a welcome one, as are analyses that
emphasize the origins of much of the Nicaraguan revolution in liberation
theology. The latter has had a clear role in the Nicaraguan case. Yet it
is important to see that this has always been related to some conception
of socialism as well. On this subject see Dodson and O'Shaughnessy, 1990,

revolutionary victory was accomplished by the Bolsheviks in Russia in 1917. Every subsequent socialist revolution in the century was fundamentally influenced by the Soviet state and the Soviet Communist Party in one respect or another. Even the Chinese revolutionary triumph in 1949, the second major socialist revolution, was fundamentally affected by its complex relationship with the Soviet Union. Surely the "revolutions" in Eastern Europe were substantially influenced by Soviet power and Soviet revolutionary theory. The Cuban revolution of 1959 and the Nicaraguan revolution of 1979 marked the only successful socialist revolutions in the Western hemisphere, though they occurred relatively late in the revolutionary cycle begun in 1917 and their relation to the Soviet structure was quite different from earlier cases of socialist revolutions. In both of these American cases the revolutionary triumphs were guided by organizations that were outside of the traditional Communist or Socialist parties: the July 26 Movement in Cuba had origins outside the Cuban Communist Party; the Sandinista National Liberation Front (FSLN for its Spanish initials) was rejected by the Nicaraguan Socialist Party (PSN) as "petty bourgeois adventurists" because of the decision to follow the path of armed struggle. In spite of the claims of broad sectors both inside and outside of the government in the United States, the Soviet Union never gained hegemony over either system.[2] Nevertheless, these two revolutions received substantial aid from the Soviet Union and Eastern Europe, both military and political, after they

---

and Girardi, 1987. On the general sense in which it is appropriate to see the Nicaraguan revolution as socialist, see Harris, 1992.

[2]The extent to which the Soviet Union attempted to control Nicaraguan developments is somewhat unclear. Important participants in developing relations between the Soviet Union and Nicaragua claim that there was a clear attempt by the Soviet Union to impose its model on Nicaragua (interview with participant in discussions between the Nicaraguan Directorate of Foreign Relations, high level Soviet officials, and persons active in the Nicaraguan Ministry of Culture, April 7, 1992). The same people suggested in an informal interview that Cuban influence started out in the same direction but that Cuban representatives soon learned that the Nicaraguan situation was too dissimilar to impose the Cuban model. /

had consolidated their revolutionary triumphs. Indeed, without this aid the Nicaraguan and Cuban revolutions would probably have succumbed to either direct or indirect military intervention from the United States. Such aid is no longer available to either the Cuban or the Nicaraguan revolution; they must survive without the aid of a consolidated and militarily powerful rearguard in Europe. They thus stand at the end of the period in which socialist revolutions are to be understood as following a trajectory determined, or at least strongly influenced, by Soviet theory and practice.

The First in a New Series?

The two American cases of successful socialist-oriented revolutions thus stand at the end of a process and at the beginning of another one. With the elimination of the Soviet Union and massive changes away from a socialist system in Eastern Europe, "really existing socialism" as it was known can no longer serve as a positive example for future development. Furthermore, any future revolutionary socialist developments must exist without the rearguard of the Soviet Union to provide aid and to constitute a sort of balance against imperialist forces led by the United States.

The most clear and immediate example of the significance of developments in Eastern Europe for future revolutionary projects is provided by the Salvadoran case. After the changes that occurred in Eastern Europe and the legal elimination of the Soviet Union, the Farabundo Martí National Liberation Front (FMLN) clearly was obligated to give up hope for a military victory and revolutionary consolidation that could, perhaps, have been accomplished with Soviet aid similar to that which both Nicaragua and Cuba received after their revolutionary triumphs. None of these three cases was dependent for its origins or for a significant portion of material aid in the revolutionary struggle itself on the Soviet Union, but the existence of the Soviet Union made at least some sort of resistance to U.S. pressure possible.

The elimination of the Soviet Union put the Salvadoran revolutionary forces in a position that no previous revolution since 1917 had faced. For each such revolution the question of the extent to which they would associate themselves with the Soviet Union was an open one, but Soviet backing in economic development as well as in resisting direct U.S. military intervention constituted a real

15

option. That option no longer exists. This new context makes it even more imperative to learn from the experiences of Cuba and Nicaragua in the sense in which each of these systems developed a path different from that followed in Eastern Europe, depending on the history and social conditions of the particular country. Both cases present examples of practices fundamentally different from many aspects of Soviet practice. The Nicaraguan case, at least, presents numerous significant examples of new theoretical perspectives on revolution that can be of use in future struggles for liberation.

The apparent Cuban and Nicaraguan trajectories are quite disparate. Future revolutionary theory and practice will, without doubt, draw from each in both a negative and positive sense. At least at this point it appears that the Cuban case will show whether it is possible to continue with a model of a one-party state guiding revolutionary developments. The Nicaraguan case provides a fundamentally different model. Nicaragua never intended to be "another Cuba" and contemporary developments in the two countries are fundamentally different. The July 26 Movement in Cuba transformed itself through a merger with the old Communist Party into the guiding political force of the revolution. It continues to protect its position as the revolutionary vanguard by maintaining a monopoly on political power. In Nicaragua, the basic guiding revolutionary organization, the FSLN, lost governmental power through an open (and universally praised) free electoral process undertaken as a result of the theory and prior practice of the FSLN itself. Far from having accommodated itself to the old communist party (the PSN) the FSLN found itself in the curious position of opposing both the old PSN and a new Communist Party of Nicaragua (PCN) as part of the National Opposition Union (UNO) coalition that succeeded in taking government power.

The election of 1990 was not held simply as a result of external pressures, though its timing was related to the ongoing negotiatons among Central American governments seeking peace in the region. The commitment of the FSLN to elections was long-standing and consistent. Indeed, in many ways the 1984 election is as significant in the development of the Nicaraguan model as the 1990 election. The early election, also praised by many international groups as a clean and fair election,[3] demonstrated that the FSLN was to follow a policy of attempting to obtain both external and internal legitimacy through an electoral process modeled on that of existing electoral democracies. No similar process has yet to occur in the Cuban case in spite of substantial international pressure on the Cuban government to undertake a free election.[4] To understand the lessons of the Nicaraguan experience and the theory which guided it we must resist the temptation, so common among anti-communist commentators, to simply enfold it in the broader revolutionary socialist experiences of the twentieth century or even of twentieth-century Latin America. Both the roots and later developments of the Nicaragua experience must be understood in Nicaraguan terms. Nevertheless we can draw some general lessons from this particular experience for developing revolutionary practice in other contexts.

While some would have it that history is over and that revolution is thus a thing of the past, the basic roots of revolutionary practice remain as they always have. While some macroeconomic indicators may suggest that there is economic improvement in the Third World there can be little doubt that poverty continues to increase as does unemployment and the unequal division of wealth. In Latin America especially, there are continuing signs of revolutionary ferment. In Guatemala armed struggle continues. The presumably stable Mexican government found itself responding to a major armed uprising in Chiapas in early 1994. This uprising, led by the Emiliano Zapata Front for National Liberation, showed a surprisingly high level of organizational sophistication. While the government of Peru has made substantial gains in war against its major guerrilla enemies, unrest and major violence continues.

---

[3]For an especially important example, see the report of the Latin American Studies Association, based on extensive observation of the 1984 election. LASA, 1984.

[4]This is not to imply that the Cuban decision is incorrect or to deny that other structures exist in Cuba that constitute serious attempts to construct a new form of democracy under the idea of "people's power." The present point is simply that the Nicaraguan and Cuban cases are different in this respect. At the time of this writing, substantial revisions of the Cuban system were being undertaken.

Although the Colombian government has been able to include some revolutionary groups in the traditional political process, others continue to be active in the countryside. The implementation of austerity policies in Venezuela, long understood as an example of stable democracy, led to several atttempts to overthrow the government, with substantial popular support. Argentina has seen major outbreaks of violence in some provinces.

Yet, insofar as future revolutions occur they cannot be expected to be modelled on the notion of state ownership of the means of production or of centralized state planning. Even in South Africa, the African National Congress, which has close relations with the Communist Party, has called for a mixed economy. It is impossible to predict what will happen in future revolutions or what course future revolutionary movements will take. Yet it is not unreasonable to believe that the old Soviet model will give way to alternative conceptions, even where socialism is seen as a revolutionary goal. In this context, understanding the Nicaraguan experience in developing a model based on political pluralism and a mixed economy as well as efforts to defend revolutionary gains even after electoral defeat of the main revolutionary party can be useful in examining new alternatives. There is much to be gained from the relative success of some elements of the Nicaraguan experience and perhaps more from the relative failures that have been experienced.

The FSLN in Nicaragua is presently engaged in a substantial practical and theoretical struggle to make sense of some of these issues. Would-be revolutionaries are well advised to pay close attention to Nicaraguan developments in the past as well as the present. If, for example, the FMLN should take power through the electoral process in El Salvador it will do well to examine the Nicaraguan experience critically in terms of the alternative forms of land ownership and state ownership that are continuing to develop in Nicaragua as "privatization into the hands of the workers" proceeds. Developments in Southern Africa, especially in Mozambique and Angola, have some similarities to the Nicaraguan experience as well, and much may be gained there from a clear comprehension of Nicaraguan theory and practice. There are more than surface similarities between the continued activity of armed groups in Nicaragua after the election and continued counterrevolutionary violence even after a clear electoral victory for the revolutionary party in Angola, for example.

Thus, while there is much that is unique to the Nicaraguan context, there is also much to be learned from the examination of its revolutionary theory and practice for making sense of continuing revolutionary struggles in the world. While the present juncture does not seem to bode well for revolution, it is to be remembered that the victory of the FSLN in Nicaragua was hardly anticipated in the late 1970s either.

The Internal Basis of the Nicaraguan Revolution

It is clear that the Nicaraguan revolution was based on internal, national developments, not on external forces. Augusto Sandino, leader of a four-year military struggle against the U.S. marines was rejected by the Communist International as a "petty bourgeois adventurer" much as the FSLN was rejected by the Nicaraguan Socialist Party (PSN). Although the PSN, the FSLN, and the Republican Mobilization Party (MR) worked together in 1964–66, Tomás Borge points out that both the PSN and the MR rejected the armed struggle which was at the root of the FSLN's position from the time of its founding. After the first Sandinista attempt to conduct a guerilla operation in the mountains of the Rio Coco and Bocay regions, the split between the FSLN and the PSN was clear.[5] This experience, as well as the defeat in 1959 of an

---

[5]Although some sources suggest that Fonseca quit the PSN (see Booth, 1985: 139); my interview with a present FSLN member of the National Assembly who worked personally with Fonseca suggests strongly that the PSN rejected the newly formed FSLN as "adventurists" soon after the first armed guerilla actions, not that FSLN leaders simply quit the PSN. Tómas Borge is somewhat vague on this subject but he makes clear that one of the original founders of the FSLN, and its first political director, Noel Guerrero Santiago, had been a PSN militant and that he was ultimately rejected by the PSN as a result of internal discussions. Borge's words are "Al incorporarse al movimiento revolucionario nicaragüense, ingresó en el Partido Socialista—cuyos dirigentes decían entonces marxista-leninistas—y allí se vio involucrada en serias discussiones que lo alejaron de su filas" (Borge, 1989: 186). He makes clear that the other militants at the time (Carlos Fonseca Amador, Santos López, Tomás Borge, Silvio Mayorga y

earlier guerilla action in which the PSN had participated,[6] led the FSLN, under the theoretical guidance of Carlos Fonseca, to re-examine the lessons of both the Cuban example (where the initial guerilla focus came into the country from outside and later established its national base) and earlier attempts to send revolutionary armed forces into Nicaragua from Honduras. Instead, the FSLN adopted the view, in practice as well as theory, that it was essential to prepare for the armed guerilla action through a long process of developing support among the population.

It is important to understand that Fonseca went back to study the historical roots of the Nicaraguan experience when he realized that there were clear theoretical problems with applying the lessons of other revolutions to the Nicaraguan case. The need to under-stand how an armed force could successfully sustain itself in the countryside led him to a deep study of the experience of Sandino. It was not sufficient to simply study the experiences of the Russians, the Chinese, the Vietnamese, the Cubans, and the Tupamaros; it was essential to root the Nicaraguan revolution in the history of struggle within Nicaragua. It became clear to Fonseca that the prevailing view in the official communist parties (here, the PSN), that Latin America was still feudal and thus must make a revolution in alliance with the indigenous national bourgeoisie, was funda-mentally in error.[7] This led him to examine in close detail the

---

Jorge Navarro) agreed with Guerrero at the time. He was giving Mayorga, Fonseca, and Borge "political instructions, as students, while he was still in the PSN" (Borge, 1989: 186). He does report that Fonseca and Guerrero had a basic disagreement about the role of Sandino, with Guerrero taking the old view of the Communist International (Borge, 1989: 187).

[6]One knowledgeable person I interviewed claimed that Ernesto "Che" Guevara was expected to participate in this action but that he never showed up. Whether this was his intention and he was somehow prevented from, or decided not to, participate must remain a matter of speculation. I have been able to find no written documentation on this question.

[7]Tomás Borge discusses this at some length, quoting Fonseca on the low level of understanding of Marxist theory in the PSN and pointing out that the first communist cell was not formed around the University in Leon

Zelaya period in Nicaraguan history and thus to fundamentally reformulate existing explanations of Nicaragua as essentially feudal.

Nicaraguan developments after the triumph of 1979, in both theory and practice, are quite distinct from those in other revolutions. Most significantly, the FSLN committed itself early in its history to the concepts of the "mixed economy" and "political pluralism." In this sense, developments in Nicaragua may be said to precede developments in the Soviet Union and Eastern Europe; it is even possible that the concepts of *perestroika* and *glasnost* were, at least in part, influenced by Nicaraguan developments. In the Nicaraguan case, the electoral defeat of the FSLN in 1990 was not merely a disaster for the revolution, although it was certainly a setback for the FSLN. It did demonstrate the victory of the fundamental idea of electoral democracy within the Nicaraguan revolution. And, unlike in the Soviet Union or most of Eastern Europe, the leading revolutionary party (the FSLN) remains the single largest organized political force in the country.

No Counterrevolution by Election

Although there are forces within the governing UNO coalition that would clearly like to make a counterrevolution by election,[8] it

---

until 1956. He makes clear the Browderist foundation of the PSN, which was formed in 1944 (Borge, 1989: 87–91). For a lengthy attack on the position of the PSN and others opposed to the armed struggle (described as "the traditional left") written shortly after the National Guard's assassination of Ricardo Morales and Oscar Turcios in late September of 1973, see Borge's reproduction of his article written to commemorate Morales and distributed clandestinely throughout the student movement (Borge, 1989: 422–37). See also Ricardo Morales Avilés (1983: 129–66) "Charla al movimiento cristiano revolucionario."

[8]The Allende experience in Chile is frequently thought to have demonstrated the impossibility of achieving revolution through the electoral process. The Nicaraguan experience may well demonstrate whether it is possible to make a counterrevolution through elections. It is, perhaps, too easy to lose sight of similarities in the two processes. Just as Allende's revolution was blocked by the existence of a judiciary, a strong parliamentary force, and police and military forces that respected the old regime, those within the Nicaraguan government who would most clearly

is clear that the revolution continues in at least two important senses. The policies of the new government are in some ways, as Minister of the Presidency Antonio Lacayo has said, a continuation of the Sandinista revolution. The refusal of the president and her administration to go along with the most extreme anti-Sandinista measures or radical measures for the reversal of the agrarian reform passed by the National Assembly under UNO leadership—in spite of substantial pressure from the government of the United States to do so—is indicative of a willingness on the part of the Nicaraguan government to maintain a degree of independence from Washington not characteristic of prerevolutionary Nicaragua. It is a measure of the continuing success of the Nicaraguan revolution that popular pressures have had to be taken into account, as when the major opposition to a new tax on vehicle operations led to a nearly insurrectionary situation in the streets of Managua and a subsequent reversal of the policies that gave rise to the protests.

While the capital city has been cleansed by its UNO mayor of murals painted during the period of the Sandinista government, many public monuments to the revolution still stand, including huge portraits of Sandino and Fonseca on the front of the major government building. Several cities, including Estelí and León (the second largest city in the country) still have FSLN mayors and the murals picturing the revolution remain in these cities. The spontaneous outpouring of masses of Sandinista supporters upon the bombing of Fonseca's tomb makes clear that the revolution continues in a very important sense.[9]

---

like to undertake a counterrevolution face the same forces from the Sandinista period.

[9]There has been criticism of the police for not reacting with more force when the demonstrators burned the mayor's office and property of Vice President Virgilio Godoy on this occasion. To put this in perspective, it is interesting to note that one of my informants, a Sandinista militant who holds office in his local FSLN organization and local community organizations in a poor barrio of Managua (he is a mechanic in a large textile factory), told me that the police "distanced themselves" from the crowd because they were afraid of the demonstrators. That this fear was not without foundation is clear from his remark that "if the police had attacked us we would have burned down Violetta's house."

22

There are clearly forces, led by, among others, Vice President Virgilio Godoy and Arnaldo Alemán (a candidate for president in 1996), that see the electoral defeat of the FSLN as an opportunity to fundamentally eliminate Sandinism it all its forms. The minister of education, Humberto Belli, clearly is attempting to do his best to alter the curriculum and the textbooks to eliminate what he sees as "onesided" views of the revolution.

But this force is not unchallenged. President Violetta Chamorro de Barrios, Antonio Lacayo, the ministry of the presidency (Chamorro's son-in-law), and other elements of UNO are clearly taking a fundamentally different approach. The transition between administrations was accomplished through a complex and detailed agreement which left General Humberto Ortega as head of the armed forces, established an agreement to privatize state holdings at least in part "in favor of the workers," prevented a massive purge of the Sandinista police force, and laid down a policy of not returning property to the Somoza family or its close associates.

UNO itself, not the FSLN, has been the strongest critic of the new administration, even calling at times for Chamorro's resignation. The very development of a basic split within the governing coalition that led to FSLN dominance of the National Assembly throughout 1993 was at least partially a result of the fact that the administration saw itself constrained to respond to popular pressures in matters involving issues as important as the privatization of agricultural and industrial properties. UNO has broken into an extremely revanchist opposition and a governing administration (backed by some members of the National Assembly) that seeks to moderate the revolution and to maintain stability while doing so. Thus the battle between revolution and counterrevolution has paradoxically continued within the coalition that brought defeat to the FSLN.

The FSLN in Opposition

The politics of the first three years of the new administration have been complex, but it is clear that the FSLN continues to play a substantial role even within the official politics of the government. The president's partial veto of a law to reverse property distributions made by the Sandinista government after the election but before the transition of power has been extremely controversial but it has been sustained by the courts and even by the National Assembly with participation by UNO members. Those advocating elimination of Sandinismo from the country refer to the property titling which occurred at the end of the Sandinista period of government as *la piñata*. Yet it is clear that other forces in the government recognize the legitimacy of much of what occurred. In the first place, the bulk of the property included in the *piñata* was clearly a matter of simply giving official titles to peasants who were benefitted by the agrarian reform. Since before the election President Chamorro has unequivocally stated that her government will not disturb titles to land given to small and medium holders (Enriquez, 1991: 174). The courts have accepted ex-president Daniel Ortega's right to the house he occupies as a result of early revolutionary confiscation. This is a reflection of the fact that many participants in the process as well as common citizens understand that many people worked in the Sandinista government for extremely low salaries and that the title to their homes and even automobiles is just compensation for their work.[10]

---

[10]A pro-Sandinista informant spontaneously complained to me about the *piñata* but readily accepted the analysis that many of those benefitted in fact had a right to their houses and cars as a result of the fact that they had occupied important government positions with very low pay and benefits (the example was of a person who had occupied a major administrative position in a non-governmental agency). This informant maintains the view that some members of the National Directorate have improperly benefitted. She cited the case of her close neighbor Tómas Borge, whom she described as having a number of *manzanas* (the common land measure in Nicaragua—approximately 1.7 acres), and a number of houses. She was unaware that all of this belongs to a foundation that is operating a nursery school and providing aid to people needing medical assistance and help in finding employment. His own home is included in the property but most of the "houses" are offices, including his own modest office, which is by no means comparable to the offices of deans in United States universities. Nevertheless, there seems to be widespread resentment about some aspects of the *piñata*. What this indicates is that the office of the presidency is refusing to exploit this issue in its own interest, preferring to work in a more constructive manner with the leadership of the FSLN. For further discussion of the importance of the *piñata* in damaging the credibility of the FSLN, see chapter 7, below.

It is true that Chamorro's opponents within her own government coalition (UNO) are outspoken in opposing what they call "co-government" with the Sandinistas. An early, and continuing, example of this opposition was contained in an "Open Letter from the Parties of UNO to the President of the Republic," occasioned by Antonio Lacayo's remarks made to the Spanish language international television network, UNIVISION, that "this government is a continuation of the Revolution that began in 1979." The letter, over the signatures of representatives of twelve of the fourteen parties that constitute UNO, cited the "Preamble" of UNO's "Program of Government," which they allege was "inexplicably suppressed from the publication by the President of the Republic of this Program." The preamble states, according to this letter:

> The National Opposition Union (UNO), conscious that our country suffers the most grave crisis of its history, fundamentally as a consequence of the dictatorial and totalitarian system and the administrative disaster of the Sandinista regime, considers that its immediate task consists in a dynamic and sustained action capable of rescuing the Nicaraguan people from the social, political and economic prostration in which it finds itself, for which the present Program of Government is proposed to the people, which contains the necessary elements for the reconstruction of Nicaragua. (*La Prensa*, April 1, 1992)[11]

---

[11]The twelve parties represented by the signatories are: The National Conservative Party (PNC), The Liberal Independent Party (PLI), The Social Democratic Party (PSD), The Popular Conservative Alliance (APC), the Liberal Constitutionalist Party (PLC), the Democratic Party of Confidence (PDC), the Popular Social Christian Party (PPSC), the National Conservative Action Party, the Democratic Movement of Nicaragua Party, the Communist Party of Nicaragua (PCN), the Neo-Liberal Party, and the National Action Party (PAN). It should be noted that UNO consists of "11 legal parties and three factions or tendencies of parties not included in UNO." Thus these three factions are a part of UNO while the party of which they are part is not in UNO as a party. (Oscar-Rene Vargas, 1990: 158). As the situation has developed it is fair

Clearly this represents a substantial political force which would like to turn back the revolution, at least as a Sandinista revolution. However it is essential to remember that these complaints are against the presidency itself, historically the single most powerful actor in Nicaraguan politics.[12] As the economic situation of the country has deteriorated and armed resistance has continued on the part of re-armed *contras* and some armed leftist groups, there have been continuing controversies that question the legitimacy of the government. From the right, the most consistent charge is that the administration is engaging in "co-government" with the FSLN. There have been continuing attempts to develop a national dialogue to the extent that at some point there has been discussion between elements of the right within UNO not only with the government but also directly with the FSLN. While few significant agreements have been both reached and instituted the disputes go forward.

---

to say that "you can't tell the players without a scorecard." That is, the alliance is fluid to the point of flowing in many different directions at the same time. It is highly doubtful that it will be able to run a single candidate for the presidency in 1996.

[12]On this point, see Oscar-Rene Vargas, 1990. His analysis was written shortly before the 1990 election based on an early poll that strongly suggested an FSLN victory for the presidency but not for an absolute majority in the National Assembly. It thus represents an interesting perspective on the larger issue from the point of view of an observer who expected and welcomed the re-election of Daniel Ortega:

> In Nicaragua the parliament lacks prestige. It is not considered as a true state power, nor are its members able to obtain an effective quota of power or of influence. The situation is explained, in part, by the predominance of a strong presidentialist regime that annuls the faculties of the legislative power.
>
> But the lack of prestige of Nicaragua's parliament is found in a system of frozen minorities, renewed in different pacts between Somocismo and the Conservatives. By legal disposition it was established beforehand how many deputies each of the two parties (Conservative and Liberal) would have in the National Assembly. (153–54)

Only future developments can make clear what will happen to the revolution but it is clear that initial reports of its death were premature, failing to take into account the extent to which the Nicaraguan population has come to be a force of its own, not always united with any particular political party. The FSLN, like other political organizations, can forget this reality only at its own peril.

The Continued Legitimacy of the FSLN

Countries and international organizations welcome FSLN representatives to meetings concerning aid to Nicaragua, negotiations about the repayment of the foreign debt and economic adjustment policies within Nicaragua. Prominent figures within the Democratic Party in the U.S. have had discussions with members of the FSLN National Directorate and other FSLN officials when the latter have visited the U.S. FSLN celebrations of events such as the victory of July 19, 1979 still draw huge crowds, as does the *Replique*, the annual reenactment of the FSLN's strategic retreat from Managua to Masaya during the last stages of the insurrection. These factors, as well as others, indicate that whatever the opinions of frustrated political actors in Nicaragua might be, it is far too early to conclude, as did an important scholar interested in Nicaragua, that "while the Sandinistas retained control over the military, the international and domestic legitimacy of the revolution they had led was gone" (Kornbluh, 1991: 344). Perhaps in the eyes of some the revolution is over when the revolutionary party no longer holds a monopoly of governmental power. It is clearly within the tradition of revolution and revolutionary analysis of the period since 1917 (not only in the USSR, China, and its allies, but also in Mexico) to adopt this stance. Yet, it is precisely this sort of analysis that must be reconsidered in light of the actual theory and practice of the Sandinista Revolution.

The Election as a Sandinista Victory

It is not clear that all is lost from a revolutionary perspective merely because an incompletely-formed political party, controlled by an organization rooted in its history as a "military political front," has lost an election.[13] Indeed Daniel Ortega was quoted by a lieutenant colonel in charge of foreign relations of the Sandinista Popular Army as having said that "we won because we lost the election and disarmed the *contras*" (LASA interview, June 26, 1992). He also summed up the strategy after the election in a famous speech as "governing from below." An army captain in the northern village of Yalí, sidearms obviously ready to use in the zone where *contras* were engaged in disarmament, made a similar point: "We consider the termination of armed forces sponsored by the U.S. to be a success of the election" (LASA interview, June 22, 1990). Alejandro Bendaña, general secretary of the Nicaraguan foreign ministry during the FSLN period, said "having lost the election does not mean having lost the revolution" (LASA interview, June 26, 1990). The newly elected FSLN vice-mayor of Ben León stated that the election constituted the passing of "government from one class to another" (LASA interview, June 17, 1990), but it is important to connect his remarks with those of Alvaro Arguello, director of the program of post graduate studies in international relations at the University of Central America in Managua, to the effect that though

---

[13]Orlando Piñeda, elected as an FSLN member to the National Assembly from Estelí, pointed out to me that, in his view, it was "fundamentally important to remember that the FSLN was born as a military political front and that it continued being one while in government." He clearly held that this explains many difficulties that the FSLN has had in developing itself as a political party. He believes that, in an important sense, it still is not really a party (interview, April 4, 1992). In an interview with the Latin American Studies Association Summer Seminar in Nicaragua, Luis Carrión, then secretary of the FSLN and a member of the National Directorate, stated that the FSLN had only "hundreds of cadre" at the time of the triumph in 1979, that "they began to construct a party after the triumph" and that "a few years after the triumph, the Front was a party." However, he described this as connected to the government as a "ministry of mobilization." He characterized the FSLN after 1982 as "a parallel organization to the state," whose function was to "harmonize and coordinate all the instruments" available to prepare for U.S. military intervention. Although he says that, after Esquipulas, it was time to make changes in the party-state relationship these were put off until after the elections. He was clear that from the origins of the FSLN it was organized as a "vertical party to do things" (LASA interview June 25, 1990).

the FSLN lost the election, it won the revolution and that the FSLN was ready to begin the process of answering the question "Can we make revolution without being in power?" (LASA interview, June 18, 1990). To put all of this in context, a seriously incapacitated veteran of the Sandinista army without employment who describes himself as a member of the FSLN commented in an informal discussion with the author that "the election was not a defeat, it was a victory, it shows that the revolution has developed democracy in Nicaragua" (interview, April 5, 1992).

People close to the bases of Sandinista organizations may not think of the continuing revolution simply as a matter of action by the FSLN. A leader of the National Workers Front said, in discussing a possible strike action, "Now we are going to test the force of the revolution" (interview, LASA Summer Seminar, June 28, 1992). A member of a base organization in Estelí involved in organizing new militias even while disarmament was the official policy of the FSLN and the government stated that "the revolution must continue forward with younger cadres or with older more experienced ones" (LASA interview June 21, 1992).

Perhaps there has been a counterrevolution, as the UNO coordinator in Estelí claimed in 1990 (LASA interview with Dr. Briolla Lanussa, June 21, 1990), but it is too simple to merely reject the opinions of so many others at all levels of Nicaraguan society. Indeed, those oriented toward the right in UNO make clear through their own complaints about the government that no counter-revolution has been consolidated. Vice President Godoy himself has said, obviously in a highly critical manner, that "what exists in Nicaragua is a prolongation of the FSLN government" (*La Opinión*, April 22, 1992, 8A). It seems that the vice president would support a counterrevolution by election but he regretfully admits that it has not yet occurred.

None of this is to say that there have been no setbacks or that the future success of the revolution is assured. Indeed, on a daily basis life has become so difficult for most Nicaraguans that basic survival is in doubt. Many, if not most, of the revolutionary advances in education, health care, and social services have been reversed. Malnutrition and starvation have returned to the countryside. Credit has not been forthcoming for production in either agricultural or industrial activities now sometimes controlled by the workers. Whether new forms of ownership can survive is a most serious question. After all, agrarian reform is as easily reversed as worker ownership of industry when new forms of economic activity meet defeat at the hands of the marketplace.

Foundations of the Continuing Revolution in Sandinismo

It is not mere rhetoric to speak of the continuation of the Sandinista revolution even though the FSLN no longer controls the government. There are substantial bases in Sandinista thought to suggest that this idea is fundamentally appropriate and it is clear that there are fundamental changes occurring within the FSLN itself that have clear meaning for future revolutionary thought and practice. After all, Sandino himself was not struggling for control of the government, but to promote national sovereignty. It was only with the development of the FSLN in the 1960s that the revolution took on the more classic form of struggling for state power. Even so, there has always been a strong current of thought within the FSLN concerned with the concept of "hegemony" in the Gramscian sense more than with mere holding of governmental offices. In the current context there are two fundamental elements of continued revolutionary struggle that are especially important in this regard—the struggle to democratize the vanguard itself (the FSLN), and the revolutionary activity of organizations such as labor unions and community organizations that are achieving substantial independence from the FSLN. The existence of armed leftist groups that have assassinated right-wing political figures and engaged in a massive assault on Estelí, calling themselves Sandinistas, is further evidence that the FSLN as a party does not always control revolutionary forces that continue to function in Nicaragua.

There is an important sense in which the Nicaraguan revolution continues even if one sees the Sandinista revolution as having ended and assumes that the FSLN and other Sandinista forces will eventually either fade away, be swept away, or become secondary to other revolutionary forces in the country. After all, prior to 1979 there were no free elections, and there was no constitutional structure that actually controlled political activity. The economic processes as well as the political processes in the country were based on arbitrary actions, not normal political processes. While many high officials in the present government were connected with the

30

contras, few of them were actually supporters of the Somoza regime. President Chamorro is the wife of one of the most famous martyrs of the struggle against Somoza, Pedro Joaquin Chamorro. Vice President Godoy was, himself, an active proponent of the anti-Somoza revolution and served as minister of Labor under the FSLN. Alfredo César, leader of UNO in the National Assembly, was at one time a Sandinista militant. When asked in 1990 whether the popular Sandinista revolution exists, he responded: "I have held the thesis of a democratic and national revolution. I think that this process was frustrated and interrupted for some years, accidently, by the course that things took. With the government of Violetta Chammoro we are retaking the democratic and revolutionary road" (quoted in Ferrari, 1990: 18). Humberto Belli, currently minister of Education, even suggested in 1990 that it would be a good idea for groups from both sides of the ideological and political sector to get together to discuss a common history of the country and a common "civic education." He further suggested that he thought that Sandinism had held an acceptable position in the period from 1980–81 until the FSLN took a "Marxist-Leninist" line and that it is gradually coming back to a democratic position. He calls the present position of the FSLN a "more potable Sandinism" (quoted in Ferrari, 1990: 19).

At a minimum, a clear political revolution was accomplished that has produced, not without some strains, an electoral democracy from a cruel dictatorship. While this is hardly a fulfillment of the FSLN's model of revolutionary success, it does establish a new arena of struggle for revolutionary forces. In the more far-reaching sense of revolution, it is clear that a struggle continues for maintaining the basic economic reforms undertaken during the FSLN's period of government, even though success in that arena, as in the political one, cannot be guaranteed. In these respects the revolution is clearly in retreat. It is only insofar as revolutionary forces can make use of the political structures and processes to protect revolutionary gains that these structures can be seen as a victory of the revolutionary government that was turned out of power through these very processes. At least for a time, governmental structures have provided an arena in which the most counterrevolutionary forces have been frustrated in several important areas.

There are also still forces active, both within and without the FSLN, that clearly are attempting to continue a struggle to make a socialist revolution succeed in Nicaragua. The question is not whether there is a revolution in Nicaragua, only where it is to be found. In the state? In the government? In the FSLN? In the actions of other organized groups?

Making Sense of the Election Defeat

Few people, either inside or outside of Nicaragua, expected the FSLN to lose the presidency in the election of 1990, although some thought that it might lose an absolute majority in the National Assembly (Oscar-Rene Vargas, 1990: 153). Most public opinion polls seemed to suggest an FSLN victory and the FSLN leadership was confident in these results, given their contacts with the base and with the masses. The UNO victory was a shock. Some people, even those not really FSLN members, describe themselves as going around like zombies for several days after the election. If there had been any desire within the FSLN to deny the results it must have been strongly counterbalanced by the fact that the elections had been so closely monitored by all sorts of international groups and agencies. It is true that the U.S. government had intervened both directly and indirectly in support of UNO but the FSLN did not try to scapegoat the U.S. Instead it asked itself what had gone wrong. Within a period of two or three months the Sandinista position was clear.[14] The people had voted for peace and against the draft; they had voted against the economic conditions and the embargo that was at least partially responsible for it. Fundamentally, the majority of the voters did not believe that it was possible to have peace and U.S. aid with the FSLN in power. But, at the same time, people at

---

[14] I visited the country in late April and early May, just before the transition took place and again in June of 1990, shortly after the new government had taken power. As early as the first visit the analysis on the part of those sympathetic to the FSLN was clear. I was, for example, briefed by a researcher in the Nicaraguan Institute of Economic and Social Research (INIES) and talked with FSLN members, sympathizers, and militants at all levels. There was little disagreement about the basic analysis. The same can be said for the more elaborate analyses received by the LASA Summer Seminar in June, which was briefed by a large number of different sources.

all levels of the FSLN soon began a process of serious and severe self-criticism.

FSLN Self-Criticism and Internal Reform

It is one thing to understand the defeat in terms of fundamentally external factors; it is another to understand how the defeat could have been so unexpected. After all, the FSLN had always prided itself on being an organization based on the masses and presumably responding to them. It was not long before the analysis of this phenomenon also crystallized. The problem was "verticalism" within the FSLN, mass organizations, and the government itself; the solution was seen as "democratization" of the processes and the practices of the FSLN.

There can be little doubt that the FSLN developed from its inception as an organization with strong "verticalist" structures and traditions. In developing an insurrection in the context of a military dictatorship with sophisticated and cruel structures of suppression, clear leadership and secure structures of command are essential. These structures also served well in dealing with the counter-revolutionary war that marked the whole period of FSLN governance. Yet these same structures impeded some important developments of the revolutionary practice of the Sandinista state. Ultimately, the FSLN came to see its verticalist structure as a problem that needed to be overcome. The electoral defeat magnified and focused the problem.

It is important to note that this analysis did not begin with the election defeat. As early as 1987 or 1988 it had become clear to the leadership of the FSLN as well as to many foreign observers that the base units of the FSLN, the Sandinista Defense Committees (CDS), (modeled after the Cuban Committees for the Defense of the Revolution), were not functioning as they should. Therefore, the charismatic revolutionary figure, Omar Cabezas, was assigned to reformulate and restructure the CDSs. His critique of their earlier functioning was clear: they were too verticalist, sending orders from the top down rather than soliciting the views of the bottom; they were too "sectarian" in the sense that they were incorrectly seen simply as support groups for the FSLN; and they were organized in a bureaucratic fashion. The solution was to "democratize" the CDS, which would eventually become "the communal movement"

(LASA interview, June, 1988). It is beyond the scope of the present discussion to detail what happened and is happening with these base committees but it is important to see that the self-criticism of the FSLN as too "verticalist" is not simply a recent invention. Very soon after the election results were known the National Directorate announced that the FSLN would begin a process of democratizing itself through holding a series of local and regional meetings that would result in the first National Congress of the FSLN, scheduled to be held sometime in the fall of 1990 but postponed until July of 1991. This process was combined with the opening of the FSLN ranks to a whole new class of members who did not have to demonstrate the traditional commitment of an FSLN "militant."[15]

The process also included early elections of new leadership of student and youth organizations, and an opening up of the meetings of the Sandinista Assembly (the official governing body composed of militants within the Front) to more public scrutiny. Since the Congress, the FSLN membership has elected new local and regional bodies, whose original members were chosen by the Congress for a temporary period of one year. The initial process was well described in *El Nuevo Diario* with regard to the Regional Committee of the Southern Autonomous Region of the Atlantic (RAAS):

> Eleven people presented themselves as candidates for the Political Committee of the FSLN in the region, among them three women . . . none of whom [the women] were elected.
>
> The elections were held in two rounds. In the first the five members [of the Political Committee] were chosen and in the second round the Political Secretary and the Financial Secretary were chosen.
>
> Electoral delegates were the members of the directorates of the neighborhoods, districts and towns of Bluefields, such as Kukra Hill, Corn Island, El Bluff, Orinoco, Laguna de Perlas, etc.

---

[15]Estimates of the number of militants before the election vary substantially but it is safe to say that they probably numbered less than the 20,000 estimated in a "deep background briefing" at the U.S. embassy in 1988.

The participants considered the elections occurred in a clean and open manner which demonstrates that a true democracy reigns in the FSLN.

In order to present themselves as candidates for director of the Political Committee the candidates presented their plans of struggle (*planes de lucha*) in which they agreed to the strengthening of the unity of the party and necessity of undertaking actions in Defense of the Autonomy Law of the Atlantic Coast regions. (April 6, 1992, 1)

Throughout the country similar processes led to the election of a substantial number of people who had not previously held the offices to which they were elected (see *Barricada*, April 9, 1992, 1).

The first Congress chose a new National Directorate, including two new members, after an open debate. There was substantial controversy about the fact that it was possible only to vote for a slate, not for individual candidates. Since that time there have been numerous open and public disagreements among the nine members of the Directorate, including an attack by Daniel Ortega against what he saw as incorrect policies relating to the FSLN-owned communications media. There have also been open criticisms of the National Directorate (primarily for failing to maintain sufficient unity). An open forum of FSLN members, lasting three nights, with about three hundred participants was held on the topic, "What kind of Sandinista Front do we want?" which included substantial debate (*Barricada International*, April, 1992, 15). The Sandinista Assembly, the highest governing body of the FSLN between sessions of the Congress, has met a number of times and has seen intense open debate about policy questions as well as about the internal operations of the FSLN itself.

There have been serious splits within the FSLN itself over several different issues. At one point in 1993 Daniel Ortega threatened to take back his seat in the National Assembly from Sergio Ramírez who occupied it since the 1990 election in place of the ex-President. The dispute arose over a piece of legislation legalizing privatization of some public services. The FSLN bench in the Assembly supported the measure as necessary to regularize a process they saw as inevitable. Pressure from the union sector was important in this matter, giving rise to Ortega's statements.

A special session of the FSLN Congress held May 20–23 of 1994 demonstrated a clear division between those united with Daniel Ortega, calling themselves the "Democratic Left" and those who supported Sergio Ramírez as leader of the group "for a *Sandinismo* that returns to the majorities" and a third group led by Henry Ruiz calling itself "outside the currents" (*Barricada International*, June, 1994, 4). The Congress rejected a proposal to create a new position of FSLN president which would presumably have gone to Tomás Borge. In a contested election for general secretary Daniel Ortega was elected over opposition from Henry Ruiz. The National Directorate elected at this Congress was expanded in size from ten to fifteen members (including several women according to a new party rule that all leadership bodies must include women as thirty percent of their membership). Sergio Ramírez was not re-elected to the Directorate although he continues as head of the Sandinista bench in the National Assembly, still occupying the seat discussed above, and as a member of the Sandinista Assembly. The new Directorate includes nine members associated with the "Democratic Left" and six associated with the group "For a *Sandinismo* that returns to the majorities." Similarly the newly elected Sandinista Assembly is divided between the two groups, with the "Democratic Left" holding seventy five percent of the seats (*Barricada International*, June 1994, 18–20).

All of this indicates that, in fact, the FSLN has responded to concerns about its past practices by opening up a substantial area of free discussion and a serious process of election of delegates and officials at all levels. In the past, public discussion of differences among the leadership was extremely uncommon and most local and regional officials of the party were chosen by higher levels of authority. What this means for the future is, of course, unclear. However, it is obvious that the FSLN's response to electoral defeat was not to close ranks and increase party discipline but to open itself up to a broadly based discussion of how it is possible to "democratize" an organization that began as a military-political front composed of a closed group of militants which proceeded to function in close relation to state officials. Although there were some precedents to this opening, such as proposing non-FSLN members as candidates for offices at the local and regional levels, the post-election process indicates a continuing revolutionary transformation of the structures of the FSLN itself. Daniel Ortega's words of April 12, 1991, before the Congress had met, still sum up the situation well:

> The electoral defeat has led us to totally change the *Frente*, and we still haven't finished adapting ourselves to the new kind of organization we are assuming. We can no longer count on the large quantity of party professionals we once had, nor can the *Frente* be the same small group that we were during the struggle against Somocismo. It must be a new organization. It's still going to take us some time to organize ourselves to be effective revolutionaries in this new stage Nicaragua's going through. What's already clear is that we have the capacity to influence the conduct of the government effectively from the grassroots, and that is what's meant by governing from below. (*Envío*, English edition, June 1991: 29)

The ongoing process of democratization is by no means complete and includes the continuing possibility of new breaches opening within the FSLN itself. On the one hand, some forces within the FSLN, most clearly headed by Sergio Ramirez, seem determined to develop the organization as a basically social democratic party functioning in the context of the institutions of liberal democratic constitutionalism. Other forces, including those headed at least at times by Daniel Ortega, while not denying the validity of this approach, seem more willing to focus on the continuing possibility of mass actions and on the necessity of the FSLN to respond to even the most militant actions of labor and community organizations. The FSLN is thus itself clearly involved in a continuing transformation.

The Nicaraguan revolution continues not only within the FSLN and in relations between the FSLN and some elements of the government; other revolutionary actors are evident in the present scene. These include armed organizations of ex-*contras* and veterans of the Sandinista army, sometimes acting in unison with each other, labor organizations, and community groups. While the basic FSLN policy is to prefer a sort of social and political stability to the alternative of mass actions, other actors are clearly not so sure that this is the appropriate path for maintaining the Nicaraguan revolution.

New Revolutionary Actors: The *Revueltos* Emerge

Even before the 1990 election a process had begun to demobilize the armed forces known as the *contras*. It is commonly held that this military force, originally consisting of former members of the National Guard under Somoza, had ceased to be a serious military threat in 1987 after the Sandinista Popular Army (EPS) had inflicted a "strategic military defeat" upon them (Barry and Norsworthy, 1991: 368). Under the auspices of the Esquipulas agreement, the Nicaraguan government had made substantial progress in negotiations with the *contra* leadership, capped by a formal agreement at Sapoá. Nevertheless, with continued aid from the U.S. government they continued to be enough of a problem that the Nicaraguan government was unwilling to abolish the military draft. The United States government continued to provide aid to the *contra* forces even after the agreements reached between these forces and the Nicaraguan government, presumably to ensure that the election would go forward. After the election a difficult process of negotiation with the new government led to a "final" disarmament of the counterrevolutionary armed force, which was largely completed by June of 1990.

It is one thing for a government to reach an agreement, it is another thing to comply with it. Clearly the Chamorro government promised much to all of those who agreed to be disarmed. They were promised land, housing, education, a role in the police force, medical aid, special representation in government ministries, in short nearly everything they demanded. Demobilization took place on a large scale.[16] Some of the former fighters, about half, opted to

---

[16]*Envío* points out that official figures from the United Nations Observer Group in Central America (ONUCA) report that 19,613 *contras* had been demobilized by July 5, 1992 even though the *contras* themselves had never claimed to have more than 12,000 fighters and the Sandinistas claimed there were only 8,000 *contras* under arms. A part of the inflated numbers can be accounted for by the benefits each individual received, including new clothes, three months' worth of food, free medical attention, and the right to participate in development poles where they could live

return to their native villages; the another half to go the new development poles as they were given this option for transportation by the International Verification and Support Commission (CIAV). Twenty-five to thirty percent of those exercising each option changed their minds, asking to exercise the other, demonstrating a shifting set of demands by individuals involved in the process (LASA interview with Arthur Garcon, head of CIAV, June 21, 1990).

After the disarmament process had officially come to a close and only small armed bands remained (they were threatened with being treated as "common criminals"), a new force arose. This force consisted of those who had disarmed but claimed that the government was not fulfilling the agreements. These groups, known as *recontras*, demanded compliance with the offers of land, education, and housing. They also often demanded basic changes in the UNO government and in the army. They took diverse actions, including the barricading of roads that had never been blocked during the war, the taking of government offices in rural areas, and the killing of individuals, especially members of rural cooperatives and police, whom they took to be Sandinistas.

This group of *recontras* was widely thought to constitute a sort of shock force for the more right-wing members of UNO, organized around Vice President Godoy. Indeed, it was widely rumored that *recontras* were responsible for violence in Managua against strikers and that they were encouraged by the right-wing elements of UNO. Humberto Ortega accused Godoy of encouraging the re-arming of ex-*contras* and Antonio Lacayo, Chamorro's minister of the presidency, agreed, suggesting that the vice president should resign (*Envío*, August, 1991: A8.)

At the same time as the *contras* were disarming, the Sandinista Army was markedly reduced, the draft was abolished, and many former members of the military found themselves among the growing ranks of the unemployed. These people, as did the *recontras*, began to complain about lack of sufficient attention to their needs and a failure on the part of the government to provide them with the land, housing, education, and medical care that they had been promised. Soon some demobilized army personnel took up arms, presumably partly in order to fight the *recontras*. They

---

and work in newly formed communities (Vol. 19, no. 108, July 1990: 40).

became known as the *recompas*, as military and police personnel were often called *compas* during the Sandinista period of government. Many, inside the government and out, came to fear that the situation would turn into civil war among these two forces and the army.

Yet many within the FSLN had immediately come to the conclusion that the former *contras* were actually not the enemy, but simply peasants who had been lost by the FSLN. Daniel Nuñez, President of the National Union of Farmers and Ranchers (UNAG)[17] said that "there are no counterrevolutionary people, only confused people, tricked people" (LASA interview, June 19, 1990), and both UNAG and the Rural Workers Association (ATC) soon took on the task of attempting to organize together with former *contras*.

By early 1992 it had become clear that many people at the bottom were uniting in their demands against the government.[18] Some of the *recontras* and the *recompas* had even come together and were commonly known as the *revueltos* (or scrambled ones, as in scrambled eggs). For example, these united forces were blocking roads throughout the northern part of the country, an action that had never taken place during the years of the *contra* war. In Jinotega, the president of the local UNAG organization reported that the combined forces were "maintaining positions without arms, at the entrance and the exit of the city" and that they pledged to stay there until the government complied with the agreements that had been made to obtain their disarmament, especially legalization of the properties assigned to them so that they could get credit in order to produce crops. Though the *revueltos* declared that their struggle was a "civic" one, UPI reported that local officials in

---

[17]UNAG was formed in 1981 when the Association of Rural Workers (ATC) decided to group small and medium landowners and cooperative members in a new organization. The ATC was founded prior to the triumph of 1979 in close conjunction with the FSLN. Both UNAG and ATC have maintained very close links with the FSLN.

[18]For a fundamentally different analysis that still sees the *recontras* and the *recompas* as fundamentally opposed to each other, see Isabel Rodriquez, "Alternativas para sobrevivir," *Pensamiento Pensamiento Proprio*, 10, no. 87 (January-February, 1992.)

Jinotega suspected that "some of them could be armed and ready to fight for their rights." There were said to be as many as three thousand of these people and they also were blocking "the entrances and exits of La Trinidad, Estelí, Condega, Palacaguina, San Juan de Río Coco, Quilalí, Ocotal, and the customs offices of El Espino and Las Manos on the border with Honduras." Quoting from *El Nuevo Diario*, UPI reported as following:

> One of the leaders of the uprising, identified as Commander Narciso, declared "we will continue blocking the highways until the government complies with the agreements signed with the National Self Defense Movement" which integrates *recontras*, *recompas* and *campesinos* who have historically demanded land in order to work.
>
> Francisco Zeledón, coordinator of the Sandinista Front in Quilalí said that 1,500 hectares of land would be needed to satisfy the demands of the "*revueltos*" and thus to "avoid a spilling of blood." ("Los 'revueltos' bloquean carreteras en Nicaragua," *La Opinión*, April 23, 1992, 3C)

As the process of people at the bottom coming together has continued to develop, a new United Peasants organization has been formed that joins elements of the demobilized *contras*, demobilized members of the army and other security forces, and UNAG.

In spite of dramatic developments, the disarmament of several new groups of armed insurgents, and a general amnesty in August of 1993, armed groups continued to exist in the countryside. The most dramatic developments included the taking of hostages in the Nicaraguan embassy in Costa Rica, the seizure of a peace-making delegation by a group of *recontras* and the consequent taking of hostages, including the vice president and several other high level UNO officials, by a re-armed Sandinista commando in Managua. Each of these crises was ultimately resolved through negotiation. Even more dramatic was the seizure of the city of Estelí by a group of veterans of the Sandinista army, calling themselves the Revolutionary Front of Workers and Peasants, who used the occasion to take funds from the local banks and to make demands for the fulfillment of promises made by the government to those

41

demobilized both from the army and from *contra* groups. The army retook the city by massive assault using both air and ground forces, recalling the infamous aerial bombardment of the same city by Somoza's forces in 1978 and 1979. Barricades were thrown up in the streets, some of them manned by citizens of the town. There were over two hundred casualties, including at least fifty deaths, some of them women and children. Many citizens of the city were extremely surprised and upset by the strong response of the Sandinista army to this event. One such individual was quoted by the Associated Press as saying "they only asked for justice, a bit of land and a few resources in order to work, to survive and to be able to feed their children and their parents" (*La Opinión*, July 24, 1993: 10A). The events in Estelí followed directly after a call by Daniel Ortega for civic mobilization and was seen by at least some commentators as a response to that call. Yet the Sandinista army, led by Humberto Ortega, undertook a dramatic repressive response.

This situation of armed conflict evidences the paradox of the post-election position of the FSLN and its relation to the continued revolutionary movement. One basic element of the agreement by which the FSLN passed power to UNO was to maintain Humberto Ortega's command of the army. The right wing of UNO and of re-armed *contra* forces has continually demanded his replacment, which finally occurred in late 1994. On the other hand, there has been substantial unhappiness among FSLN members and supporters with Humberto Ortega, beginning with his decorating a U.S. military attaché with the country's highest military medal, the Camillo Ortega medal, named after Humberto and Daniel's brother who died in the insurrection. This discontent was clearly heightened in many quarters after the assault on Sandinista veterans wearing the FSLN's red and black kerchiefs in Estelí. The paradox is that these same actions clearly contribute to the stability in the country and reduces Humberto Ortega's standing among his fellow Sandinistas. As *La Opinión*, a Los Angeles, California, Spanish-language newspaper not generally sympathetic to the FSLN put it in an editorial shortly after the incident in Estelí:

> The bloody episode of the capture and retaking of Estelí perfectly illustrates the paradoxes of the present situation in that country. The rebels were, it appears, mostly Sandinistas. It has even been speculated that

they acted on the stimulus of a discourse by ex-president Daniel Ortega. With this, Sandinismo would appear to have taken up the banner of anti-governmental inconformism that is so extensive in the country.

The ferocious counter attack of the army, commanded by another Sandinista, Humberto Ortega, Daniel's brother, also leaves the Sandinistas in a good situation as it dissipates doubts with respect to the decisive manner in which the government will deal with any type of insurrection. The logical reflection that arises in this respect is: If they deal with the Sandinistas like this what can others expect?

Unfortunately military force is never sufficient to eliminate manifestations of social discontent. There is a lack of effective response to the problems that motivate such expressions of disconformity. On the contrary, the possibility that the situtation can degenerate into a war of all against all is much too great. (July 24, 1993)

Whether the situation will deteriorate to this extent remains an open question. What is not in doubt is that the FSLN, like the government, is faced with a situation in which popular forces continue to act in dramatic ways in order to protect what they take to be revolutionary necessities.

In a sense there appears to be the possibility of revolutionary developments not under the control of any existing political force. The government, with the aid of the FSLN, has been able to defuse some of the problems with armed groups through a series of negotiations and amnesties. Other groups remain active. Many of these are the result of individual acts of discontent in which some strong man unites with a few of his associates into an armed band seeking money, land, and a payoff from the government for once more giving up their arms. The existence of such armed bands has been a feature of Nicaraguan history for over a century. Yet mixed with these groupings in the present context is a clear sense of general grievances in the countryside, leading to the continuing possibility of popular-based groups to which a systemic political response is essential both on the part of the government and any political party, including the FSLN, that pretends to represent popular demands.

Outside of the military context, popular pressures to maintain and even deepen revolutionary gains have been extremely important. The actions of organized labor have been perhaps as significant as those of armed groups.

Labor as an Independent Revolutionary Actor

The FSLN, as well as the government, has had to deal with outbreaks of revolutionary forces organized in massive strikes. The largest union organizations in the country during the Sandinista years were closely associated with the FSLN, combined into the Sandinista Workers Federation (CST). In the last few years of the Sandinista government economic policies placed great burdens on the organized working force. There were substantial layoffs of government workers. Wages, especially for government employees and teachers, were held at low levels in spite of substantial inflation. This situation presented a good opportunity for alternative labor organizing. It was taken advantage of especially by unions associated with the political opposition, often aided by the AFL-CIO, the United States government, and other conservative forces that opposed the Sandinistas. Nevertheless, nearly two-thirds of organized workers during the Sandinista period were in unions affiliated with either the CST or ATC (Barry and Norswothy, 1991: 383). The Nicaraguan government, while it was controlled by the FSLN, was able to maintain a shaky labor peace, largely due to its influence in Sandinista unions. With the change in government the situation altered dramatically.

Strikes broke out among government employees soon after the change of government in 1990. Health workers and teachers engaged in lengthy strikes, including hunger strikes and seizures of work places. Strikes, sometimes involving massive demonstrations and confrontations with police, took place throughout both the old state sector and the private sector. Farm workers organized by the ATC engaged in the seizure of state farms and demanded privatization in favor of the workers. In early January of 1992, workers at Aeronica, the state-run airline, became aware that 49 percent of the airline was to be sold to TACA, the Salvadoran airline company. They demanded immediate delivery of the 20 percent share of the company they felt was their due, in accordance with the agreements of the past year, and a role in the negotiations with TACA. When their requests were refused they placed an airliner across the runway of the international airport, blocking traffic for a few hours. Fifty-seven of them were put in jail for acts of "terrorism" (*Barricada International*, March, 1992: 4). Sugar refinery workers undertook a two-month strike during the *zafra*, or sugar-cane harvest, of 1992, succeeding in obtaining substantial ownership of the refineries and somewhat better wages and working conditions. They also engaged in at least somewhat successful protests in 1993 and again in 1994.

The tables have clearly turned since the days of the Sandinista government. Now the newly formed National Workers' Front (FNT), which includes the CST and twenty-one other labor federations, is actively opposed to much government policy. The old anti-government unions, now largely grouped in the Permanent Workers' Congress (CPT) and the National Workers' Confederation (CTN), find themselves in support of the government, or of UNO opponents of the government, in many cases and opposed to the FNT's actions. Both the CPT and the CTN, for example, opposed the two national strikes of May and June of 1991 (Instituto de Estudios Nicaragüenses, 1991: 64–65).

These two earlier strikes set the model for labor relations in the period of the new government. In spite of claims on the right, it is clear that the strikes resulted from the action of the unions themselves. They were not instigated by the FSLN, as such. Nevertheless, when the situations became critical, FSLN leadership, headed by Daniel Ortega, entered negotiations with the government and was able to produce results acceptable to the unions and their members. In the second strike these results were not obtained until after people in many areas of Managua had constructed barricades in the streets in support of the strikers, which were often removed and rebuilt. Violence took place, including the shooting of several strike supporters by armed civilians thought by many to be re-armed *contras* supported by Vice President Godoy. A pro-Sandinista radio station was destroyed by a fire set by opponents of the strikers. Later, especially in the case of the earlier strike, union leaders and the rank and file complained about lack of compliance with the agreements.

As the Chamorra presidency has gone along such strikes have continued, not always dominated by the FNT. In September of 1993 transport workers, including taxi, bus, and truck owners, as well as the owners of private vehicles, objected to a new tax on vehicle licensing and a raise in the price of fuel. As transport came to a halt the city of Managua took on the appearance of a city involved in insurrection with armed citizens occupying barricades thrown up in the streets in a manner reminiscent of the insurrection that overthrew Somoza. A police officer and at least one civilian were killed by gunfire. Ultimately, negotiations conducted under the auspices of the National Assembly led to a reversal of government policy. Some critics of the government from within UNO, including Francisco Mayorga, president of the Central Bank during the early Chamorro period, attributed the action to the Ortega brothers and saw it as a contest of wills between them and President Chamorro (*La Opinión*, September 25, 1993: 7A). Yet it is clear that this action was independent of the FSLN, organized by the National Transport Commission. Once more, popular forces were unwilling to comply with government actions they considered damaging to their interests without substantial opposition, including resorting to massive public displays that threaten the stability of the government.

The role of the FSLN in these labor actions is an interesting one. It seems clear that the FSLN national leadership is committed to maintaining a substantial degree of stability in the country, fearing that if the new government is unable to maintain itself the FSLN will be blamed for bringing it down. Yet the FSLN also must respond to the forceful demands of those sectors to which it has been historically committed. Clearly this is a double-edged sword. Every time strikes or civil disturbances break out right-wing forces accuse the FSLN of creating "anarchy and chaos" and thus of attempting to overthrow the constitutional order. Even though it is at least sometimes clear that these actions spring from other sources, the FSLN will be held responsible for what happens. Under these circumstances, and given the fact that many community and labor leaders involved in these actions are FSLN militants, it is incumbent on the FSLN national leadership to attempt to bring together the leaders of the actions and the government to reach some solution, at least temporarily. This leads to further criticism by the right, as well as from some at the base that the FSLN is selling them out by playing the role of pacifier rather than leader of revolutionary forces.

Sandinistas in the Streets

A good example of this dynamic was produced when, the very day after ceremonies had been held to commemorate the death of Carlos Fonseca, his tomb (a national monument, including an "eternal flame" that was extinguished for a time by the Managua city government on the orders of Arnaldo Alemán) was bombed and partially destroyed. Historical collaborators with the FSLN as well as militants from local base communities spontaneously went to the streets, without any official call to action by the leadership. They quickly began repairing the tomb on their own, though the army soon announced that it would undertake the project. They began to look for targets of their anger, working in several different groups. They felt sufficiently angry that had the police not "distanced themselves" from the demonstrators they, at least according to one participant in the action, "would have resisted violently and burned down President Violetta's house (interview with local FSLN base militant, a father of nine, in Monseñor Lezcano, a working-class sector of Managua, April 9, 1992). Ultimately a large rally was called at which Daniel Ortega gave a militant speech that ended in calling on the people to go home and to continue the struggle in a peaceful manner. The response of the right was to allege that Ortega was calling for more chaos while some people felt that he had simply calmed down the crowd unnecessarily.

All of this makes clear that revolutionary forces continue to act in Nicaragua, whether the FSLN wants them to or not. The FSLN must respond to these forces, just as must the government. The president and administration have found it necessary to deal with the FSLN as a legitimate force. The FSLN is thus put in the strange position of accommodating itself to government policies while at the same time making strong demands for the maintenance of the gains of the revolution as understood by the popular sectors. It is clear that FSLN leaders, at least members of the National Assembly, see this as at the same time a "pragmatic" posture and one that simply assures the existence of institutions to respond to popular demands (interviews with Carlos Zamora and Orlando

Piñeda, members of the National Assembly, April 1992). Yet here the FSLN is not itself the revolutionary force, it is responding to revolutionary forces almost by trying to pacify them.

While it is impossible to predict the future, the situation as it exists has deep roots in the theory and practice of the revolution that has been developing from the time of Sandino. Understanding the theory and practice of the FSLN can serve as a guidepost in making sense of what occurs as the process develops. The following analysis is an attempt to determine the major aspects of Sandinista theory, its successes, and the contradictions and problems to which it has given rise during the period when the FSLN controlled the government and the state. The first part of the analysis will focus on the development of the theory in relation to practice, the second part on problems that arose in the actual practice headed by the FSLN.

2

DEVELOPMENT OF THE POLITICAL
IDEAS OF THE NICARAGUAN REVOLUTION:
FROM SANDINO AND FONSECA
TO THE TRIUMPH

While the early formation of the ideas of those that led the FSLN to revolutionary triumph was substantially influenced by Marxism, the unique character of the Nicaraguan revolution is a result of its connection with the struggle in the mountains of northern Nicaragua from 1927 to 1933 led by Augusto C. Sandino. Sandino and his small army fought fundamentally to free the country from domination by the United States. As Carlos Fonseca began to formulate ideas of his own, independent of the views of the Nicaraguan Socialist Party, he looked to Sandino for guidance. Sandino himself was more a fighter than a theorist but his numerous writings, mostly descriptions of events in his armed struggle, have been a source of much inspiration for the FSLN. It is clear that Carlos Fonseca paid a great deal of attention to whatever he could learn of Sandino and his ideas. It is the unique blending of this study with other ideas, including those derived from Marxism, that constitutes the foundation of Sandinsta theory. Yet there is no clear agreement about the relationship between the ideas of Fonseca and Sandino.

Fonseca and Sandino

Whether Fonseca's ideas and practice deviate in a serious way from that of Sandino is a politically charged question. Some would allege that while Sandinismo is a genuine Nicaraguan view, the FSLN has perverted it into purposes fundamentally inconsistent with those of Sandino and many who have followed his thoughts and actions (see Zelaya, 1985: 6ff.). Thus, it is possible to allege that Sandino's struggle represented a truly nationalist response to conditions of foreign domination and yet that contemporary Sandinismo, as represented by the FSLN, is inconsistent with Sandino's own legacy,[1] or that Sandino's real views were fundamentally different from those that were attributed to him by Fonseca in some other way. Indeed, one of the most thorough and interesting recent studies of the relationship between Sandino and Fonseca casts the question in terms of Fonseca "reconstructing Sandino" (Palmer, 1988: 97–101).

Here Fonseca will be treated as a student who set out to learn *from* Sandino, not to use Sandino simply to teach others.[2] Fonseca, as Sandino before him, was an actor who was looking for theoretical guidance and was willing to develop a theoretical perspective of his own as a result of such a search. Tomás Borge puts this perspective

---

[1]See Donald Hodges' intelligent discussion of this issue in relation to Eden Pastora and Jeane Kirkpatrick. He points out in a concise manner the difficulties of their analysis, yet his own view shares a certain logic with theirs. He holds that we should understand Sandino as an anarcho-communist whose views are in substantial contradiction with Marxism-Leninism (Hodges, 1986: 292–93).

[2]Here, as elsewhere, it should be understood that I am not denying legitimacy to other interpretations such as those of Palmer or Hodges, as a matter of intellectual history. But for the purpose of understanding the political ideas of the FSLN as a practical political matter it seems reasonable to think of the question from a fundamentally different perspective. It is interesting in this context to note that Fonseca in 1975 referred to attempts by others, specifically Pedro Joaquin Chamorro, to use the image of Sandino for purposes opposed to those of the FSLN, fearing that these were related to the possibility of plans for late attacks on the FSLN from those who claimed the banner of Sandino but did not agree with the FSLN (Fonseca, 1985: 174). This point, as well as others made in the analysis from which it is drawn, do make clear that Fonseca was aware of the necessity to tone down the use of radical, especially Marxist, language, to "search for patriotic expressions and those against exploitation made by representatives of past national culture and to make such citations widely known" (173). This does not show that Fonseca *only* used Sandino for this purpose but it makes clear that it was one element of his work. It is notable that Sandino did the same with Zeledon.

well when he says that "Carlos saw in Sandino and his ideas not an eternal symbol, not an abstract symbol, but a guide for the comprehension of Nicaraguan reality and its revolutionary transformation" (Borge, 1984: 57).

Fonseca was influenced quite early in his revolutionary activity and theoretical understanding by the position of the Nicaraguan Socialist Party (PSN). His trip to the Soviet Union and Eastern Europe at the age of 21 while still a law student in León led to an ebullient description of the Soviet Union ("*Un nicaragüense en Moscu,*" in Fonseca, 1985: 29–96). He had read Marx, Engels, Lenin, and Mao as well as numerous liberal writers, including John Steinbeck (Humberto Ortega in Fonseca, 1985: 19) and was clearly a Marxist of some sort very early in his revolutionary activity;[3] he speaks of creating a "communist cell" at the university in 1955 (at the age of 19). He says that he was considered a militant in the "Communist Party" (referring to the PSN) at this time though he says that its actual influence was weak (Fonseca, 1985: 290–91). Yet, as was the case with Sandino, his views and those of the official Communist Party were always in tension. He told the National Guard interrogators who had arrested him on his return from Moscow that he was not a "communist" but that he didn't "hate communist ideas, I am in agreement with the Marxist philosophy." He went on to elaborate that he agreed, for example, with the Brazilian Communist Party in its anti-imperialist program but that he disagreed with the "politics followed by the Communist Party of Hungary until before the counterrevolution of October, 1956." He further proceeded to say that his disagreement was due to the fact that the major objective of the latter party was to "servilely copy the methods used by the Russian communists" (Fonseca, 1985: 242).

It is not unreasonable to assume that Fonseca went to Sandino as much to make sense of his own practical and theoretical dilemmas as to develop an "ideology of Sandinismo" to manipulate

---

[3]In his declaration to the National Guard upon being held for questioning on his return from Moscow in 1957 he speaks of having "repeatedly read" a number of books, including Lenin's *Leftwing Communism, an Infantile Disorder, The Communist Manifesto*, a summary of *Capital*, Engels' *Origin of Private Property, the Family and the State*, as well as Mao and other authors, apparently when he was 17 or 18 years of age (Fonseca, 1985: 241).

others. There was not some already developed view that he wanted to mimic. On the contrary, he clearly wanted to make sense of the reality in which he was working in the context of a generalized sense of Marxian theory. His genius was evidenced partly by his willingness to make sense of Marxian ideas by looking to Nicaraguan history as much as to other experiences. The figure of Sandino was the primary Nicaraguan precedent for what he wanted to do. He speaks of having heard of Sandino when he was ten or twelve years old. He also had been told that a distant relative who had been active in Sandino's movement had been assassinated in the massacre of Sandino supporters (1985: 293). Borge says that when he and Fonseca had formed the first "Marxist cell" at the university in Léon, Fonseca said that "Sandino is a kind of road. It would be frivolous to reduce him to the category of one more ephemeral annual disturbance." The response of the leader of the group, Noel Guerrero Santiago, who had been in the PSN, was to say that Sandino "struggled against foreign occupation, not against imperialism" (Borge, 1984: 20; and 1989).[4]

Thus Fonseca was not only aware of Sandino at this time but also of the fact that the PSN, and thus the international Communist

[4]It is of passing interest to note that in the earlier work (1984) Borge refers to the person involved in this discussion simply as "a man from Leon who lived in Mexico and about whom we never knew whether he was a coarse fellow *(charro)* or a Marxist militant." In this work he says that "we were recruited through the Socialist Party and Carlos directed the first Marxist cell of Nicaraguan university students." Here he says that the three students were Carlos Fonseca, Silvio Mayorga, and Tomás Borge. In the later work, *La Paciente Impaciencia*, Borge goes into a great deal more detail, including the claim that Noel Guerrero Santiago was at that time the political leader of the FSLN (*"El mando político en 1963 estuvo centralizado por Noel Guerrero Santiago,"* 186). He notes that Guerrero left the FSLN after charges involving misuse of money, that they didn't know where he was, although they thought that he was probably in Mexico. He further notes that they no longer considered him a traitor, merely someone who was "victimized by personal weaknesses" (187). This is interesting not only in terms of the dispute about Sandino but in terms of the exact historical relationship between the PSN and the early FSLN. Clearly the later work is the product of more intensive reflection and analysis. It appears that Borge wants to assert that the FSLN had already split from the PSN by 1963.

movement, held him in some disrespect. To go back to study Sandino in this context, especially after the rebuke of his political instructor at the time, was to look independently at a Nicaraguan phenomenon, not merely to resurrect a nationalist symbol for use by the pre-existing Marxist movement. Borge points out, through the use of a quotation from Jaime Wheelock's book (1986b), that at the time of the conversation about Sandino the organization was called simply the "National Liberation Front." Fonseca's study and writing on Sandino was important; it led to the name change "Sandinista Front for National Liberation." In this context Borge says:

> Our vanguard—the FSLN—, born into humble swaddling clothes, torn by the initial sufferings, surrounded by darkness, anxiously desired (*requería de*) a visionary, a guide, a mystic, a generous man, a leader who made himself great by forgetting himself and by the mastery with which he joined (*conjugaba*) critical energy with a brotherhood that was in each cell of his singular stature. Carlos Fonseca was the principal founder of our dreams, the head, from once to forever, of the Sandinista Front for National Liberation. (1989: 184)

Lessons from Cuba

It is universally recognized that the triumph of the Cuban Revolution in 1959 was a major inspiration to those struggling against the Somoza dictatorship. The Cuban case made clear once again that armed struggle was possible. According to Fonseca, the quarter century of Somocista rule had led to sporadic rebellions but not to "revolutionary consciousness, nor organization" because Marxism did not "penetrate Nicaragua" until the Cuban Revolution led to Marxism "seizing a broad sector of the Nicaraguan youth" (Fonseca, 1985: 293).

Yet it is not always sufficiently understood that the first Nicaraguan response to the Cuban struggle led more to defeat than to victory. As Fonseca said in 1968–69, although the period immediately following the Cuban revolution marked the "gestation period of the armed revolutionary struggle," from 1959 to 1962 armed struggles each led by a different group "reflected the clear anarchy that plagued the insurrectionary revolutionary struggle"

(Fonseca, 1985: 159, 160). During this period, according to Fonseca, elements that came to form the FSLN "vacillated in presenting a clearly Marxist-Leninist ideology" partially because of the position of the PSN in opposing armed struggle (1985: 161–62). It does not stretch the imagination to suggest that among the FSLN itself this reflected the question of how to square its own Marxism-Leninism, developed within or close to the PSN, not only with the Cuban case but also with what they could learn from the theory and practice of Sandino.

Writing in one of his carefully developed chronologies in 1972, Fonseca pointed out that the year 1965 marked a momentary interruption in the armed revolution, even though it was pretended at the time that it was simply a period of "accumulating forces." He attributed this to a "decrease in the discipline of many revolutionary militants" (1985: 378). Undoubtedly the FSLN and Fonseca learned anew from the Cuban experience that armed struggle could defeat even an overwhelmingly stronger enemy but they also could see that this lesson had its own origin in Nicaragua (Fonseca, 1985: 179). It wasn't that the Cuban experience taught a lesson not applicable to Nicaragua, it was that the Nicaraguans must look to their own history more clearly to see how the lesson applied. The FSLN shared the enthusiasm created by the Cuban triumph as did numerous other revolutionary groups throughout the world. Yet the death of Che and the failure of numerous attempts at armed struggle which blossomed from the Cuban example must have led the FSLN to look for its own success in an understanding of the Nicaraguan experience itself.

Thus it is all too easy to understand the use of Sandino by the FSLN as a simple copy of the use of Martí by the July 26 Movement in Cuba; what is at least as realistic is that the FSLN looked to Sandino because he presented an historically relevant figure to make sense of their own situation, a figure who had a real resonance in their own consciousness and that even preceded their exposure to Marxist or socialist ideas. It isn't that Castroite revolutionaries in Nicaragua dreamed up a connection with Sandino to fool the Nicaraguan people; indeed, in a manifesto written in 1964, Fonseca pointed out that he and other FSLN cadre had been fighting even before Fidel Castro was in the mountains (1985: 315). Rather, revolutionaries in Nicaragua who were encouraged by Cuban success looked to the experience of Sandino to understand the situation in their own terms. The question is what Fonseca had to learn from Sandino as much as it is how he could use stories about him to teach others.

Politics, the Armed Struggle, and the PSN

From 1963, when the predecessors of the FSLN were defeated in armed struggle at Rio Bocay and Rio Coco, until the action at Pancasán in 1966, the FSLN limited itself, in practice, largely to "legal work among the masses." What this experience demonstrated, according to Fonseca, was "that the revolutionary armed struggle (urban and rural) is the motor of the revolutionary movement of Nicaragua. The armed struggle is the only thing that can inspire revolutionary combatants in Nicaragua to complete the tasks that the revolutionary directorate determines, whether they be armed or of some other revolutionary quality" (Fonseca, 1985: 162).

Fonseca's basic critique of Sandino was that he was unable to combine his correct military strategy, also based on the rebellious tradition of Nicaragua, with a correct political strategy (see, for example, Fonseca, 1985: 353). Fonseca's explanation of this phenomenon is a key ingredient in the philosophy of the FSLN. On this matter Fonseca spent a great deal of theoretical energy, even though commentators (especially those working in the English language) usually fail to follow up on this lead to the real connection between Fonseca and Sandino. Many prefer to see Fonseca as simply using Sandino's ideas in an ideological manner (Nolan, 1984: 17–18; Hodges, 1986: 161ff.; and Palmer, 1988). If we assume that Fonseca and the FSLN knew what to do and that this included using the image of Sandino to rally support for their cause among a broad mass of people on basically nationalist grounds it may make sense to simply explain the relation between Fonseca and Sandino in this way. A more reasonable assumption is that Fonseca undertook a serious historical examination of Sandino (and much else in Nicaraguan history) in order to help understand what was to be done.

After over ten years of armed struggle following the Cuban triumph, with no clear end in sight, the question was how to make sense of the Nicaraguan situation in terms of the Marxian theory Fonseca and most of the other FSLN leadership shared. In Marxian theory it is not enough to simply say that a revolutionary attempt failed because there was something wrong with the strategy of the leadership; it is necessary to explain why such strategy was followed and why it failed. Palmer is willing to dismiss this question by simply alleging that

> Like all historical protagonists, Sandino could not have been expected to comprehend fully or voice his role. Only after a few more turns in the wheel of history could his real historical purpose and significance be understood. Moreover, only FSLN members—the Nicaraguan nucleus of the "generation of the Cuban Revolution"—with their Marxist hermeneutical skills were deemed capable of understanding and fulfilling Sandino's struggle. (1988: 99)

Similarly Nolan discusses "the progressive process of truth making itself known to those whose actions constitute the motor of the process" (1984: 107). All of this simply begs the question. What we need to know is what Fonseca and his *compañeros* thought they found out from their analysis.

The prevailing analysis within the PSN and the pro-Soviet international Communist movement was that Sandino was a "petty-bourgeois *caudillo*" (Palmer, 1988: 95). As Fonseca points out, shortly before Sandino's assassination the Anti-Imperialist League condemned his "betrayal of 1930." Fonseca explicitly sees the position of the Anti-Imperialist League as a precursor to the position of Earl Browder (Fonseca, 1985: 406). It is important to see that Fonseca, though he had earlier connections with the PSN, considered it an economistic group which merely organized "small groups of workers to demand salary increases" (Fonseca, 1985: 376), and which had a "chronic tendency to act at the tail of the traditional political bands controlled by the exploiting classes" (1985: 375).

The major dispute between the PSN and the FSLN was, of course, the question of whether to take up arms. At the risk of parodying the position of the PSN and other Latin American communist parties in general, it may be said that their view was that Latin America, in most cases, was basically feudal. Thus the process of change required a substantial role for the newly developing national bourgeoisie which could help usher in capitalism and liberalism. The role of the Communists was to join in a united front with the liberal national bourgeoisie to obtain progress through the electoral arena. The FSLN, as had the July 26 Movement in Cuba, rejected this analysis. It is impossible to understand the dynamic of the theoretical development of the FSLN or of the July 26th Movement without taking into account the basis of their rejection of the "official" view and the new theoretical synthesis they developed to make sense of their own struggle.

Fonseca's View of Nicaraguan History

In his introduction to the second volume of Fonseca's collected works, entitled *Viva Sandino*, Jaime Wheelock writes that:

> Carlos understood the necessity of synthesizing the experience of the Sandinista Front which was accumulated in over ten years of permanent struggle and of deepening the same in the original antecedents of the new deeds (*gesta*), that is to say in the fertile teachings of our War of Liberation headed by Sandino. . . . Carlos worked in preparation of the *Cronología* for more than a year wanting to precisely provide to the militancy a practical instrument that would aid in understanding the roots of our cause, the form in which Sandino and his detachment victoriously confronted a formidable army, the validity of the Sandinista cause and, principally the political, ideological and military context in which it should constitute the foundation of our platforms of struggle. (Fonseca, 1985a: 15)

He further characterizes Fonseca's work as being constructed in accordance with "his penetrating vision that integrated an indispensable dialectical portion to make sense of the Sandinista deeds and to extract their lessons" (Fonseca, 1985a: 15). Fonseca's analysis is not the work of someone who is attempting simply to develop an "ideology" by which to manipulate other political actors, it is the activity of a truly creative Marxian theorist, looking for strategic guidance from the history of the social system within which he works in the attempt to promote revolution.

At first sight it appears that Fonseca's chronology is merely another long-winded Nicaraguan history lesson that begins with the promulgation of the Monroe Doctrine on December 2, 1823 and ends with the first Tri-Continental Conference in 1966. Even worse, the introduction to the chronology, entitled "Viva Sandino," reveals that the reader is to be treated to a history lesson that begins with Columbus in 1492. Yet reading the work carefully makes clear that it is a full-blown piece of Marxian historical research. It provides the reader with a fundamentally new understanding of how Marxian theory can make sense of Nicaraguan history in the context of "neocolonialism."[5] This, as well as reading the earlier chronology, called "The Chronological History of Nicaragua," shows that Fonseca has developed a view about the relationship of U.S. imperialism, class struggles in Nicaragua and the history of Nicaraguan politics that provides clear lessons for future FSLN activity and self understandings.

Sandino often railed against the "magnates of Wall Street" and the "bankers of America" (see, for example, Sandino, 1984: 277). His "Plan for the Realization of the Dream of Bolivar" took the form of a proposal to be considered by a conference of twenty-one Latin American states. In it he affirms that he is "deeply convinced . . . that North American capitalism has arrived at its final stage of development, transforming itself, as a consequence into imperialism" (1984: 341). Sandino was especially concerned about the U.S. interest in an inter-oceanic canal or railroad through Nicaragua, and the concomitant commitment of the U.S. to preserve its investment in the Panama Canal through building naval stations and through maintaining a monopoly of the right to construct any system of transportation across the Nicaraguan isthmus. Indeed, he

---

[5]It appears that this term makes its first appearance in Fonseca's writings in *Nicaragua Hora Cero*, originally published in 1969 to replace what he earlier referred to as the "semi-feudal and semi-colonial" status of the country. Here there is insufficient time and space to fully explore the implications of this change of phraseology but it is possible to suggest that it reflects a move from a rather traditional Marxism to what Hodges calls "the New Marxism" (1986: passim). One problem with such an analysis would be that Fonseca states in a later essay in which he also uses the term neocolonial that Latin America had "feudal societies" as late as 1932 (Fonseca, 1985a: 67).

proposed that the Latin American presidents should reserve to their own capital the right to build a canal as well as a naval base in the Gulf of Fonseca (1984: 349). In any case he thought that if the United States were to be allowed to build the canal with its own capital, the twenty-one Latin American states should demand that this be accompanied by a treaty which would require the United States to forego, in Sandino's words, "all North American interference in our Republics and refrain from interfering in our internal affairs, agreeing as well that the United States of North America should not foment rebellions against the Governments of Latin America, Continental or Antillian that do not want to convert themselves into hand servants of the governments of the United States of North America" (1984: 340).

It is hardly surprising to find Fonseca alleging, as did Sandino before him, that the role of the United States was a significant fact in Nicaraguan history and contemporary Nicaraguan life and that the question of the inter-oceanic route was of prime importance in this phenomenon. What is important is that Fonseca was able to provide a sophisticated and subtle analysis of the relationship of this fact to political and economic reality within Nicaragua itself. This analysis is embedded in Fonseca's discussion of Nicaraguan history.

From his perspective, the question is why Nicaragua, even at the time of Sandino, lacked a clear socialist or working-class based analysis of political reality in spite of its clear tradition of political rebellion among substantial elements of the working population, especially the peasantry. His answer has several elements, each of which relates to why there had been no real liberal tradition in Nicaragua.

The first fundamental element in Fonseca's explanation relates to the fact that the interests of the great powers in Nicaragua had been, even since the time of the Spanish conquest, fundamentally related to its geographical position. It is especially important that communication between the Atlantic and the Pacific oceans is made possible by Nicaragua's geography (1985a: 23–24, 27–30, 33, 36–40). In his view, this helps explain why the single Central American state that was created shortly after independence was broken asunder into the several states that exist today and and why Francisco Morazán, president of the Central American Federation at the time of its dissolution was executed (thus preventing him from restoring unity among the Central American Republics (1985a: 28). It also explains, in Fonseca's analysis much of nineteenth century Nicaraguan political history. Furthermore, it explains a great deal about what he sees as the way in which the incipient class conflict which began in the latter half of the nineteenth century was resolved in Nicaragua.

Although the revolt against the Spanish in Nicaragua had some elements of "an uprising of the multitudes," the extreme wealth of the "reactionary" landlord sector (made possible by the fertility of Nicaraguan soil) was such as to make possible their domination of the post-independence period. Thus, until the last half of the nineteenth century, although substantial political violence continued, it was simply a question of fighting over governmental "booty" (1985a: 26–27).

After 1855 and the expulsion of William Walker, the U.S. adventurer who seized Nicaragua by force of arms, declared English the official language and legalized slavery, Nicaragua, according to Fonseca, "remained under the yoke of the landlords, represented politically by the conservative oligarchy" though the "incipient" bourgeoisie came to play some role in the process. Partially as a result of the addition of coffee to the traditional ranching element of agriculture in Nicaragua in the last few years of the nineteenth century and in much of the rest of Central America at an earlier date, the feudal system began to break down and liberal ideas were "inexorably" diffused through the country, even though the conservatives were able to generally prevent the "realization of the liberal reform that Nicaraguan society required" (1985a: 33–34). In this context Fonseca notes that the so-called War of the Indians of 1881 was both a "visible symptom of the decomposition of the feudal sector" and a significant "antecedent" of Sandino's war, which involved similar people fighting in roughly the same area. Indeed, he alleges that FSLN fighters as well as Sandino's men heard stories of this earlier struggle as they fought in the mountains around Matagalpa (1985a: 34). Tomás Borge makes much of the fact that those involved in these rebellions, which took place in the home province of both Borge and Fonseca, painted themselves in red and black, colors also worn by Sandino's fighters and the colors of the FSLN flag (Borge, 1989: 32–33).

In 1893 the liberals, through an open war with the "popular mass" fighting on their side, succeeded in taking power and "establishing a regime which began the liberal reform" (1985a: 35).

This was an exclusively bourgeois liberalism, according to Fonseca, though it was aided in its military campaigns by *campesinos* and the broad masses. The lack of a working class, except to a minimal degree on the Atlantic coast among miners, and agricultural and commercial workers, meant that socialist ideas (typically brought by European working-class immigrants into other Latin American countries) were absent from the Nicaraguan context. Thus, according to Fonseca, the whole period that preceded the Cuban Revolution was marked by the fact that "the liberal bourgeois method would, during much of the time, be the only instrument of analysis of the national problems" (1985a: 35). The primitive agricultural character of the bulk of the economy was a fundamental element of the situation.

Thus, it would appear, the process of liberal bourgeois development had begun in Nicaragua in the late nineteenth century. Nicaragua was not, as some would have it, a country where feudalism had always dominated; bourgeois liberalism had its own impact. Perhaps, Fonseca seems to suggest, the "bourgeois social democratic process would have continued its natural evolution" if it had not been for the direct intervention of the United States government. As he puts it:

> The new breaking out of Yankee aggressions against Nicaragua since 1909 signified the imposition of a great historic frustration in the process of development of Nicaraguan society. The political change operating in 1893 constituted the most important political step registered in Nicaraguan affairs aside from the emancipation from Spain and the expulsion of the filibusterers. (1985a: 38)
>
> Because Zelaya threatened the canal interests of the United States, it intervened and granted power once again to the oligarchy that Zelaya had overthrown with popular backing. It meant that Nicaragua would not be left to itself to develop on its own terms, but rather that it would have to develop in a condition in which it was the "prey of the growing North American monster." (1985a: 39)

Internal Nicaraguan political life thus came to reflect a peculiar situation in which the old feudal class maintained political hegemony simply because of its connection with the political and strategic interests of a dominant foreign power. The death of Diego Manuel Chamorro in 1923 while he held the office of president led to a short period in which Bartolomé Martínez attempted, through the *"Transsacción"* to build a conservative-liberal alliance and to reduce direct American presence. The coup of 1925, headed by Emiliano Chamorro, was an attempt to break this alliance in the interests of the "most closed oligarchy." Here, the liberals, specifically Juan B. Sacasa (whom Fonseca describes as a recent liberal whose clan had shared conservative domination of the country with the Chamorros throughout the nineteenth century) and José María Moncada, were, according to Fonseca, representing the interests of an "atrophied bourgeoisie" (1985a: 42). The U.S., of course, supported Chamorro or, more exactly, his presidential designee, Adolfo Díaz.

The Constitutionalist War represented the last vestiges of revolutionary action on the part of the liberals, headed by Moncada and Sacasa. As all other incidents of political violence in Nicaragua, most of the fighting was done by *campesinos* in accordance with the tradition of political rebellion characteristic of Nicaragua. However, this time there was an additional element, represented especially well by Sandino, "a worker of peasant extraction" in Fonseca's words (1985a: 42). Sandino, who had travelled to Mexico where he was exposed to workers' struggles and the Mexican Revolution as well as "the gusts of the proletarian wind of the Bolshevik October" (1985a: 43) joined in the Constitutionalist struggle. Although his strategy of fighting in the Segovias was originally rejected by Moncada, he ultimately succeeded in developing a successful guerilla war against government troops. He was aided in this strategy, according to Fonseca, by the fact that the *campesinos* of the Segovias, where he chose to fight, were threatened by the growth of coffee culture on the part of *latifundistas*, the owners of large agricultural estates (1985a: 44).

The war itself, however, was not officially led by such elements; it was headed by Moncada. Once again, liberalism in Nicaragua was fundamentally affected by the direct intervention of the United States. This time, however, the leaders of the Liberal Party were not simply defeated, they were bought. Fonseca alleges that the treaty of *Espino Negro,* through which Moncada agreed to lay down arms, represented "the burying of the Nicaraguan national bourgeoisie as a revolutionary class which opted to associate itself with the feudal and reactionary classes and indissolubly fused itself with them" (1985a: 47).

Fonseca's critique of Nicaraguan history convinced him that the national bourgeoisie was not a new element of Nicaraguan life constituting a valuable part of a coalition to struggle against a basically feudal regime, but rather an old actor on the scene which had lost its revolutionary credentials once and for all in 1927. The peculiar conjuncture of events in which the bourgeoisie had fused itself with the class which preceded it as the major economic force was not merely a result of the working out of Nicaraguan class relationships on their own terms; it was a result of direct intervention by an imperial power. Though the imperial power certainly derived economic benefits in the traditional sense from this relationship, its main interest was strategic and political.

Thus a sort of simple-minded picture, held by some "Marxists," of the role of the national bourgeoisie as a progressive force in battling imperialism is seen as a barrier to making sense of the real revolutionary situation in Nicaragua. Here we have a concrete case in which Fonseca is avoiding what he elsewhere terms "economic materialism; a falsification of Marxism" (Fonseca, 1985: 184). His historical analysis seems to take into account the fact that a simple reduction of revolutionary possibilities to economic categories can make sense neither of history nor of present practice.

In the historical analysis as so far developed, Fonseca has made clear that the real forces with which Sandino had to contend were fundamentally insurmountable. Sandino thus does not appear as simply a proletarian fighter who lost. He appears as a man working in an historical context both within Nicaragua and within the world in which he could have never succeeded in making a revolution even had he held a consistent and appropriate political strategy, although he could struggle in a meaningful manner.

Sandino's "partial victory" in expelling the U.S. Marines showed that guerrilla combat and strategy could succeed in Nicaragua even against overwhelming odds. The problem was that his fundamentally military organization could not produce a corresponding political development. Among other things this meant that Sandino was "forced, in spite of the fact that his personal temperament never inclined him toward arrogant individualism, to imprint an individual stamp to the central command of the anti-imperialist resistance." Fonseca insists that this was due "essentially to the objective and subjective conditions of the space and time" in which Sandino acted (1985a: 64).

Much ink has been spilled over what Sandino's exact ideas were and how they relate to socialism of various kinds. Fonseca clearly thought that Sandino's failure to create a socialist system was due to factors outside of Sandino's control. He was a worker, he had been exposed to socialist ideas, he expressed his interest in the proletariat and in creating a classless society, but these things were not enough. The issue is not whether Sandino had particular ideas, but what ideas could have resonance in the population at that time, in that space. In Fonseca's view, one fundamental element of the situation was that, properly speaking, "class consciousness did not exist" in Nicaragua (1985a: 48). Not until the Cuban Revolution in 1959 did Marxist ideas come to have any resonance in popular sectors of Nicaragua and Fonseca indicates that even as late as 1971 it was possible to discuss whether a "true workers movement" had arrived in Nicaragua (1985a: 35).

Fonseca also points out that the relationship between Sandino's struggle and the contemporary revolutionary movement both inside and outside Nicaragua were of substantial significance to the ultimate outcome for Nicaragua in the early 1930s. Here Fonseca strongly criticizes the "utopian pacifists within Nicaragua" but emphasizes even more strongly the relationship between Sandino and the international communist movement. Far from suggesting stronger links than really existed between Sandino and contemporary socialist movements, Fonseca asserts that "the progressive content of Sandino's ideas was not justly appreciated at any time by the nascent Latin American revolutionary sector" (1985a: 69). He attributes Sandino's break with the Mexican Communist Party to a "closed sectarianism" which marked the position of the party and says they engaged in "the most absurd conjectures, in the name of an aberrant dialectic" (1985a: 71).

Here Fonseca is not interested in simply throwing stones, suggesting that people should have acted differently; he seeks an explanation of the problems in something more than mere individual or group will. He says that there has been no real analysis of the "attitude of the international revolutionary movement towards the

Sandinista resistance," that one should be undertaken and that its "lessons can serve to avoid old errors in new times and to extend due solidarity to countries, that since they are small are lashed by the reaction. This logically makes solidarity more urgent" (1985a: 71).

There are fundamentally four factors in Fonseca's analysis of the failure of the international revolutionary movement to make proper sense of Sandino's movement. They are:

1. A failure to understand the international conjuncture of forces. This included a failure, especially on the part of parties in the Caribbean and Latin America who took a "dogmatic" view, to understand that the United States was the fundamental imperialist threat in Latin America. It was also a result of the fact that there was a "lack of flexibility" in combining the needs of local struggles with the need to defend the Soviet Union.

2. The anti-imperialist movement was at an early stage in those countries, especially in East Asia, where it ultimately succeeded.

3. Many intellectual revolutionaries misunderstood the tactics that led to his minimal demands because they looked upon Sandino, the worker-peasant, with an attitude of intellectual vanity. Fonseca asks: "Couldn't it be that the professors in revolutionary programs elaborated on desk-tops didn't want to understand the genial efficacy of a tactic of struggle, the guerilla tactic, that the *campesinos* could undertake in the mountain ranges of Nicaragua?" (1985a: 73).

4. The international struggle in colonies and semi-colonies had not yet made clear the "fundamental importance" of rural armed struggle. (1985a: 72–75)

At the same time he alleges that Trotskyists engaged in "anti-Yankee demagogy" but that under the circumstances, this merely served to confuse the situation. He criticizes the American Popular Revolutionary Alliance's (APRA) view as "petty bourgeois." Finally, his point is that all revolutionaries "have a complete right to express opinions in accordance with [their] own criteria about a particular situation, but an opinion should never be used as a pretext for refusing to occupy a place in the trench" (1985a: 74).

Upon completing his analysis of revolutionary criticisms of Sandino, Fonseca makes some reference to the attitude of "pacifist utopians" within Nicaragua as simply representing the general view of Nicaraguan intellectuals. His essay ends with the statement that hegemony in the intellectual movement in Nicaragua remains dependent on a clique of the military and the oligarchy in the form of the "Confraternity of Catholic Writers and Artists," suggesting that liberalism has never managed to obtain serious intellectual stature in Nicaragua. He points out that though Ernesto Cardenal is related to this group he may well be "the exception that proves the rule." Here he seems to be suggesting that the problem with theory in Nicaragua is that it has never had a substantial native root capable of making sense of the revolutionary reality. He states that "Nicaragua was ideologically maintained at the level of a cavern, Marxist ideas without domestic retouching could not break the seven frontiers (Guatemala, El Salvador, Honduras, Costa Rica, Panamá, and two oceans) that in the manner of walls, seven walls prevent penetration into confined Nicaragua" (1985a: 85).

None of this was of merely academic interest to Fonseca. He was involved in a long-standing and difficult armed struggle which confronted many of the same issues, especially in relation to the position of other leftist groups. As Victor Tirado puts it, Fonseca's major contribution was that he created an understanding of how the ideas and lessons of Sandino should be united with those of Marx, Lenin, and Che Guevara, and what this meant for how the FSLN must act in relation to the history of Nicaragua. Speaking of Fonseca's contribution, Tirado López says:

> he never wanted the Sandinista National Liberation Front to be a sect dedicated to repeating formulas alien to our history and to our people.
>
> All of those who repeated dogmas, those who had never understood in what sense the old political routines had to change remained in the middle of the road and got nowhere. They counselled us that we should deviate from our road, that we should follow them. The facts have shown the uselessness of this advice. We thanked them but we believed that this advice was useless today, as it had been yesterday. (1986: 52)

The reformist advice of the old left was to be rejected in favor of armed struggle. But it was also true that the armed struggle, represented by the fighting at Rio Bocay and Rio Coco, for example, had not really made sense in terms of the idea that the guerilla force was a *foco*, as that term had come to be understood since the Cuban Revolution. Tomás Borge says that Fonseca claimed that these actions were not based on a "guerrilla foco; that the FSLN was born with the vocation of exploited classes to which they were bound from the placenta" (1984: 29). In this sense, a new theoretical and practical synthesis was essential. Armed struggle, not legal political action and alliances, was seen as the only correct strategy, yet the *foco* conception of armed struggle didn't provide the right model. The key to the new synthesis was Fonseca's class analysis in relation to Nicaraguan experience and the role of Sandino.

The fact that the legal political struggle did not take place in the context of a national bourgeois hegemony meant two things. On the one hand, it meant that the struggle could not be conceived of as a worker-peasant alliance in direct fight against the bourgeois ruling class, which could cover itself with liberal legitimacy. The point was not to take up arms against the bourgeoisie but against the dictatorship. It was not Somoza that counted, but Somocismo. This was because a popular struggle against Somoza as the representative of a foreign influence could have a resonance similar to that of Sandino's struggle against the U.S. Marines. The armed struggle was thus a struggle of national liberation that could lead to revolutionary change because there was no legitimate national bourgeois system of hegemonic power.

On the other hand, the weakness, or lack, of a national bourgeoisie as a coherent class meant that the success of the liberal opposition, which wanted to remove Somoza but leave the basic system intact, was doubtful. It was possible to engage in strategic alliances with liberal opposition forces, recognizing that they ultimately lacked the capacity to direct the historical process, so long as the armed struggle continued.

Of course, the fact that a well articulated structure of classes did not exist implied that the proletariat as well as the bourgeoisie was weak or nonexistent.[6] This was what led the traditional left to argue for alliance with liberal forces. Fonseca claimed that in the Nicaraguan context it was possible to develop an ultimately proletarian revolutionary program by depending upon the role of an armed vanguard action. Given Nicaraguan history, such a vanguard might be able to sustain itself on the basis of a direct relationship with the peasantry and yet to understand the ultimate proletarian character of revolutionary action in the twentieth century. Nicaraguan history and contemporary practice had shown that the strong tradition of armed rebellion based on the peasant masses could sustain armed struggle if the guerrillas could establish a proper relation with the peasantry itself. The point was not to build a peasant army but to build relations with the peasantry which made it strategically and tactically possible to maintain the armed action of a small but disciplined vanguard. The peasant base was not, in itself, sufficient to carry the revolution through to triumph but it was an essential element in sustaining the capacity for armed struggle. The peasantry could not substitute for the proletariat but, in alliance with other workers, it could maintain the possibility of revolutionary change. The analysis below will suggest that a failure to fully make sense of the complexities of this reality ultimately led the FSLN to lose substantial support in the countryside, providing a social base for the counterrevolutionary forces that plagued revolutionary Nicaragua. At this point in the discussion, however, it is essential to spell out Fonseca's views as they relate to the context within which he worked.

It was not simply a matter of waiting for the proletariat to come into being, nor of assuming that the urban working class would simply learn from the struggles of the peasantry. On the contrary, Fonseca thought that the actions of the FSLN vanguard had to lead the broad mass of Nicaraguans to support revolutionary action. The vast and overwhelming majority of the Nicaraguan people were victims of the whole system, not merely of Somoza, and it was essential to point this out as well as to make clear that armed resistance was possible. In this context, students had a special role

---

[6]For an earlier analysis in which I argue that a broad sense of the working class as a revolutionary actor is necessary to make sense of the Nicaraguan Revolution, see Wright, 1988.

in the process. As Fonseca explicitly says in a message from the FSLN to student revolutionaries as early as 1968:

> The industrial proletariat in our country is very young and currently, in the overwhelming majority, unorganized into unions, a situation which limits its capacity to fight. At the same time the peasant movement with classist demands dates only from recent years. For this dialectical reason the sector of the people consisting of students is that which has received revolutionary ideas with the most enthusiasm at this stage. (1985: 135)

Fonseca's major contribution to the theory of the FSLN struggle was to recognize the subtle and complex character of the manner in which class relations could work themselves out in the Nicaraguan context and the consequentially complex nature of the relationship between the rural and urban struggles. The revolutionary vanguard as an armed "detachment" of the people had the function of maintaining armed struggle to promote the heightening of class consciousness and the recognition of the possibility that victory against the dictatorship was possible. But it also had the vital function of teaching the population about the nature of the reality in which it lived. It is in this context that Fonseca's advice to guerrilla fighters who were training others to use weapons to "also teach them to read" has special relevance to his understanding of the strategy of ultimate victory. It also helps to understand the meaning of his claim that "to search for the people is not sufficient: they must be trained in order to participate in the revolutionary war" (1985: 166).

In this sense the weakness of the bourgeoisie was an essential element in making it possible to develop a popular conception that could support revolutionary activity. The traditional opposition had been based on the conservative oligarchy, as had intellectual hegemony in the country. Thus it was not necessary to go through the stage of combating liberalism as an ideology—it had never really become a force. As Jaime Wheelock points out, the "bourgeoisie had never had in its hands the centers of rationality and logic of the system. These were in the hands of imperialism and its local expression, Somocismo" (Wheelock, 1984: 34). In this sense the fact that the ideas developed by the FSLN came from a clandestine source was, perhaps, an advantage. For those in the population who suffered from the repression of the regime, Sandinista ideas came to be their own not only for lack of a viable alternative but also because the regime defined any opposition as Sandinista. As José Luis Balcarcel puts it:

> The dictatorship and imperialism that sustained it persecuted and repressed everything that opposed it or that it didn't identify with its own interests, considering it Sandinista. Sandinista ideology extended and consolidated itself as the anti-dictatorial and anti-imperialist position and as that which called for a change of existing conditions inasmuch as the popular classes and the middle sectors regarded as contraband those ideas (with the secrecy which being clandestine imposed upon them) which were opposed to the imperialist and dictatorial imposition at which they directly struck. (1980: 117)

Thus a climate developed in which intellectual opposition was transformed into practical opposition as students and others were recruited into the active vanguard, often going to the mountains to be trained as guerilla fighters. Being subjected to the proletarianising experience of guerilla struggle in the mountains (and thus learning, if they hadn't experienced it before, the real deprivation of the vast majority of Nicaraguans) increased their class consciousness. At the same time, the presence of urban workers gave the peasantry the sense that the urban population could produce those who would share the real conditions of *campesinos* in the struggle against the dictatorship. Thus the educated taught the ignorant and the ignorant taught the educated. Through a genuinely dialectical process a consciousness of common struggle was created.

In this context, Fonseca's basic class analysis led to a sophisticated conception of revolutionary strategy. The experience of Sandino was an essential element in making sense of the possible dynamic; through the peasants' actual memory of a figure that students had come to know in their attempts to make sense of Nicaraguan reality a common sense of identity was created. The point was not to spout classist phrases, but to work with a complex class dynamic to build revolutionary possibilities through practical alliances. In this context it was not necessary to "reconstruct" the legacy of Sandino; rather, it was necessary to learn its essential lessons in building a military vanguard with a clear relation to a popular political movement for fundamental alteration of the old political system.

As mentioned above, Fonseca's elaboration of the class base of Nicaraguan history took place in the context of the apparent military defeat suffered by the FSLN at Pancasán in 1966. Henry Ruiz notes that Pancasán was "considered to be a military defeat but a victory of a political character." This is not only because it "reverberated in the memory of the people who heard its echo in the Nicaraguan soul and the Sandinista Front began to propel itself into all corners of the country" (leading to a large number of new recruits into the organization), but also because it made it possible for the FSLN leadership to become clear about the role of armed struggle in their overall strategy (1980: 10, 11). Ruiz points out that at this time the handful of cadre were able to make sense of their basic strategic position. In this context he indicates that Fonseca made clear that the point was not to use military action to strike at Somoza's person. On the contrary:

> Carlos maintained that Somoza was like a precious jewel given in pawn in which all the contradictions of our people were glued together, where national liberation was a bit confused with liberation from the dictator, where the economic contradictions with the bourgeois sector of our country concentrated; in synthesis, dictatorship and oppression of classes had a well defined profile in Somoza. Thus, meditating a bit on what I'm saying, the model of action and the general lines of Nicaraguan revolutionary theory were what were discovered. (1980: 14)

None of this meant that armed struggle as the road to victory was to be abandoned. On the contrary, it meant that the FSLN had become clear on the point of armed action by the vanguard.

The armed actions of the vanguard not only made them the center of anti-regime action, it also allowed them to develop a capacity to control what they believed would be an ultimate insurrection against Somoza so as to produce a genuine change in the system. According to Jaime Wheelock, between 1972 and 1974 Fonseca thought that the process of creating an adequate military-political apparatus to make the revolution would pass through a number of stages among which were "the initial constitution of a small detachment (*destacamento*); later the effective armed struggle where the vanguard could prove itself and, after that, all of the works of penetration and organization of the different popular sectors to arrive finally at the popular insurrection" (Wheelock, 1986: 103). Thus the point of the military vanguard was not to function as "an army defeating another army," ultimately the vanguard was not "to convert itself into an army but to be the head of the armed people" (Wheelock, 1986: 104, 106).

The task of the military-political vanguard was to organize in all possible ways to create mass organizations that could ultimately lead to an armed insurrection with the FSLN at its head. Much of the history of the period after Fonseca's death can be best understood in terms of the process through which the FSLN learned to create and organize within a broad structure of mass organizations and to supply direction to insurrections such as that in Monimbó, which arose, as it were, spontaneously from the population.[7] Clearly Fonseca provided a theoretical guide that was put into practice and altered the reality and self-understanding of the Nicaraguan Revolution as it developed.

Fonseca's view was that the FSLN itself was to be a small vanguard group of the most dedicated individuals who could guide the process to completion. It could count on the rebellious tradition represented by Sandino (in which each member of the vanguard would also follow Sandino's model of perfect personal conduct and willingness to sacrifice). It would have to understand the broad popular nature of any successful struggle given the objective class conditions of Nicaragua, as well as the opportunities for creating working class unity in practice.

One of the most significant failures of Sandino's struggle was his failure to build an organization that could outlive him. Although Fonseca did not think Sandino could have really done much else in his situation he was careful to make sure that unipersonal leadership

---

[7]On the relation between the more or less spontaneous development of the insurrection and the three tendencies within the FSLN, see Molero, 1988.

would not be characteristic of the FSLN. Jaime Wheelock writes that Fonseca

> aided also in forging a determinant sense of anti-*caudillismo*, of equality amongst us. Carlos was the forger of the Sandinista Front, its craftsman *par excellence*. His authority was transmitted to the organization in such a sense and in such depth that the militants felt the authority from the beginning as an organic substance, not bound to persons. Carlos lived obsessed with the continuity of the FSLN, of the struggle. I believe that he saw the danger of his possible disappearance and this influenced him, of course. (Wheelock, 1984: 13)

Contemporary Consequences of Fonseca's Theory

Combined with the objective result of mass organizing across a broad front, this sense of multiple leadership within the organization and a recognition that a mixed economy was essential at the present stage of Nicaraguan history has had substantial consequences in contemporary developments. It explains much about the meaning and practice of pluralism in revolutionary Nicaragua, for example. It also makes sense of the continued dynamic of the role of mass organizations in Nicaragua.

Finally, the above analysis should explain the fact that the paintings of Sandino and Fonseca are of equal prominence on the face of the governmental building in Managua. Sandino was not merely put there by Fonseca, nor is it merely that each gave his life in valiant struggle. Neither could have found such a place without the other. Any careful observer, of whatever political persuasion, should ultimately understand that it is impossible to comprehend the "socialism" of the Nicaraguan Revolution on the model of any other existing system. As both Sandino and Fonseca understood, Nicaragua must be understood on its own grounds. Those who refuse to understand this basic fact will always see what happens there as a mystery and will never know why Fonseca holds such a substantial position in the minds of Nicaraguan revolutionaries. Revolutionaries around the world who take due account of this fact will understand that foreign models must be studied but that such study alone can never lead to comprehension of the lessons that Sandino and Fonseca have to teach. Those who would make political change must not merely study theory, they must act with full commitment to the slogan: "Patria libre o morir!"

In bringing together the concepts of revolution derived from the study of Marxism and a number of different socialist revolutions of the twentieth century on the one hand and the Nicaraguan historical experience of revolutionary armed struggle under Sandino on the other hand, Carlos Fonseca Amador was able to inspire the FSLN to follow the path of ultimate victory. This path was not an easy one, hundreds of militants and untold sympathizers as well as Nicaraguans caught in the violence against their will lost their lives, even more were injured. Yet the FSLN followed the basic guidelines laid out by Fonseca that suggested three fundamental things. They were:

1.   Armed struggle is a necessary element of any revolution in Nicaragua. A long tradition of armed struggle among the rural population can aid in developing this struggle in the present. A guerrilla force may be built based on close collaboration with the peasantry.
2.   There must be careful preparation for such struggle, carried out by a vanguard of disciplined revolutionaries. These people must not only fight in the mountains but also must organize on a consistent basis both in the cities and in the countryside. In this context it is important to recognize that many rural workers are peasant farmers and wage workers at the same time. The building of links between the urban proletariat and the peasantry requires substantial urban work as well as maintenance of the rural armed force.
3.   Ultimately a prolonged general strike and an insurrection will bring down the dictatorship.

The Three Tendencies and Theory

Significantly, the division of the FSLN into three tendencies, the "Prolonged People's War" group, the "Proletarian Tendency," and the "Insurrectional" or *"tercerista"* faction, can be understood as each group focusing on one element of Fonseca's triple message, holding that the others did not sufficiently value that element.

Fundamentally, the Prolonged People's War (GPP), headed by Tomás Borge, Henry Ruiz, and Bayardo Arce, held the view that it was essential to maintain the guerilla in the mountains, understanding that this was related to the forging of genuine revolutionary cadres from mostly urban "petty bourgeois" backgrounds, and from student backgrounds. Henry Ruiz put it as follows:

> The mountain was like a crucible. There the cadre were really discovered. Carlos Fonseca was obsessed with tempering the cadre in very difficult circumstances and I can say, without downgrading anyone or trying to offend those *compañeros* who weren't in the mountains, that really the cadre that were forged there are the true examples of the revolution. (Ruiz, 1980: 18)[8]

From this perspective it was essential to maintain the struggle in the mountains and to continue to live with the *campesinos* in order not to lose their confidence (Ruiz, 1980: 14). This is not to say that the GPP had no interest in urban actions. Indeed, one of the most important urban actions, the taking of the house of Chema Castillo, was led by people from the GPP, especially Tomás Borge. It was precisely in this context that the division between the three tendencies developed (Molero, 1988: 23-24). The GPP may be characterized by the view that the struggle was necessarily to be prolonged and that its continuation required the maintenance of the armed contingents in the mountains. This emphasizes the first of the points listed above.

The "Proletarian Tendency" group was headed by Jaime Wheelock, Carlos Nuñez, Luis Carrión, and Roberto Huembes. The

---

[8]The first issue (dated May and June, 1980) of *Nicaráuac*, a "cultural journal" representing an FSLN perspective, contains three basic interviews, one with each of the leaders of the three old tendencies. They are: Henry Ruiz, associated with the GPP; Humberto Ortega, a leader of the Insurrectionists or *terceristas*; and Jaime Wheelock, from the Proletarian Tendency. The interviews do not directly address the issues of the earlier divisions. It is interesting, however, that Tomás Borge begins his chapter on the divisions within the movement with the same quote from Ruiz that I have reproduced here (Borge, 1989).

National Directorate expelled Wheelock from the FSLN as the group came into existence, a fact that all parties were later to regret. The position of this tendency is well described by María Molero:

> The Proletarian Tendency held the view that the guerrilla war in the mountain no longer [1974] constituted the backbone of the anti-Somocista struggle and that it was necessary to first form "a solid nucleus of proletarian organization and organic connections between the proletariat and the *campesinos*" [note to mimeographed document]. In consequence the proletarians were to maintain, as they had been doing for years before, their organizational forces in the urban nuclei of the Pacific and in some rural areas close to Managua. (1988: 24)

This is not to say simply that the Proletarian Tendency was interested only in urban issues. In fact, Jaime Wheelock was to become the head of the agrarian reform in the revolutionary government. It is true that Wheelock's analysis depends substantially on the idea that a good deal of the rural workforce in Nicaragua under Somoza was as much a proletarian as a peasant group (Wheelock, 1980). The consequences of this view in later practice are the focus of much of the analysis of agrarian reform below.

Shortly after the division between the two tendencies discussed above, a new group, the *tercerista* (third way), or Insurrectionalists, arose as a formal group, led by the brothers, Humberto and Daniel Ortega, and Victor Tirado. This group clearly foresaw that the insurrectionary phase was now possible. Their actions were marked by building alliances throughout Nicaraguan society, including with revolutionary Christian groups and the most advanced elements of the Nicaraguan bourgeoisie. The Insurrectionalists were quick to mobilize around spontaneous uprisings in Monimbó and Matagalpa, among other places.[9] They were especially able to focus on the third element of Fonseca's

---

[9]It is interesting to note that Humberto Ortega emphasizes quite strongly the spontaneous uprising, especially of youth, that occurred in Matagalpa immediately after the FSLN, under *tercerista* leadership, took the National Palace by force (1980).

teachings in developing broad coalitions to undertake the final insurrection.

Formal unity between the three tendencies was achieved only four months before the final revolutionary triumph. Molero sums up the experience of the three tendencies and their ultimate reconciliation as follows:

> *The accelerated rhythm of the mobilization of the masses, the evident crisis of the regime and the experience of the insurrection of September itself* [which the *terceristas* had launched after the taking of the National Palace and the uprising in Matagalpa] *made it impossible to postpone the unification of the Sandinista Front.* Various factors made it possible to obtain this unity relatively rapidly: insurmountable difficulties had not been produced among the three tendencies, none of them had constructed a new Sandinista Front and in practice the work of each of them had complemented that of the others. (1988: 29; emphasis in the original)

Ultimately the unity of the three groups was brought about through the insight that events showed the necessity of each element in the struggle. Theoretical differences that had arisen from serious investigation of practice were resolved in practice itself. As this objective unity became more obvious in the struggle it also became more obvious that victory was near and that it was possible for all elements in the FSLN to contribute to that victory. It also became clear that FSLN unity would be essential in constructing a revolutionary government.[10]

---

[10]In addition to the discussion in Molero cited above, a good source for understanding the issues that divided the tendencies and the degree to which the National Directorate, at least, understood them to be fundamentally overcome is Invernizzi, Pisani, and Ceberio, 1986. This book consists of interviews with Humberto Ortega, Jaime Wheelock, and Bayardo Arce. The third chapter is explicitly devoted to discussion of the three tendencies but the first two chapters contain interesting remarks related to this issue as well. Especially important in this regard are remarks regarding the role and activities of the National Directorate, such as Humberto Ortega's claim that "there are really no problems in working

FSLN Principles of Government

As the FSLN moved from a military-political group dedicated to seizing political power to an organization that could organize Nicaragua into a new state it was essential to further refine and develop the theory that was to guide practice in government. The "Historic Program" of the FSLN, presented to the people of Nicaragua by Carlos Fonseca, was to provide guidance to the new government but it was, of course, essential to develop a theoretical position that could be used to put this into practice in the actual situation in which power was taken.

For purposes of making sense of how to govern, the FSLN drew four fundamental principles from the work of Fonseca and his understanding of the lessons of Sandino. The Governing Junta of National Reconstruction agreed, under Sandinista leadership, that these fundamental principles had guided it in putting "into practice a form of government" that was characterized by those principles. Three of these (excluding popular participation, which was presumably contained in Article 2) were to ultimately be guaranteed by Article 5 of the Nicaraguan Constitution.[11] They were:

> 1. Political pluralism. The ultimate success of the Sandinista Front in guiding the insurrection and in obtaining the position of the clearly leading political force within it was based on the fact that the FSLN, especially through *tercerista* guidance, had worked with many sectors of the population in defeating the dictatorship. The origins of the members of the FSLN as well as those who came to constitute the new provisional government were diverse; they were "plural" in virtually all senses.
>
> 2. Mixed economy. A simple analysis of capitalism, feudalism, and socialism had obviously been long since overcome. Fonseca's understanding of the fact that Nicaragua was not, in spite of Browderist interpretations, simply a feudal country and that it had also never really developed its own

---

as a collective directorate because we already had the experience of the tendencies" (41).

[11]Molero suggests that these were derived from the *tercerista* programmatic platform (1988: 30).

capitalism surely made it clear that a simple feudalism-capitalism-socialism path was not a rational way to think about the future development of Nicaragua. The complexities of dependency, as they were so well understood in the scholarship of the 1960s and 1970s, had clearly become known to the militancy of the FSLN. It was not reasonable, nor was it responsible, to simply believe that the FSLN was the vanguard of a proletarian revolution. Everyone recognized that the proletariat was but a minor fraction of the Nicaraguan population. A complex class structure in a revolution based on unity among people from various class positions suggested more that it made sense to see the FSLN as the "vanguard of the people."

3. Popular participation and mobilization. This calls for more than simple representative democracy. The inclusion of the mass organizations in the Council of State clearly manifested this conception. In Article 2 of the Constitution this is spelled out as follows: "The people exercise democracy, freely participating and deciding in the construction of the economic, political and social system what is most appropriate to their interests. The people exercise power directly and by means of their representatives, freely elected in accord with universal, equal, direct, free, and secret suffrage." What is significant in this language is the notion of the direct exercise of power that is seen as additional to representation through elections. Here we clearly have instantiated the notion of participatory democracy.

4. International non-alignment. This is a clear result of the fundamentally Bolivarist conceptions of Sandino as distilled through the modern understanding of Fonseca. It was clear that the U.S. government and large U.S. economic entities were a significant part of the problem for Nicaragua. But it was also clear that Nicaragua must seek its own road. After all, experiences with the traditional parties allied with the Soviet Union had been unsatisfactory.

Understanding practical developments and their theoretical bases as well as the resulting theoretical disputes under the ten years of FSLN government requires close attention to the development of these principles in practice, the contradictions to which they gave rise, and especially to their relation to class analysis. The FSLN began as a clearly Marxist organization, committed to the development of socialism; it grew through alliances with non-Marxist forces into a governing organization committed to pluralism and a mixed economy. The insistence of the new state on maintaining a status of international non-alignment was seen by the United States as simply a cover for further Soviet penetration of the Western hemisphere. Thus the Nicaraguan experience is full of contradictions due not only to the complexity of the class situation in Nicaragua itself but also to the profound implications its revolution was seen as having in the world as a whole. The period of the FSLN guiding the Nicaraguan revolution through control of the state was a living experiment in an attempt to construct a truly democratic and revolutionary socialism. Its successes and failures are important to gaining an understanding of how it may be possible in the future to improve on this model.

FROM CORPORATIVIST PLURALISM
TO ELECTORAL DEMOCRACY

Upon taking power in 1979, the FSLN proceeded to construct a government of "national reconciliation." Rather than simply taking power from the old state and constructing a new state in its own image, the FSLN clearly felt that it was essential to unite with other groups in the new state and the new government as it had in the last period of the insurrection. In one important sense this was a surprising move. The FSLN had a great part of its theoretical origins in Marxism-Leninism and had consistently seen itself as a "vanguard" party.

The Vanguard and Pluralism in Marxism-Leninism

In Marxist-Leninist theory from its origins in Lenin's *State and Revolution* it is clear that the "vanguard" exists in two fundamental senses. Marx's theory suggests that socialist revolution will take place first in the most highly industrialized states. Lenin claimed that it is possible to make socialist revolution first in countries such as Russia that were the victims of a new phenomenon, imperialism (Lenin, 1939). In this context it is clear that the industrial working class, or "proletariat," which Marx had seen as the vast majority that would constitute the revolutionary actor, was relatively small. Thus, in the context of anti-imperialist revolutions, the proletariat constituted the "vanguard" of all exploited classes, even though it was not the largest class actor, a position actually occupied by the peasantry. Further, since this revolutionary upheaval took place in a condition where the working class, with its class consciousness, was not predominant, it was essential for the party to function as a "vanguard" in making sense of the situation. Thus the tradition of Marxism-Leninism, from the Bolshevik Revolution forward, had suggested that the vanguard party should guide political developments in representing the interests of the most advanced elements of the working classes. While some alliances with other groups and even parties might be possible, the general expectation was that the vanguard party was to guide political action through control of the state. Ultimately, this led in a number of cases to an explicit constitutional recognition of the leading role of the Communist Party.[1] Thus many people expected the FSLN to take direct control of the state and to create a system modelled on that of the Soviet Union or Cuba. Indeed, many opponents of the system, including the U.S. embassy, alleged that this was, in fact, what happened.

What actually occurred was far different. The concept of pluralism guided the process in Nicaragua from the start and continues as a fundamental element of FSLN theory even after defeat in the elections of 1990. As noted above, some FSLN spokespersons even see the electoral defeat as a victory in the sense that it proves that the FSLN was able to establish a pluralist democracy. In the Soviet Union and Eastern Europe, attempts to develop pluralism (which occurred after the FSLN had already committed itself to the concept) within the world of "really existing socialism" have apparently led to the abandonment of socialism altogether. Whether this is the ultimate result in Nicaragua remains to be seen.

---

[1]Actual experience, including early Soviet experience, was a good deal more complex than this, including the fact that the Bolsheviks early on worked in combination with other parties. Developments in China, Yugoslavia, Cuba, and other systems were also much more complex than this model might suggest. Nevertheless they approach the more or less stereotypical explanation much more closely than the Nicaraguan model. For an analysis that sees the Soviet model as the real foundation of FSLN ideas, see David Nolan, 1984. Nolan served in the U.S. embassy in Managua for some time until he was expelled as *persona non grata* in the late 1980s. His book is generally highly regarded even by some scholars sympathetic to the Nicaraguan revolution.

The Development of the Concept of Pluralism
in Western Liberal Thought

In an odd sense the history of pluralism as a concept parallels its actual development in the Nicaraguan context. The idea of pluralism originated among the "guild socialists" in early twentieth-century England and has become a concept promoted by quite conservative forces in the United States as definitionally equivalent to capitalist-based electoral democracy. The first manifestations of the concept in Nicaragua included a substantial representation of interests, not unlike guilds, in formal governmental bodies and the concept has evolved in practice so that it supports, at least in part, an electoral system that is moving towards the interest of the bourgeoisie. To understand these developments more clearly it is helpful to examine both the development of the concept of pluralism in U.S. academic and political discourse and its practical development in Nicaragua.

"Pluralism" came to represent the key concept of political science in the United States by shortly after the middle of the century. The term had taken on a very different meaning than it had for the guild socialists; it came to be used as a descriptive term for the "advanced" North American and Western European systems. "Pluralism" was the view that developed political systems were the result of social systems marked by a high degree of social differentiation that produced "cross-cutting cleavages," a pattern contrasted to polarized social systems. In a pluralist system, or a "polyarchy" as Robert Dahl christened it, there was said to be rule by a group of minorities, not by any single elite. The circulation of elites and a political system marked by a number of alternative access points to political decision-making assured that such systems could remain stable while responding to a number of different interest groups.

Pluralism as defined in the preceding paragraph began as a clear critique of conservative theories on one hand and of populist theories on the other. Behavioral political science began with the assertion that "traditional" political analysis focused too much attention on the role of political institutions. The traditional emphasis on the Constitution, the division of powers in the institutions of the United States government, and especially the role of formal legal institutions was, according to behavioralists, an aspect of a normatively loaded analysis that was based on political conservatism. The new "behavioralist" movement emphasized the individual and social groups that mediated between individual interests and governmental institutions. Although pluralism was allegedly a politically "neutral" analysis it was clearly associated with liberalism.

Yet pluralism was also a critique of populism. Populism, as Dahl understood it in his *Preface to Democratic Theory,* falsely asserted that it was both possible and desirable for the majority to rule. Democratic institutions, in the populist view, were to reflect the will of the people as a whole. Pluralism denied that there was such an entity as the "people." On the contrary the pluralist view was that political rule was always based on coalitions of minorities. Socialism would seem, in this analysis, to be even further from a rational analysis than populism. Just as there was no such thing as "the people," there were no classes as understood by Marxists and other socialists. The concept of "socio-economic groups" came to replace the concept of class in serious social analysis.

In spite of the fact that pluralism had clear origins in American liberalism it came under attack from the left as a "conservative" view beginning in the early 1960s. It overemphasized stability, it ignored the significance of the general social environment, which created "hegemony," and it thus failed to understand the role of economic elites in supposedly "advanced" political systems, according to its leftist critics. Many left-leaning social scientists came to emphasize some sort of neo-Marxian analysis in opposition to pluralism. More fundamentally, the left as a whole adopted the concept of "participatory democracy," which had its origins in the Port Huron Statement, the founding document of the Students for a Democratic Society (SDS).

It is ironic that pluralism was a basic element of the revolutionary theory of the FSLN. The FSLN has its roots in Marxist theory, which emphasizes class analysis and therefore would seem to be antithetical to the concept of pluralism. The irony is magnified by the fact that the FSLN also has roots in the new Marxism, which is often associated with student movements in the United States. That movement was, at least in academic terms, closely associated with the rejection of pluralism as a theory to describe the politics and social structures of the United States and Western Europe. Pluralism, as a theory describing North American and Western European polities was roundly rejected on the left, especially in political science circles, as a "conservative" analysis that neglected the class hegemony in the systems it presumably analyzed. Participatory democracy was urged as an alternative to pluralism by both academics and activists. How then can we explain that the FSLN should adopt the concept of pluralism as the foundation for its own theory and practice?

The FSLN, Pluralism, and Hegemony

One possible explanation is simply that the adoption of language making reference to pluralism was a device to cover the real Marxist orientation of the FSLN.[2] It is clear that by the time of the FSLN triumph in 1979, the term "pluralism," whatever its real origins in political terms, had become a standard-bearer for the political right in the United States in terms of criticism of "totalitarian" or "closed" political systems. The latter were conceived of as primarily the systems of the "Soviet bloc" and China. The right-wing critique of Nicaragua was at least partially framed in terms of the claim that the FSLN was a "totalitarian" party and that pluralism was absent in the system. The view that the FSLN adopted the language of its objective enemies to describe itself as a method of covering its true position, besides betraying the paranoid fantasies of those political observers who suggest that somehow all "communists" must function in terms of nefarious schemes,[3] neglects the reality of the development of the FSLN and its theories.

---

[2]In an interview, Orlando Piñeda rejected such an analysis in a very interesting manner. He was describing the Marxist roots of his own thought and that of many other Sandinistas when a young woman who had introduced him to me suggested that the language of pluralism was introduced to cover the fact that the FSLN had a Marxist orientation. In her view, the anti-communism of the Somoza period had made Marxism "the devil." He quickly and forcefully corrected her on this subject, obviously in order to instruct her that her view was incorrect, more than to impress me as the interviewer.

[3]For an especially interesting variant of this sort of analysis in relation to Nicaragua, see the ex-dictator's analysis in Somoza, 1980.

An alternative possibility is that the FSLN understood a fundamental criticism of the concept of pluralism offered by the left in the U.S. and thought that it was possible to develop a genuine pluralism in Nicaragua that would combine pluralism with participatory democracy under the guidance of a vanguard. Critics of pluralist theory have often suggested that what this theory fails to recognize in the United States is a sort of dominance of the system as a whole which prevents numerous issues from being processed through the political system. This notion is similar to the concept of "hegemony" developed by Antonio Gramsci. The FSLN seems to have held that pluralism with "hegemony"—based on the role of the FSLN itself as the "vanguard of the people"—could produce a transition to a fundamentally different sort of social, economic, and political system. It is thus useful to examine the concept of hegemony, its relationship to the FSLN's concept of pluralism, and its actual political practice in Nicaragua.

Gramsci's notion of hegemony suggests that particular social orders function within the context of domination by particular classes or social groups.[4] Such hegemony is not simply a matter of the imposition of state power. Rather, the concept suggests that a context of broad social, ideological, and political relations provides the basis for possible action; the "rules of the game" within which a pluralist order functions are developed in such a manner as to favor the social groups that actually hegemonize the system as a whole.

Traditional theories of political pluralism as an explanation of political reality within developed political systems, most notably that of the United States, have been frequently criticized for failing to take into account the fact that these systems function in the context of hegemony in a civil society that serves the interests of dominant economic groups. Control of civil society provides the possible parameters of social and political action. Within the United States, for example, this has meant that socialism is not a viable option for political practice. This is not because socialist groups are repressed by open state power but rather because the serious advocacy of basic change away from capitalist relations is not consistent with the

---

[4]For explicit discussion of Gramsci in the Nicaraguan context, see Vargas Lozano, 1988 and Salazar, 1988.

rules of the game within the civil society. Most Marxist theorists would suggest that such hegemony typically serves the interest of a particular class; in capitalist systems, the bourgeois class. Thus, hegemony in a socialist system would presumably be exercised by the working class, or the proletariat. The traditional notion of the Communist Party serving as "the vanguard of the proletariat" can be understood as an explication of the notion of possible hegemony in a socialist system. Yet it is important to see that this is not simply a question of "who governs" in the political sense. Lenin held that the state was simply an instrument of coercion in the hands of the dominant class. Gramsci's view was that this restricted interpretation of the state was insufficient to make sense of possible strategies for obtaining and maintaining power. The hegemony of a particular class was maintained by a much more complex structure than simply coercion in the hands of the state.

While the FSLN clearly understood the Gramscian notion of hegemony, it does not see itself as the vanguard simply of a particular class. Rather it sees itself as a force based on the "logic of the majority," or as the vanguard of "the people." It may at first sight appear that this is only a hidden reference to the replacement of bourgeois hegemony by the hegemony of another class, simply called "the people" in order to avoid Marxist-Leninist terminology while maintaining it in practice, or merely the adoption of the language of the "people's democracies," so common in Eastern Europe. Closer examination shows, however, that the FSLN's view is a good deal more sophisticated and complex than this analysis would suggest. The FSLN's view is that there never was bourgeois hegemony as such in Nicaragua. On the contrary, hegemony was exercised by a foreign power, namely the U.S. Only in the later years of the struggle against Somoza did the national bourgeoisie even attempt to exercise hegemony (Jaime Wheelock in Invernizzi, Pisani, and Ceberio, 1986: 191–92; and Wheelock, 1984: 23–42). Thus the FSLN was not the vanguard of a single class, but of the "broad popular majority." The point was not, as some left opposition parties in Nicaragua would have it, to create the dictatorship of the proletariat. Rather, it was to create a set of rules of the game that would allow all sectors of the society, including the bourgeoisie, to function without creating a bourgeois hegemony.[5] It is in this context that the concept of a "mixed economy" is combined with that of political pluralism and of a vanguard party representing "the broad masses of the Nicaraguan people." If the vanguard party could aid in creating mass organizations that played a substantial role in actual decision-making at all social and political levels, pluralism could be combined with participatory democracy to maintain the hegemony of popular forces.

Thus in Nicaragua the FSLN seems to have combined the concepts of a vanguard party, hegemony based on participatory democracy, and political pluralism to create a fundamentally new model of transition to some sort of socialist justice. In discussing the reality of democracy in the Nicaraguan revolution, Coraggio and Irvin show awareness of this theoretical tradition when they state that "pluralism is not exclusively about political parties. The essence of pluralism is that it allows for a diversity of views that enriches political and social practice at all levels, not merely at the level of political parties" (1985: 33). The Nicaraguan experience demonstrates that this aspect of pluralism has deep roots in the experience of the FSLN both prior to the triumph and afterwards.

Plural Actors in the Anti-Somoza Struggle

Although from its founding the FSLN represented a vanguard of a few individuals organized in a relatively centralized manner, it never pretended to be the only relevant force struggling against the dictatorship. Indeed, in many cases the FSLN found itself confronted even with armed uprisings, the most notable being that in Monimbó, which were not primarily a result of its own organizational work. Without going into a detailed account of the struggle against Somoza we can note here that numerous forces, including organized Christian groups, student organizations, labor

---

[5]This seems similar to Mao's analysis of class relations in pre-revolutionary China. Yet I have been unable to find specific reference in Sandinista literature to this fact. It is difficult to believe, in light of the sophistication of much of the analysis of theorists and actors within the FSLN, that this similarity has gone unnoticed by them but it remains the fact that little, if any, direct reference is made to Mao's analysis in this context.

unions (often associated with other leftist parties), and national bourgeois groupings (notably those grouped around the leadership of *La Prensa*), were serious forces that engaged in anti-regime activities. While the FSLN made efforts to organize within these groupings they were not necessarily under its direct control. Thus the participation of a plurality of forces was a fundamental aspect of the uprising against Somoza. Ultimately, of course, the FSLN as an organized armed force was able to lead in the process of destroying the Somoza regime and organizing a new system.

The FSLN's capacity to lead diverse forces demonstrated its vanguard role in practice. But this was not a result of the fact that the FSLN somehow guided or controlled all other forces from the top. Rather it was that after many years of valiant struggle and many deaths, the FSLN captured the public imagination as the genuine representative of the revolution. It was not that the FSLN commanded but that it led through its exemplary action. In this context it is interesting to note how the population in many cases depended upon the FSLN to provide arms and leadership once the insurrection was in full bloom. One participant in the insurrection in Monimbó said that after they had begun to fight with the Guard

> we knew that the Sandinista Front would come, but there were those of us who imagined that they were going to come here in columns or something.
>
> It wasn't until later that we noticed that we were the Sandinista Front; that they came to orient, but that we were the ones, beside them, that had to fight. This was the day when the red and black kerchiefs began to come out. For the first time everyone began to participate in the fight. (Maria Chavarria, quoted in Arias, 1981: 154)

As a result of this sort of phenomenon many people came to think of themselves as Sandinistas in a sense other than formal membership in the FSLN. It remains the case that the statement *"soy Sandinista"* (I am a Sandinista) by no means necessarily implies party membership. One way a group can gain hegemony within civil society is to develop broad popular identification with its symbols. The symbol of Sandino has deep popular roots within twentieth-century Nicaraguan experience and one of the main sources of its hegemony is the FSLN's identification of its struggle with that of Sandino's army, those who alone were unwilling to trade their guns for "ten Yankee dollars."[6]

During its first few years the FSLN was a purely closed military vanguard but, according to Jaime Wheelock, new objective conditions in 1973–74 made it possible to begin to work with other organizations (1986: 66–67). The willingness and capacity of the FSLN to direct developments so as to include people from all social groupings (other than the direct confidants of Somoza and the National Guard) led to the development of pluralism in practice under the leadership of the vanguard party. The formation of the three tendencies within the FSLN is often discussed in terms of the desire on the part of the *terceristas* to engage in broad alliances in opposition to the other tendencies. Marvin Ortega affirms that the first call for pluralism was "by the *terceristas* with the call for a 'common front of National Unity' in 1977—not just of the left" (1986: 18).

Yet none of the groupings had ever denied the viability of certain alliances and the necessity to work with numerous organized forces. It is essential to remember that the split was overcome by the formation of the Directorate, which contained three members from each of the tendencies, in itself a pluralist resolution of the conflicts of the past. It is instructive that none of the groupings has called for a rejection of the sort of pluralism that the *terceristas* initiated. Although Bayardo Arce argues that there is not "pluralism in the vanguard" in ideological terms (Invernizzi, Pisani, and Ceberio, 1986: 58) it is clear that the FSLN learned the necessity of uniting a plurality of forces in order to engage in successful political practice.

The long vanguard tradition of the FSLN combined with its common struggle with popular forces and even with representatives of the national bourgeoisie and its allies gave it the controlling position in the final struggle against Somoza. It might thus appear that the only question, once Somoza lost power, was who would seize that power. A traditional understanding of a revolutionary vanguard might suggest that the vanguard should seize state power

---

[6]For a general discussion of the conscious incorporation of the Sandino story into FSLN theory and ideology, see Palmer, 1988.

in order to transform civil society. In the context of a socialist vanguard, which the FSLN has never really denied that it represents, this would suggest that the state power, which has maintained a bourgeois civil society, should be seized by the vanguard and directed towards its proper purposes.

Pluralism, Hegemony, and the Revolutionary State

However, as noted above, according to the FSLN's view there really was no "bourgeois hegemony" in Somocista Nicaragua. Power within the state was far too personalized to be understood in this sense. A broadly based coalition such as that which was ultimately victorious was possible because many elements of the bourgeoisie had their own interests in the ousting of Somoza.

It is easy to move conceptually from the recognition that Somoza and the National Guard were involved in massive repression of the population as a whole to the view that a strong state existed which was headed by Somoza. More serious examination of the situation, however, makes clear that no strong or well-organized state as such existed, though it might make sense to speak of an authoritarian regime. In this sense there was also a political system through which formally organized political power was exercised. Within the political system there was a constitutional form which included a regular system of elections, a division of powers, the protection of constitutional rights, and so forth. The political system, however, in the Sandinista view, lost all legitimacy with the "electoral farce of 1967," in which massive fraud was associated with the election of Anastasio Somoza Debayle to replace his brother. The FSLN had not participated in supporting the candidate of the Conservative Party, Fernando Agüero although other opposition groups, including the PSN had done so, according to Wheelock. From then on, in Wheelock's words, "it began to be seen clearly that there were two great camps in the country: that of the Somocista dictatorship and the bought-off coalitions of the right on one hand, and, on the other, that of the revolutionary left whose vanguard is the Sandinista Front" (1986: 61). Though not everyone shared this view, it prevailed.

Those who hoped for a solution within the political system (seen as the formal rules of the governmental institutions) as well as those who hoped to see a solution at the level of the regime with

91

"Somocismo without Somoza" were equally frustrated. The struggle was at the level of the state itself.[7] Thus, the task of the FSLN was not merely to organize a political system in order to replace the political power held by the existing regime, but to create a fundamentally new state. This was not a new aspect of the FSLN's view; they had always been involved in a revolutionary struggle to fundamentally alter social relations in Nicaragua, not merely to get rid of Somoza. Jose Luis Coraggio describes the situation clearly. Under the heading "Hegemony as Political System," he writes that:

> It is clear that certain capacities and styles for the construction of a new society were prefigured in the struggle for power. In its struggle against Somocismo the FSLN combined the armed struggle with counter-hegemonic methods in order to actively accumulate forces and to strengthen its legitimacy and, *in defeating the regime to defeat the bourgeoisie in its aspirations of gaining social hegemony "without Somoza" at the same time.* After the triumph and as a result of this trajectory space remained open for all social sectors to actively participate in the new national project *under the revolutionary hegemony.* (1985: 36–37; emphasis in original)

Many people have wondered why the FSLN did not move immediately to elections after the triumph in 1979, given their clear popular support. When asked to address this question, Jaime Wheelock pointed out in 1983 that to have done so would have been merely to continue with the system as it had existed under Somoza when elections had been held regularly, but given the way in which they were conducted, the Liberal Party and the Somozas always won. To simply have held an election that the FSLN could surely win in such a context would have been to legitimize the old process, in which "elections were absolutely without prestige" (Wheelock, 1984: 78). Before an election could be meaningful it was essential

---

[7]For the "political system-regime-state" system of categories that are at the basis of the language used here, see Edelberto Torres-Rivas, 1985. While the present project does not allow for an extensive elaboration of these concepts I believe that they are extremely useful in making sense of actual political developments within the context of political change.

to construct a new system of, for example, voter registration, which had not existed in the past. The FSLN, in Wheelock's view held that "it was not necessary to have elections because it was felt that, in the first place the revolution was a perfect consultation with a much higher democratic quality; and in the second place, because it was not the task of the moment, national reconstruction was the task given highest priority" (1984: 78).

In the present context it should be clear that the point was not merely to move forward as the leading force within the existing structure of hegemony, within the state as it already existed, but to fundamentally transform that state.[8] In this context three fundamental phenomena require discussion to make sense of the practical development of the newly synthesized concepts of pluralism and vanguardism. The first is the creation of the Governing Junta of National Reconstruction with three FSLN and two non-FSLN members and of the Council of State as an aspect of pluralism. The second is the development of "participatory democracy," especially through the creation of mass based "popular organizations." The third is the role of the army and the popular militia.

The Governing Junta of National Reconstruction

One of the first steps taken by the FSLN was the creation of institutions that were clearly distinct from the FSLN as an entity. As the vanguard, the FSLN felt that it should provide direction in a situation in which there were few remaining institutions of any sort. When asked what the role of the National Directorate was, Bayardo Arce commented:

> In the beginning we were deeply involved in everything, because of the lack of institutions: someone had to decide. The only visible authority, recognized by the revolutionary practice, was the National Directorate. But one of the first things that we did was to define a functional role. Thus a government, a military structure

---

[8]See Humberto Ortega's discussion of this in relation to Sandinista conversations with U.S. congressional representatives, in Invernizzi, Pisani, and Ceberio, 1986: 81–82. Also quite revealing is Jaime Wheelock's analysis developed in *El Gran Desafío*, (1984: 77–82).

and a security organization were created. The National
Directorate reserved for itself the definition of the
general lines for the political economy, military doctrine,
agrarian reform and external action. (Invernizzi, Pisani,
and Ceberio, 1986: 42)

It is notable here that the Directorate *created* a government, it did
not choose to *become* the government, though it clearly felt
sufficiently strong to do so had it wanted to. It is also notable that
it neither dissolved itself nor created the FSLN as a party in the
first few months.

The first major step taken in creating the government was to
form a Governing Junta of National Reconstruction in exile in early
1979. Its function was to serve as the new executive organ, a
function that it formally exercised following Somoza's flight from the
country. Although its members were effectively chosen by the FSLN
Directorate, the first Junta included two prominent figures from the
non-FSLN revolutionary leadership, Violetta Barrios de Chamorro
(widow of the assassinated editor of *La Prensa* and later president
of the country) and Alfonso Robelo Callejas from the Nicaraguan
Democratic Movement, as well as three FSLN representatives. That
this was not merely a formal cover for FSLN domination is indicated
by the fact that although only three votes were required to pass a
measure in the body it operated on the basis of consensus
(apparently meaning unanimity in practice) from its inception.
Rafael Cordoba Rivas, the last non-FSLN representative commented
on leaving the Junta that it always operated "with mutual respect"
(cited in Diaz Castillo, 1985: 12). Though its membership rapidly
changed with the resignations in 1980 of Violetta Chamorro and
Alfonso Robelo (who became a major leader of the counterrevolutionary forces), it is instructive that they were not simply
replaced by FSLN representatives. On the contrary, the positions
were occupied by Rafael Cordoba Rivas of the Democratic
Conservative Party and Arturo Cruz Porras, an international banker
and representative of the bourgeois opposition to Somoza.[9]

---

[9]A good brief history of the formal governmental developments from
1979 through 1984 is provided in John Booth, "The National Governmental System," in Walker (1985: 29–44).

From the point of view of making sense of pluralism in connection with the role of the vanguard what is important about the composition of the Junta is that it shows that the FSLN did not merely choose to impose its unilateral conceptions upon other elements of the revolutionary movement. Even though all of the members of the junta recognized the real control of the FSLN Directorate as the "vanguard" (Booth, 1985: 187), the FSLN clearly used the Junta as a way not only of bringing other forces along but of determining the situation with respect to the views and demands of those outside the FSLN. That is to say that the FSLN clearly recognized that it could not represent everyone, though it could serve as the vanguard of the people.

The view of the FSLN as a vanguard suggests that it will favor some interests over others. This is explicitly understood to mean that other parties are necessary to represent the less favored interests so that political decision-making can function in a manner that takes into account the full range of social interests while continuing to "privilege" some sectors. Bayardo Arce said: "The Sandinista Front knows that it can not represent all sectors of the country equally because we prefer (*privilegimos*) the worker, laborer, *campesino* sector. In a society such as ours that is based on political pluralism and the mixed economy we know that there have to be other interests that need their own political expression" (Invernizzi, Pisani, and Ceberio, 1986: 90).

The Council of State: Functional Representation

The organization of the Council of State, which shared legislative authority with the Junta from May of 1980 until after the 1984 elections, further indicates that the FSLN clearly understood pluralism to require representation of various interests in a number of ways. Pluralist theory requires that organizations exist that can "articulate and aggregate interests" within the political system. The Council of State represented not only political parties and movements (eight in number in 1982–83) but also "popular organizations," labor organizations, guilds, social organizations, and private sector business organizations. Thus a plurality of groups had formal representation, including many that functioned as vocal opponents of the FSLN position within the formal political structure. Pluralism thus had a clear role in the actual development of the political system itself.

Opposition activity was not only a way for the FSLN to come to understand and adapt itself to the views of organized groups within the political system. These groups had clear influence on the actual course of policy. Most notable in this respect is the large role played by the opposition in developing within the Council of State the most fundamental legal structures through which political competition is to be expressed. Both the Law of Political Parties and the Electoral Law were the subject of substantial give and take, resulting in the opposition influencing the final result in a serious manner.

The Mass Organizations and Pluralism

The same was true, to some degree, with developments between the elections of 1984 and 1990, even though, or perhaps as a result of the earlier election, functional representation no longer existed. In the formation of the constitution of 1987 there were numerous hearings held throughout the country that led to substantial changes in the final document. The national women's movement (AMNLAE) played a substantial role in the debates. They were unsuccessful in obtaining either constitutional provisions or legislation to meet such demands as the legalization of abortion but they played a large role in the development of policies related to these issues. Similarly, UNAG was instrumental in developing agrarian reform policies with a fundamentally new direction than those that had earlier existed. Even since the election of 1990 the FSLN has had to respond to the demands of these groups as much as to direct them as has been shown above.

At first sight the several references to "mass organizations" closely related to the FSLN might seem to call into question the genuinely pluralist character of the developments in question. Yet serious reflection shows that the promotion of mass organizations by the FSLN is not only consistent with pluralism, but in some ways is its most clear expression. This is especially true in cases where pro-FSLN mass organizations succeeded in making major changes in FSLN policies or proposals. The AMNLAE succeeded in 1983 in obtaining participation for women in the Patriotic Military Service in opposition to the proposals of the FSLN in the Council of State.

The farmworker's union (ATC) was instrumental in obtaining approval for the recognition of land seizures that the FSLN had originally opposed (Mondragon and Molina, 1986: 12).

Two of the fundamental elements of pluralist theory are that no one wins all of the time and that those who are best organized, whose interests are "aggregated and articulated," have the best chance of obtaining favorable results. Yet if there is any sense in which revolution and pluralism are to be compatible the fact must be taken into account that interests are not automatically organized. This is especially true for those interests that have been least represented in the previous regime. If a new system of hegemony is to develop that can assure that the least privileged sectors of the old system are to become full participants in the new society, those sectors must be organized. This will not be in the obvious interests of those who benefitted from old structures, as can be seen clearly in the fact that when the FSLN expanded the Council of State to represent those previously unrepresented, Alfonso Robelo resigned from the Junta.

The CDS

It is in the development of mass organizations and their function in revolutionary Nicaragua that the theoretical synthesis of pluralism and vanguardism through the concept of participatory democracy is most clear. Here, in the interests of brevity, I will discuss only one example of how this functions, the development of the Sandinista Defense Committees (CDS), now known as the communal movement. Originally the CDS was seen as appropriate to both rural and urban areas. Indeed, in 1979–80 there was a massive mobilization to use this structure as the basis for local power in the rural areas. The mobilization is described in one major source as follows:

> It was a gigantic mobilizing force, the *comarcal* (small rural units) representatives of the church were involved, the *campesinos* and natural leaders came down from their *comarcas* to the Municipal Board and they made their mules available so that the new authorities could go to the most remote areas to become familiar with their problems. On foot, by mule, in little motor-driven

canoes, the representatives of the new power went to all the *comarcas* and organized open assemblies with the whole population. In many cases the delegates of the word convoked them and many of them were therefore elected as CDS directors. In these assemblies the people found, for the first time in history, the possibility of engaging in dialogue, of discussing their problems, complaints, denunciations, etc. with the new civil authorities. (CIERA, 1989, 6: 75–76)

The same source makes clear that the CDS in the rural areas were subsequently replaced in their functions by "class-based" organizations. Yet as an element of urban and semi-urban organization, the CDS was to serve a fundamental function in connecting neighborhood concerns with government and party officials. They were, for a time, the most important source of participatory democracy within the structures of Nicaraguan pluralism. Everyone within a neighborhood was encouraged to participate in the CDS as a community action group, though it was clear that they were dominated and usually led by members of the FSLN.

Although the CDS was successful in many ways during the early period, especially in working with the literacy campaign and in organizing work brigades both for harvests and for local projects, they came under severe criticism by the middle of the 1980s. Omar Cabezas was assigned in 1988 to work with the CDS to overcome perceived problems within the groups. Cabezas held that the most serious problems of the CDS in practice had been that it was:

1. Marked by a vertical processing style in which orders are seen as "going down" from the top.
2. Too closely identified as an FSLN support group and thus too "sectarian."
3. Overly bureaucratic in its methods and style. (LASA interview, June 23, 1988)

It is ironic that what critics of Sandinista "pluralism" identify as the features of the CDS that make it an instrument of totalitarian control are precisely those that Cabezas sought to alter by "democratizing" the organization.[10]   This is because in fact the role the CDS could have properly served for the FSLN and the Nicaraguan government was to articulate demands on the government.   But the FSLN preferred an organization of community participation to an instrument of its own policies.   It is not unreasonable to conclude that what it sought to do was to give real life to "mass" organizations so that they could genuinely play the sort of stabilizing role that organized groups normally play in a pluralist system.   This requires a substantial degree of autonomy for such organizations, aided by organizing resources from the vanguard, not a tight system of centralized control.   This is how a living pluralism must work.

Since the elections of 1990, the communal movement has continued to reorganize itself, especially in terms of attempting to bring those who voted for the UNO and now regret it into activities for community improvement (interviews with communal leaders, Managua and Estelí, April, 1992).   As will be discussed in the following chapter on contradictions in practice in the working out of pluralist theory, it is clear that the base community organizations failed in their function of providing information to the leadership of the FSLN about the extent to which people were inclined to vote for the UNO coalition.   Thus, perhaps the best way to understand this experience is that the FSLN failed to create the sort of institution it preferred and in fact was unable to reform the institutions that existed in such a manner as to fulfill their theoretical role.   What is odd here is that it appears that the critics of the CDS were somewhat justified in their criticisms of the practice but that this practice was *not* what the FSLN preferred.

---

[10]Critics of the FSLN who accused it of totalitarianism often saw the CDS as an instrument of the FSLN by which to control the local population.   The argument partially depended on the fact that the CDS was inspired, at least in part, by the Cuban Committees in Defense of the Revolution, which were also alleged to have this function.   Whether or not it is true that the Cuban organization played the role its critics assumed, it is clear that the CDS in Nicaragua did not simply follow the Cuban model.   Any serious attempt to make sense of the role of the CDS must resist facile comparisons to other groups as a replacement for serious analysis of the Nicaraguan experience.

The communal movement survives and is an important element in the continuation of the Sandinista revolution in local communities. When, for example, a volcanic eruption occurred in Léon in 1992 one of the first announcements on Managua radio stations was that the local communal organizations in Managua were to meet to prepare community response for aid in Léon. Similarly, local communal organizations have been mobilized to aid in the campaign to deal with an epidemic of cholera and were used in vaccination campaigns by the new Ministery of Health. Thus the role of the CDS in participatory democracy continues as a real aspect of life even after the electoral defeat of 1990.

The Military and Hegemony

Of course, even the most naive and friendly observer of the Nicaraguan revolution must recognize what its most outspoken critics emphasize most strongly in the reality of the FSLN vanguard, namely, that much of its base is in the military. What distinguishes the FSLN from all other historical forces in Nicaraguan politics is the fact that it began as a small military vanguard and ultimately succeeded in directing a broadly-based insurrection. The FSLN used its military strength as a small unit to develop relations with the population as a whole, which came to support the FSLN to a substantial degree because of its military capacities.

Hegemony in the struggle was obtained by this vanguard because, not in spite, of its military characteristics. The leaders of the FSLN are known as *commandantes* (commanders), the military, the militia, and the police forces were known as "Sandinista" during the ten years of Sandinista rule. Individual military and police personnel were commonly called *compas* (short for *campañeros* or comrades) until the transition to the new government. With the new government the *compas* have become the National Police and have changed their uniforms from a military to a civilian style. The militias have been abolished. Yet a fundamental element of the transition agreements left the army as the "Sandinista People's Army" and left its command in the hands of Humberto Ortega. This last element of the agreement has become a centerpiece of opposition claims that the Chamorro adminstration is "co-governing" with the Sandinistas. It appears that this agreement was essential for the FSLN to maintain some degree of hegemony in the social order. Without the continued existence of armed forces responsive at least in part to their concerns, the FSLN apparently felt they could not be secure from the sort of revenge that they themselves had not taken on the old members of the National Guard. This fact and continuing disputes within Nicaragua and between the Nicaraguan government and the United States about the role of the army and the character of its leadership make it especially important to understand how the FSLN saw the role of the military during their period of governance.

The merging of the concepts of vanguardism and pluralism, through an understanding of the role of hegemony in every social system, must take account of the role of the military as a social and ideological vanguard as well as simply a means of national defense and social control. It is tempting to suggest that the military aspects of the FSLN would have faded away if it were not for the *contra* war and direct military threats to the new revolutionary state. But, as Peter Marchetti points out, to think in this manner is to fail to take into account the reality of war that has faced all systems in transition in this century. Revolutionary transformations, especially those involving national liberation, will be opposed by substantial forces that have benefitted from the prior regime or fear the example that the revolution represents. We must, if we are to make sense of situations such as that in Nicaragua, "take the fact of war seriously" (Marchetti, 1986: 305). It is not possible to abstract war or its concomitant military and security organizations out of the process of developing and maintaining hegemony in contemporary revolutionary contexts. To do so is to ignore one of the essential features of the phenomena under consideration. The ultimate defeat of the FSLN in the 1990 election to which the continued military draft undoubtedly contributed, needs to be understood in this context. It is doubtful that the FSLN or the Nicaraguan government anticipated such a long and drawn-out guerilla-style war. Indeed, all appearances suggest that an all-out U.S. intervention was considered at least as likely an event. In any case the fact that the FSLN in government was continuously under pressures that made the military a major focus of activity must be considered a fundamental factor in ultimately making sense of the experience. In the present context it is important to see that the notion of the military as an extension of the population as a whole played a substantial role in Sandinista thought and practice.

The substantial military organization in Nicaragua under Sandinista governmental control was essential to maintain the very existence of the system in which hegemony was possible, but also because it promoted pluralism in its own way. It is important to remember that under Somoza the National Guard was an organization which came to be seen as clearly separated from the people as a whole.[11] It was not merely a tool of the dictatorship; it was its instantiation. The military struggle against the Somoza regime was a popular one, it was not merely a confrontation of the FSLN army against its military opponent. The development of armed struggle was not based simply on the creation of a Sandinista army to confront and replace the National Guard, it was the expression of popular will to create a sovereign Nicaraguan state. Jaime Wheelock points out that the FSLN was "conscious of the fact that it was important not to convert itself into an army but to be the head of an armed people" (1986: 115).

With the success of the insurrection it became clear to the FSLN that it was essential to construct a new army and security apparatus that would have a fundamentally different relationship with the population than did the old National Guard. As Torres and Coraggio put it: "In the light of other failed revolutionary experiments it was considered that a popular and revolutionary army politically oriented towards the defense of the revolution was a necessary safeguard for the possibility of carrying out an effective democratization and social transformation in Nicaragua" (1987: 33). Thus the point was not simply to put the FSLN military force in charge. It was to create a genuinely popular military force. The "people's army" was to serve as an instrument of hegemony not only in the simple sense of defending the national sovereignty and eliminating the remains of the old military force, but more importantly in the sense of integrating the people as a whole with a military force that it could see as its own.

---

[11]This should not be taken to imply that the National Guard only recruited from existing elites. Quite the contrary. Many of its recruits came the most humble of *campesino* backgrounds. Somoza himself was not of sufficiently high social status to be admitted to the exclusive La Terraza club, a nightclub in Managua. However, members of the Guard were, once recruited, intentionally isolated from their fellow citizens not only economically but socially.

Fear of the army or the police was virtually non-existent in the population as a whole, especially in the urban areas, during the ten years of Sandinista rule, though there was some concern expressed by opposition forces, especially in relation to the armed units of the Ministry of the Interior. Some degree of opposition to the army also developed in the countryside as the *contra* war progressed. Yet these problems did not generally spill over to the population at large. The point of the fact that there was a Sandinista army and a Sandinista police is not that they served simply as an instrument of the FSLN but that they served as an intermediary between Sandinismo, meaning popular support for the general revolutionary practice, and Sandinismo as represented by the FSLN as the vanguard.

The development of a popular Sandinista militia which handed out up to five hundred thousand modern weapons to the population (organized in local groupings) was a similar measure. It not only provided for effective military action against a *contra* force that focused on civilians but it provided for a practical sense of people's participation in the revolution. To be a member of a militia or the army did not mean that one was a part of the FSLN. Bayardo Arce claimed that the most generous estimates would lead to the claim that 12 percent of the army were members of the FSLN. On the other side of the equation, he said that only 59 percent of the members of the FSLN were either reservists or members of the militia (Invernizzi, Pisani, and Ceberio, 1986: 84). Nevertheless, to this day many Nicaraguans proudly wear their distinctive militia hats as a sign of their identification with the revolution.

Thus it is merely a flight of fancy or ideologically motivated nonsense to suggest, as did "high level western diplomats" in "deep background briefings," (as they insisted they be called in a LASA interview), that the FSLN *was* the army or that the role of the Nicaraguan military was analogous to that of the Salvadoran, Guatemalan, or even Chilean militaries. On the contrary, the Nicaraguan military situation guaranteed broad scale popular participation, even among those who would have preferred to abstain.

Of course the military also aided in maintaining the hegemony of the existing state through its capacity to prevent a fundamental change through military action. In this respect its role is little different from that of the military and the National Guard in a system such as that of the United States. In subsequent chapters it will be shown, however, that the role of the military, especially of the draft, ultimately presented serious contradictions in terms of continued Sandinista control of the government.

Events since the transition in 1990 show that the concept of the Sandinista army continues to have substantial resonance in relation to the nature of hegemony in Nicaraguan society. The major substantive criticism of UNO forces that challenged the president's continued support for Humberto Ortega's role as head of the Sandinista Popular Army before she announced that he would be removed was that the army not repress the actions of the *revueltos* in demanding the fulfillment of agreements they had reached with the government (*La Opinion*, May 23, 1992: 7A), or in repressing strikes and land seizures. Clear demands were thus made by the strongest enemies of the FSLN that the pluralist character of the new government should not accept certain elements of Nicaraguan political life as legitimate actors. Among these elements are strikers and those who have seized land. It is not merely accidental that the struggle for hegemony in the present period focuses substantially on issues involving the military and the police and how they are to respond to strikes and land seizures. These institutions were consciously structured by the FSLN as elements of revolutionary hegemony. As the drama plays itself out in contemporary Nicaragua the Chamorro administration sometimes has responded to the need to maintain stability within a revolutionary hegemony and has refused to make changes in the military institution or to use the military and the police against protestors. At other times it has responded more to the desire of its erstwhile political partners and to the apparent desires of the United States government and its own most right-wing sectors to attack Sandinista hegemony by attempting to obtain direct control over military institutions. The police and the army have both been caught in the crossfire of these shifting policies. The detailing of events in this respect could well be the basis for a major study in itself. What is clear is that the present struggle often centers around the relationship between the security forces and the population as a whole.

In this sense the FSLN reliance on the military as a fundamental element in maintaining popular hegemony within a pluralist system can only be seen as farsighted. It is interesting to note that a meeting of the presidents of all Central American countries felt called upon to demand that the U.S. continue to supply aid to Nicaragua without regard to changes in the military institution because international cooperation is a "fundamental element for the consolidation of peace and democracy in the region" (*La Opinión*, June 7, 1992: 1A, 6A). Clearly the Central American presidents, in the context of the UNO electoral victory of 1990 and the peace accords between the FMLN and the government of El Salvador, believe that the development of pluralist democratic systems in the area depends on the U.S. not attempting to eliminate key social actors through the manipulation of foreign aid. Among these actors in Nicaragua is the Sandinista military.

What occurred in Nicaragua, and probably is occurring in other revolutionary movements, including the Salvadoran one, is a merging of the concepts of pluralism and vanguardism in the practice of developing a consciously structured system of "popular" hegemony to produce a system that combines participatory democracy with the electoral and representative institutions that are characteristic of other pluralist systems. The Salvadoran experience must take place in a context where revolutionary victory was not won on the battlefield but where revolutionary hegemony can only be obtained through the ballot box. In Nicaragua, revolutionary hegemony was gained through the force of arms and is presently being contested in the electoral and political arenas. The theoretical and practical problems to which the establishment of hegemony through guidance of the state by a vanguard party that established a structure of pluralism in the Nicaraguan experience is the subject of the following chapter.

Whatever may have been the problems encountered by the FSLN, it is clear that it made a substantial effort to creatively develop an alternative to existing models of socialist practice. There can be no doubt that the aim of much of the FSLN leadership, from the time of Fonseca to the present, was to unite Marxist concepts with the practice of revolution to develop a new model of a democratic, yet revolutionary, transition to socialism. Only the future actions of revolutionaries throughout the world can make clear to what extent the path remains open to further development of this model. Understanding both the successes and the failures in the Nicaraguan experience can be useful in attempting to make sense of future possibilities in Nicaragua and elsewhere.

PART II

Theory and Practice in the
Consolidation of the Revolution:
A Critical Analysis

The FSLN united the concept of pluralism with the concept of the vanguard to create a new form of participatory democracy. The vanguard could maintain hegemony in a pluralist system, resulting in a transition to a more just political and social order, socialism. The fundamental theoretical problem with this notion as it developed in Nicaraguan practice is that pluralist theory assumes a plural society not marked by sharp social divisions; the FSLN worked in the context of a fundamentally polarized society, attempting to create a sort of social pluralism that had never existed in the past. The Sandinista notion was that a conscious vanguard could create and then maintain hegemony, in the Gramscian sense of the term. In this process, new forms of participatory democracy could ultimately assure the functioning of the system in the interests of the broad popular majorities.

Nicaragua could not become a pluralist system simply with Somoza and his allies removed from power. Thus the task of the FSLN as presumed hegemonic agent was to create social conditions that would make a pluralism possible that favored the poor.[1] In the course of practical political and economic developments some of the problems created in attempting to fulfill this theoretical notion became clear. Perhaps the most serious of these problems is that it

---

[1]It is tempting here to use the phrase "with a preferential option for the poor," which derives from liberation theology. The whole question of the relation between liberation theology and Sandinista theory is a complex one but it is clear that Sandinista theory and practice combines Marxism and liberation theology both in theory and in practice.

is difficult to develop important organizations to articulate the interests of previously unrepresented social groups that are truly independent of the vanguard that attempts to stimulate their development. When the newly developing organizations are stimulated by the party and the state they may become demobilized as independent actors, submitting themselves to state and party control in the interests of national unity.

Pluralism works insofar as the organization of interests is independent of state and party control. If, on the other hand these groups are treated as inseparable allies of the state and the party, paradoxically, groups that represent less revolutionary forces receive more favorable treatment from the state than groups allied with the revolution. The more conservative forces constantly threaten to refuse to support the newly developing legal and political system, and to attempt to alter it in their own interests. The newly created organizational forces that favor revolutionary developments thus become agents to convince their members to accept the new party and state rules even when they produce immediately harmful results for the individuals that make up the organizations themselves. The result can be a sort of de-legitimation of the new organizations as revolutionary actors in the eyes of their constituents. As this occurs the leaders of such groups become less capable of articulating their constituents' demands to the party and the government. Through playing a participatory role the groups may end up as agents simply of participatory administration rather than as elements of a participatory democracy that determines the broad shape of social and political policies.

In the Nicaraguan case this analysis explains, in great measure, the FSLN's failure to realize the weakness of its support in the election of 1990. The leaders of mass organizations did not receive accurate information about voters' intentions from those who had, for one reason or another, come to see those organizations more as administering the will of the party and the government then as channels for articulating their grievances to the top. Thus, the leaders of the state and the dominant party were sheltered from complaints and resentments that had developed in their own fundamental base.

This was especially true in the sphere of political economy. Within the broad area of the political economy these developments had special significance in agrarian reform policies and practices.

Ultimately, some of the contradictions that arose in these areas had a substantial impact on the election results of 1990 and on the ways in which the revolutionary process developed after the FSLN lost governmental power. The first chapter in this part, chapter 4, examines these developments in the period from 1979 until 1985. Chapter 5 consists of a political and economic balance sheet for this period. Chapter 6 considers the period from 1985 until the transition of power in 1990. The final chapter develops the theoretical lessons that can be learned from the Nicaraguan revolutionary practice as a whole.

Generally the first period of FSLN governance was marked by an attempt to develop a new political, economic, and social system in order to create a "new Nicaragua." In this period many of the roots of the problems that would surface later were established, though their full effects were not yet evident. Mobilization for change and to resist both external aggression and internal counter-revolution (backed by external forces) was still sufficient to provide support for the FSLN, the new hegemonic agent. Further, programs such as those providing free health care and universal education helped maintain support for the revolution among the poor, as did those that subsidized both consumers and producers of basic foodstuffs. The "social wage" provided by these measures was useful in avoiding excess demands for high wages, which would have done damage to both private producers and the state, while at the same time providing a basic improvement in the quality of life of the poor sectors of Nicaraguan society. In addition, policies such as easy access to credit on the part of all agricultural producers maintained substantial support for the FSLN in the countryside. Nevertheless this basic policy was also very costly in macroeconomic terms. The major costs produced by these policies did not begin to be fully paid until after the electoral victory of the FSLN in 1984.

In the period from 1985 to 1990, marked by the U.S. embargo and the loss of aid from the decomposing Soviet and Eastern European system, the full consequences of earlier programs became clear in the context of continued external pressures. The period was officially described as one of "survival" and much of the government and FSLN effort was devoted to attempts to deal with the inter-national situation, both in military and in economic terms. Economically the period was marked by attempts to counteract the macroeconomic consequences of earlier programs; the time had finally arrived where choices had to made between different possible constituencies. Ultimately, an economic adjustment plan was implemented that produced serious problems in maintaining the support of poor sectors of the society, especially in the urban areas. The FSLN followed a basic policy of prioritizing the countryside over the city after 1985 and of giving substantial aid, especially in terms of land titling, to private producers in the countryside rather than continuing to emphasize state farms and cooperatives as the base of agrarian reform.

In this context, developments in the mass organizations made evident, at least in retrospect, the changing composition of the forces that could make successful demands on the state and the party. Efforts to deal with these problems were undertaken but were insufficient to provide the FSLN with a clear understanding of the popular sentiments that were to lead to the electoral results of 1990. On the organizational level in this period the CDS and the ATC came to be less significant actors than, for example UNAG. Especially important in this respect was the problem of how to maintain an adequate military force to deal with actual and potential armed threats while at the same time maintaining production and consolidating the gains of the past. Here the CDS, the CST, and ATC played a substantial role in providing human power to staff the ranks of the army and the militias but received little in return for their efforts.

The basic policy was to attempt to defuse the counter-revolution by, on the one hand, providing land to individual small producers and, on the other hand, by pursuing accommodations with the organized representatives of the increasingly disloyal opposition, especially with the High Council of Private Enterprise (COSEP). The concept of *concertacíon*, which called for a national dialogue between the FSLN and opposing sectors of the society, was fundamental in this situation.[2] The FSLN, and therefore the

---

[2]In the Central American context the term *concertación* refers to an attempt to reach agreements among basically opposed parties in the interest of national development. Although the term is difficult to define it is well and broadly understood by Central American Spanish speakers. Typically, a process described by this term involves meetings between groups and organizations with very different agendas and the government to engage in dialogue in order to reach some agreement about policies.

government, consistently attempted to de-polarize the situation both internally and externally by adjusting to the loudly proclaimed complaints of the internal opposition and of the United States.

By the end of the second period, 1985–90, the government was involved in serious negotiations with the *contras* in an attempt to obtain peace, even though it had always denied that it would do so, demanding instead to negotiate with the United States government. The election was advanced by several months in accordance with the Arias peace plan in order to show that a full pluralism, based on free elections, existed in Nicaragua and with the hope that after such elections U.S. aid to the *contras* might cease. Open U.S. aid to the opposition forces was allowed during the election. All of this was structured in part so as to influence the 1990 congressional elections in the United States. The FSLN felt that a Democratic party success in these elections could reduce U.S. pressures on Nicaragua and finally end the *contra* war. While this was a policy of accommodation that makes sense in pluralist terms, its ultimate consequence was the unexpected loss of governmental power by the FSLN.

The analysis below will suggest that developments in the period preceding 1985 revealed some fundamental theoretical and practical contradictions in the model of a pluralist vanguardism that were to have their full effects in the later period. The basic problem is that pluralism and participatory democracy come into conflict in practice in such a manner as to tend to demobilize revolutionary forces, especially in what was seen as the fundamental base of the revolution, the working class. Undue influence was therefore given to those who continuously threatened to withdraw from the pluralist game and to create fundamental instability in the system. To some extent these problems relate to the increasing aggressiveness of the U.S. against Nicaragua in the later period and the forms that this aggressiveness took. After all, those involved in trying to reverse the Nicaraguan revolution took their understand-

---

It does not imply that political disagreements will cease but that there can be some degree of reconciliation of apparently incompatible groups. In the Nicaraguan case such agreements are often made quite formal and are referred to in subsequent discussions as binding by the parties. For an attempt to define the term in an economic context, see Martínez Cuenca (1992: 21–22).

ings of how to do so from the basic lines of policy that were developed in Nicaragua during the early period. The target was known through how the system had developed in the first five years and there can be little doubt that there was a conscious effort to take advantage of those contradictions that had developed in the model.

Especially important in this respect is the fact that the FSLN had seen the workers on state farms and in the cities as the fundamental foundation of revolution and had counted on them to continue to sacrifice short-term gains for long-term revolutionary goals such as participatory democracy, in which the working class would ultimately obtain hegemony in the system. In this process the small-to-medium individual producers had been assumed to be fundamentally different from workers in the "more advanced" large-scale farms of the Pacific coastal region and workers in the cities. The FSLN thus accepted it as a basic reality that there were class differences between peasants and agricultural workers as there were between wage workers and those in the informal economy in the city. The wage workers, urban and rural, were seen as having a clear class identity and it was thought that they could be counted on to support the revolution and the FSLN on the basis of their objective class interests. FSLN practice reveals the view that small and medium producers and those in the informal economy had to be appealed to in terms of their individual interests and were to receive attention in a different manner than the real proletarians. Thus, for the former group participatory democracy came to mean sacrifice and for the latter, pluralism came to mean a series of continuous demands for greater attention. The problem with this is that as the latter groups became more clearly isolated from the former they also began to see the possibilities of receiving attention for their needs from other sources, including internal right-wing forces and the United States government through its policies in support of the counterrevolutionary war.

4

CONSTRUCTION OF NICARAGUAN PLURALISM BY THE VANGUARD: PROBLEMS OF A CONSCIOUS HEGEMONIC AGENT

The Theory of Advance to Socialism: Pluralism and a Mixed Economy

Basic Sandinista theory held that there was no bourgeois hegemony within Nicaragua. On the contrary, the international bourgeoisie was represented, even if indirectly, by the Somoza regime itself. Without Somocismo, so the leaders of the FSLN thought, it would be possible to deal with national bourgeois elements by simply incorporating them in the larger social order while maintaining their role in production; the existing hegemonic system was eliminated with the defeat of Somoza. It was essential to develop an alternative hegemony within the context of international non-alignment, a mixed economy, internal pluralism, and participatory democracy.

The first step in creating such a situation was to reinforce the notion of Nicaragua as a sovereign nation-state. The FSLN was a "national liberation front"; its function was to create a genuinely Nicaraguan reality. Yet, not simply any national consciousness would do. The struggle of the FSLN to prevent a simple bourgeois political revolution had been clear from the beginning. The vanguard was to produce an alternative hegemony in the interests of the "people," or "of the broad majorities." Thus, nationalism was not the only goal; it was to be a nationalism that was combined with a process of social revolution. Clearly there was no intention to simply maintain existing economic structures. The seizure of Somoza's properties and those of his closest allies was not undertaken simply in order to distribute them to new elites. The

113

nationalization of the banks and of foreign trade made clear that there was not to be a simple temporary intervention of the state in the economic order. The idea was to use state control of the economic heights as a fundamental element of social transition. While there may have been some disagreements at the level of the National Directorate about the character of the "transition" in question (Molero, 1988: 36) and about the relative roles of central planning and market forces (Martínez Cuenca, 1992: 11), there can be no doubt that there was agreement that there should not simply be a free play of existing economic forces. Some groups and classes were to control the process, not others. Pluralism was to be united with participatory democracy through the development of mass organizations that would play a substantial role in policy making and implementation, thus representing the "majorities" in different forms.

The Sandinista position was well articulated by Jaime Wheelock, who wrote:

> What has to be dealt with theoretically is whether it is possible for a bourgeoisie to exist that only produces, without power, that can limit itself as a class to a productive role, that is to say, that can limit itself to exploiting their means of production and that can use these means to live, not as instruments of power, of imposition.
>
> I think that this is possible in Nicaragua. We received a country with an incomplete capitalism and an incompletely formed class which, moreover, never directly held political power. But the revolution has broken the logic of imperial domination in a Latin American country; when this is broken apart other very important factors are also smashed: the psychology of security for example. The bourgeoisie was accustomed to being the belligerent force and dominant in ideology, culture and society and now they do not dominate; here those who speak, those who provide the model, are the workers and peasants, the student leaders, the union leaders, the ATC, the CST, the Sandinista front, and none of them represent the bourgeoisie. (Wheelock, 1984)

This does not mean, however, that the FSLN was intent on following pre-existing models of socialism. Wheelock suggested that socialism had changed from what was suggested by prior models and from the ideas of the thirties and that the FSLN did not want to impose any particular "brand" of socialism. It looked to France and Spain as much as to other countries for its model of socialism. Socialism, in his view, is a mode of production still "in diapers" and it could not be expected that it would simply immediately replace capitalism. After all, he says, "it took a long time for feudalism to defeat slavery and for capitalism to defeat feudalism" (Invernizzi, Pisani, and Ceberio, 1986: 22).

Humberto Ortega, in the context of the same interview from which these words of Wheelock are drawn, pointed out that it would not be "dialectical" to simply follow a pattern of "appealing immediately in the political order to a radical transformation of an orthodox type" (Invernizzi, Pisani, and Ceberio, 1986: 21).[1] Rather, he argued, it was essential to find a new model of transition, not to follow any older model in detail. Moving from one system, dependent capitalism, to another one, socialism, was not simply a question of immediately changing domination of one class by that of another, as some have thought was possible in past models. The reality of dependent capitalism includes the fact that widespread hunger is a problem. Solving the class problem would not, in itself, "resolve the problem of poverty" (Molero, 1988: 36).[2]

---

[1]Molero interprets Ortega's remarks to suggest that socialist transformation must wait until the next century and that the immediate task of the FSLN and the government it controlled was simply to promote national liberation and to wait for the next century for transition to socialism (1988: 36). While a literal interpretation of his words might suggest this, in context it is clear that his point is that Nicaragua must find its own mode of transition to socialism.

[2]Given the method of citation used by Molero, which does not include page numbers, it is difficult to locate the precise quotations that she draws from Invernnizi, Pisani, and Ceberio. However, it appears that this language is not exactly what Ortega said but rather a pasting together of several different remarks. Nevertheless, I quote her language here on the grounds that even given these words her interpretation of their significance is not the only possible one.

Ortega's general point was that what can be done at any particular moment depends on existing conditions. He did not say that actions being taken at the time were insignificant in promoting a socialist transition, only that other methods used at other times and other places could not be simply followed in these conditions. It is instructive to note some of his examples:

> If Marx, Bolívar or Sandino were at the head of the Nicaraguan government, they would have been doing the same things we are doing and not what Elí Altamirano from the Communist Party or the socialists say. They hold that what should be done is to break relations with all the capitalist countries, to confiscate all of the property of the capitalists, smash them and make a dictatorship of the worker-peasant type with alliances only within the socialist camp. But it would still have to be determined with what part of the socialist camp, if with the Soviet Union, with China, with Korea, Albania, I don't know with what part they would do it. (Invernnizi, Pisani, and Ceberio, 1986: 20)

Ortega also pointed out that he didn't think that there had to be a political bureau, a central committee, and a secretary general in the party simply because these forms had been adopted elsewhere (Invernnizi, Pisani, and Ceberio, 1986: 21).

The initial government was, as Molero suggests, a government of "national reconstruction." As such it did not involve the direct elimination of a national class that had constructed an autonomous system of domination. In fact, the state had been in the hands of an elite that was dependent on an international bourgeois class, not a bourgeois elite itself. The whole social and cultural reality in Nicaragua was subjected to the hegemony of the United States. Thus, obtaining national liberation, especially in the Latin American context, was not simply a matter of breaking political dependency on the United States; it was also a matter of constructing new political, economic, and cultural hegemony. It would not have been correct to have simply declared all Nicaraguans who owned a medium or even large agricultural estate or a business to be enemies of the state, nor to allow them to control politics; it was essential to begin a process of economic construction using the few resources that existed without allowing those with wealth to control developments. Utopian schemes or imports from other models could not serve to create a new world out of whole cloth—existing fabrics had to be re-knit into new designs.

Pluralist systems seem to work so well in maintaining stability in basically capitalist systems because they are fundamentally based on markets. Markets function in relation to economic interests. In pluralist theory the government plays the role of referee among different groups, it does not set the rules of the game. It provides multiple access points for different interests to influence governmental policy. Stability in the system requires that interest groups form in a non-polarized pattern simply as a result of existing conditions and that the articulation of interests reflect memberships of individuals in multiple groups. If some one center controls all of these activities or if there is polarization in which all of those with similar interests line up against all of those with different interests, the system will be unstable.

Of course, the basic revolutionary plan was not to maintain stability, it was to make a revolution. In this sense the FSLN was to control instability in order to eventually produce a fundamentally new system in which a different structure of interests would exist than that which is characteristic of bourgeois pluralist systems. The idea was to create a socialist hegemony through a guided process of social and economic change in which the national bourgeoisie would never gain hegemony, though it could play a substantial role in national economic development. From a system of external "imperialist hegemony" combined with an internal corrupt dictatorship, the FSLN hoped to be able to create a national system with a fundamentally new orientation. Pluralism was to combine with a mixed economy to produce a new national group that was exclusively aligned neither with existing capitalist nor existing socialist states. The goal was, thus, not merely to create a new national stability based on existing internal forces that could participate, as do most other Latin American states, in an old system of international economy. Rather, it was to create a new model of national autonomy within which Nicaragua would occupy a fundamentally different role in the international sphere than it had heretofore.

Jaime Wheelock discussed this vision in the clearest manner. He suggested that it was essential to understand the past in terms of imperialism. As a producer of primary agricultural goods and an importer of finished goods, Nicaragua had been submitted to an international order in which it was fundamentally dependent on the United States, even to the extent of lacking its own indigenous class structure. The only way to move towards national independence was to change Nicaragua's role in the international division of labor. Wheelock succinctly spelled out the strategy of the FSLN as follows:

> The first thing that we plan to do in our national strategy of struggle against backwardness and dependency is to change the role that Nicaragua has played in the division of labor. That is to say that we plan to cease being a country that sells our primary materials in raw form—as in the old agro-export model—in order to move to a better level in which we industrially transform these original primary materials and put them into the market with an additional value created by secondary industrial processing. (1986: 48)

This was not to happen simply by letting things take their natural course; after all, no other Latin American country had gotten to this stage. Yet it was not to happen simply through state-directed central planning, either. The intention was to guide the process, taking into account existing productive capacities and existing social forces. A certain degree of central planning was to be combined with a guided pluralism to produce a fundamental economic transition. Participatory democracy through the creation of mass organizations that were involved in the setting and implementation of policy was to be combined with pluralism. The question remained to what degree each element of this complex formula should be emphasized.

As the process developed over the ten years of FSLN government there were a number of shifts of emphasis. Fundamentally, however, at least in the area of economic policy, central planning played a larger role in the beginning of the process than it did in later years and there was a gradual, though by no means even, process of development towards letting market forces play a larger role.[3]

Curiously, although the early period was marked by more of an emphasis on central planning than the later period, it was also marked by less coordination of economic policy. It took at least five years for the FSLN-controlled government to develop clear coordination between different governmental units involved in the making of economic policies. One critique of much of the economic policies related to food production cites the following example of coordination problems: "The process of making decisions in pricing policies was consequently complex and slow. In the case of meat and milk, for example, the process of setting prices involved four different ministries at the minimum, six administrative steps and six months of negotiations among diverse government branches before it was possible to arrive at a new price" (Biondi-Morra, 1990: 317).

Although some of the earliest actions of the FSLN were marked by their extremely pluralist character, especially in the formation of the new government, it is clear that there was a plan of political economy that depended as well on substantial central control of the process by the FSLN. The basic strategy was to develop central control of many economic decisions, to place control of Somoza-owned properties in the hands of the state, and to

---

[3]Alejandro Martínez Cuenca, part of an FSLN team that began to work on economic issues prior to 1979, minister of Foreign Trade from 1979 to 1988, and minister of Planning and Budget for the remainder of the FSLN period of government, presents a clear set of arguments on this subject. The thesis of his work is that the origins of the February 1990 electoral defeat of *Sandinismo* are found many years before that election. "We failed to give sufficient importance to the wearing down of the economy—not only a product of the war. The conceptual differences around centralism versus a market economy took too long to be cleared up inside of *Sandinismo*. That failure to clear up this dilemma on time led to losing valuable time at very crucial moments when Nicaragua was becoming integrated into the world market" (1992: 11). The present analysis differs in important respects from that of Martínez Cuenca but also owes a good deal to what he has to say. It should be remembered that he was, in good measure, the architect of the economic reform plans of much of the last few years of the FSLN period of government and thus may be a bit too interested in setting the blame for loss of FSLN support on earlier actions.

promote organization of workers as a new social and political force. At the same time, production by private property owners was to continue. Most marketing of agricultural goods was to be centralized in state hands and there was to be a system that guaranteed both good prices to rural producers and a supply of basic commodities at low prices for urban consumers. Furthermore there was to be enforcement of minimum wages and the development of a "social wage" through provision of education and health services by the state.

The understanding of the FSLN was that half of the labor force consisted of *campesinos* and artisan workers and that the majority of wage labor was employed seasonally. Half of the entrepreneurial sector was controlled by the Somozas or their close allies and most of the rest was subordinated to the Somozas through their control of banking and the processing of agricultural goods.[4] Expropriation of Somoza's properties would not negatively affect the majority of the population and it would provide the state with control of the heights of the economy. As Valpy Fitzgerald, an important British adviser to the Nicaraguan government on economic affairs, put it: "limiting expropriation to Somoza's properties would not only be politically legitimate but would also guarantee control over the whole business sector, maintaining intact 'private' property. It was hoped that capitalism could be gradually reduced to the point where it would play an essentially administrative role with guaranteed margins of utility" (1989: 30).

The remaining national bourgeoisie could be controlled by the fact that it would constitute an economic sector under the control of a larger state sector. Some of the powerful tools for this purpose included maintenance of banking control through the nationalization of the banks, state control of most commerce (including that in imported inputs, in export crops, and in basic consumption goods), state regulation of exchange rules, and control of credit by the state. These would not be substantially different in many ways from the

---

[4]Martínez Cuenca points out that there was a substantial overestimate of the weight of Somoza's properties in the national economy. He says that, in fact, the expropriation of Somoza and his allies "only affected between 30 percent and 40 percent of production, and in the countryside, less than 20 percent of the property" (1992: 57). Some of the consequences of this miscalculation will be noted below.

controls that existed, in practice, under the prior regime, though they were now to serve a purpose other than the enrichment of the dictator. There were also to be new union organizations in both the state and public sectors. The state would control salaries and production norms. The forces of public order were under FSLN control. All of this combined so that, as Fitzgerald so aptly puts it, "it was thought that it was possible to 'encircle' private capital and subject its dynamic to the state" (1989: 32).

Fashioning New Rules for the New Economic Elite: Separating Patriotic Producers from Counterrevolutionaries

Thus, in pluralist terms, the idea was to establish a set of rules of the game that would favor fundamental economic transition without eliminating the class of private producers that had been alienated from the old regime. However, it would have been unrealistic to expect to share governmental power with bourgeois representatives such as Robelo and Chamorro and to think that they would simply acquiesce to these new rules. After all, anyone with even the dimmest Marxist understanding recognizes that political and economic power are interconnected. The national bourgeoisie had not united with the FSLN in the struggle against Somoza simply in order to take a later subordinate role. Further, it would have been unreasonable on their part to simply have allowed the FSLN to proceed to organize labor unions, woman's organizations, community organizations, and others without some degree of resistance. The participatory democracy implied in the organization of these groups would clearly limit the effective participation of already organized bourgeois groups.

Indeed, these problems gave rise to early political disputes that were to have substantial impact on the whole period of FSLN rule. When the FSLN decided to change the Council of State to include the mass organizations that had been promoted by the Front, Robelo left the Governing Junta and Chamorro followed soon thereafter, citing problems with her health. It had been easy enough for Robelo to join in the enthusiasm for a new order in the beginning. Indeed in some respects he took a strong role in promoting a system that placed substantial restrictions on economic activity. Alejandro Martínez Cuenca, who served as minister for

121

Foreign Trade from 1979 to 1988 and as minister of Planning and Budget from 1988 until 1990, remembers that early on in the process Robelo had been more radical than many people in the FSLN. He had, for example, insisted on a policy that salaries should be set so that no one would earn more than ten times what the lowest paid worker received. Martínez Cuenca understood this as follows: "Robelo's radicalism is explained to me as the typical euphoria of a capitalist who got on the train of the revolution and turns out to be more papist than the Pope. Robelo even demanded to be the one to read the decrees in public which nationalized the bank and foreign trade. But, in the end, during the hard times, these people could not consistently defend the whole of the revolutionary positions" (1992: 28).

It was easy enough for an individual like Robelo to agree to, even to be enthusiastic about, substantial economic reforms. When the FSLN insisted, however, on introducing new actors into the decision-making process he could not agree to continue in the government. To have done so would have been to isolate himself from his own political and economic base. It is one thing to be enthusiastic about policy issues, it is quite another to concede basic capacities to influence future policy decisions to those who represent fundamentally different interests. As long as the rules of the game allowed Robelo and the modern entrepreneurs he represented to have a substantial role in maintaining and developing new rules he was willing to play. When the FSLN acted to introduce fundamentally new players in the game of hegemony, Robelo refused to play any longer.

The original government of national reconciliation thus did not last very long. It stretched the limits of pluralist possibilities to expect a major interest group to simply allow the FSLN to act as the vanguard. Robelo's new Movement for Nicaraguan Democracy (MDN) united with the major business organization, COSEP, and several of the traditional political parties to call for elections to be held in 1982. When they tried to take to the streets to enforce this demand and were prevented from doing so, COSEP issued a document highly critical of the FSLN. It accused the FSLN of "having deviated from its original governing program," claiming that "the FSLN is, in fact, the executive and legislative power of the nation, that the Armed Forces are in the service of the Front," and that the reason for not holding elections was simply to allow the

FSLN to have time to consolidate its control. They claimed that there had been serious restrictions on democratic liberties. The document stated that the FSLN had not respected the idea of the mixed economy and concluded that "The FSLN has destroyed national unity and is consolidating its bases to implement a communist political and economic project in Nicaragua with a totalitarian state and with the consequent restrictions of all the liberties of the citizens" (quoted in Molero, 1988: 57).

The struggle had begun over the basic rules of the game. It now could not be doubted that political forces opposed to the FSLN project would go beyond merely asserting their economic interests. They were making clear that rules of the game that would ultimately lead away from capitalist relations would not be tolerated. Vocal demands, national and international, were made for respect for "human rights." FSLN (not governmental) support for local groups that organized to prevent a large MDN rally was used to call the legitimacy of the system into question. New rules of the agrarian reform announced in July of 1981 led to further vocal protests from the bourgeois sector.

Finally, in September of 1981 (by which time the *contra* war had begun), a state of social and economic emergency was declared by the government. Four COSEP leaders were arrested for having disseminated a document both nationally and internationally which made extremely strong claims against the FSLN and the government, asserting that Nicaragua was in a state of chaos and that there was a plan to eliminate the private sector. Three of them were sentenced to six months in prison, though they were later pardoned before serving the whole sentence.

Molero correctly sees these arrests as a case of the FSLN setting the limits of allowable discourse. She says:

> What did this measure mean? Is it simply a demon-
> stration of force? It can't be ignored that there was
> another important fact that entered into it: the death in
> a gunfight, during this same time, of the business leader
> of COSEP, Jorge Salazar, while he was driving a vehicle
> full of arms for the counterrevolution. Though this was
> not made public at the time they had strong suspicions
> about the possible relation of the three people detained
> and Salazar. In this sense, the detention would be,

above all, a preventive warning to establish clear limits to attitudes that the government was not disposed to tolerate. (1988: 60)

Those, like Robelo, who joined with the armed resistance in an attempt to turn over the table on which the game was played were no longer to be considered as players—they put themselves outside the limits of the game.

In one sense, of course, this constituted progress in the process of transition. The national bourgeoisie lost out to the FSLN in the contest for hegemony and the FSLN could now proceed with the attempt to fundamentally alter the economy and to develop participatory democracy alongside pluralism. On the other hand, the legitimacy of the regime as a whole was now cast into doubt in both the national and the international arena. The enemies of the transition now could decry the regime as illegitimate, as "totalitarian." There were two ways to do this. One was to remain within the country and take up the role of a "disloyal opposition," a role to which much of the national bourgeoisie had been accustomed under Somoza. Violetta Chamorro took this route. The other was to go over to the armed opposition, as Robelo ultimately did. When even Sandinistas such as Eden Pastora and Alfredo César went over to the counterrevolutionary forces it became clear that it could not simply be assumed that those sympathetic to the national bourgeoisie would agree to stay in the game. Thus it was essential to attempt to keep as many of these people as possible within the ranks of "patriotic producers" rather than to have them simply slip into open counterrevolutionary action.

This divided the right in its opposition to the fundamental policy of transition and thus had its political value. But it also created a new center competing for ideological hegemony among the population, decrying the loss of citizens' rights and making it more difficult for the government to proceed with its basic economic plan. From this time forward COSEP would share leadership of the major opposition forces within the country with *La Prensa* and the Church hierarchy.[5]

---

[5]For an examination of the role of the Church in the process of competing for hegemony that provides substantial historical background, see Williams, 1985.

The FSLN now found itself in open competition for political hegemony, a situation that it has never been able to overcome. Yet it did not simply become another actor equal to all others. It still controlled the state, including the police and the military. It was still the only substantial organized political force that could compete directly for governmental power; none of the traditional political parties was able to consolidate a significant following, as would be shown in the election of 1984. Even with the substantial aid of the United States, the forces around COSEP could not consolidate sufficiently to even seriously contest the 1984 election and were thus forced to follow a policy of abstention from the election.

Those who remained as producers in the national economy generally continued to be favored by governmental policies in economic terms. As time would show, the rupture with a substantial segment of the national bourgeoisie at this stage not only led to capital flight on the part of those who decided to give up the national project altogether but to a lack of investment and some degree of capital flight on the part of those who remained. Furthermore it would produce an ideological basis for opposition to the FSLN outside of the national bourgeoisie itself. Eduardo Baumeister and Neira Caudra aptly describe the position of this sector (based on data through 1984) as follows:

> All in all, the capitalist sector is in a sense "on hold," producing with generous credit and little of their own working capital. It is neither investing nor augmenting the area under production (except for the single private sugar plantation). Its economic logic focuses on accumulating foreign currency and the subsequent deterioration of farms and plantations. If they invest at all it is in agricultural machinery, the purchase of which is subsidized by the state. (186)

The fundamental response of the FSLN to the national bourgeoisie's reluctance to invest in production was to continue to provide economic policies, such as cheap credit, prices for products that guaranteed profits for large producers, and substantial flexibility in economic dealings with large producers. The FSLN was presumably treating them "fairly" in relation to other producers and continually reiterating guarantees that property in productive use would be safe from expropriation in the hope that it would keep large producers operating. It would appear that, at best, early FSLN policy neutralized a certain sector of the national bourgeoisie, at least in the sense of not driving them all into the growing counter-revolution. Yet the logic of pluralism required continuing to offer substantial economic incentives to large private producers.

Participation of the Masses in Pluralism

Of course, during this period the FSLN had been working as well on the consolidation of its own base. At the same time as some elements of the national bourgeoisie were being isolated from the game, new institutional actors were beginning to play a substantial role. "Mass organizations" that constituted the real base for much FSLN support were both created and reformulated during this period. Indeed, as has been noted above, the basic political rupture caused by changes in the Council of State was partially a result of the fact that the FSLN insisted on giving these organizations an official role within it. The basic groups involved here were women (AMNLAE), community organizations (CDS), agricultural workers (ATC and later UNAG), urban workers (CST affiliated unions), and the youth (Juventud Sandinista).

If these organizations had been able to develop autonomously the FSLN's role as vanguard would have become less significant than it did, or would perhaps have even withered away. However, events show that this was not accomplished. In fact, these organizations largely remained dependent on the FSLN itself and were unable to develop in an autonomous manner; the pre-existing organizations among farm workers and women were demobilized as independent institutions and put to the work of mobilization in the interests of the state. In this latter role the mass organizations came to play a substantial administrative role; through "participatory democracy" that turned into participation in administration they were demobilized as agents in a pluralist system. In order to develop this theme and to lay the groundwork for understanding later events in terms of the dynamic of the mass organizations it is helpful to examine in detail how some of these groups developed.

Sandinista Defense Committees:
Towards Demobilization

Problems with the Sandinista Defense Committees were discussed briefly in the previous chapter. The present discussion will provide some explanation of how some of the problems identified there arose. One of the basic elements of the policies of the first five years of the revolutionary government was to maintain a social wage, rather than to simply raise wage rates to benefit workers. This included provision of education, of health services, of housing, and of a system of food supply that guaranteed all Nicaraguans access to basic commodities. The CDS was involved to some degree in all of these activities, as well as in organizing defense.

In the area of food supply, the role of local CDS leaders was substantial. On visiting the leaders of a CDS it was common to discover that they also ran the food supply system through which distribution of basic commodities at a very low guaranteed price was assured. At the official level, the CDS also played a substantial role in the system of product distribution. Thus, the local CDS leader served as a sort of local merchant or chose who would be the merchant, at least with respect to the delivery of the basic supplies at low prices. Where this was not the case, the CDS served to denounce those who sold outside the official channels or at higher than established prices.

Until 1982 Sandinista policy was to maintain a free market with price controls only on basic commodities. A system was created in 1982 beginning with sugar, and was greatly expanded in 1984, that guaranteed each individual a certain quantity of basic consumption goods. The items supplied in this way were mostly food but also included goods such as toilet paper and soap. It is important to remember that although this system is often described as a "rationing" system, since it establishes a minimum amount of basic commodities that could be purchased at a low controlled price, it actually was not strictly a rationing system. The same goods were available in the free market but there prices were not controlled in practice (though they were at most times legally controlled). Many people, probably most, found the supplies allowed to them at the low, controlled price, to be inadequate for their needs. They also found that they were supplied in outlets that were not open at convenient hours, could not sell in small quantities, and would not offer credit (Collins, 1985: 128). Some supplement of the basic allotments was thus commonly purchased through alternative channels.

While this system of supplying "basic needs" can be justified on many grounds, it produces concomitant problems. Some sense of these problems can be seen by thinking through the relationship between the basic food supply system and the public perception of the role of the CDS, which was deeply involved in the management of the system in the urban areas (Serra, 1991: 51).[6]

On the one hand, the addition of an official supply network to an open, more or less "free," market has value in maintaining the ideology of the mixed economy. Not everything is controlled by the government. Local shops that do not participate as vendors through the official system can still exist to supply many other services. The large informal economy of buyers and sellers of fruits, vegetables, daily necessities, candies, soda pop, and so forth can easily co-exist with the official system. If only the most basic supplies are provided to everyone the government is, furthermore, freed from attempting to regulate the sale of what amounts to luxury goods, thus simplifying the process.

On the other hand, any leakage of goods from the official supply channels into the open market de-legitimizes the process in several ways. Most importantly, it tends to produce, as it did in Nicaragua, apparent government repression of the free market under the claim that it is really an illegal "black market." On this basis the government in Managua attempted in several different ways to deal with the biggest problem, the traditional *"Mercado Oriental,"* or Eastern Market, an area of open markets and other

---

[6]The "ration card" system was not implemented for most commodities until 1984 and thus some of the following analysis does not fit as precisely as it might into the periodization used in this and the following chapter. Nevertheless, the general role of the CDS in working with the Ministry of Commerce (MICOIN) and the National Basic Foods Corporation (ENABAS) not only with the ration card system but also with the system by which only some stores, people's stores or *tiendas populares*, were able to obtain a guaranteed supply of goods at official prices, is especially useful in making sense of the dynamic by which the CDS was gradually demobilized.

shops located on what used to be the eastern edge of the city. There could be no doubt that a substantial black market in basic goods at much higher than official prices functioned in this market at both the retail and wholesale level.

One response to this problem was the opening of other, more official, markets that provided services to vendors and to purchasers that were more hygienic and more easily regulated. The large *"Mercado Roberto Huembes"* is a prime example of this strategy. The Eastern Market simply sprawls for blocks through its area. Much buying and selling is more or less informal and some of it, including food sales, takes place in very poor hygienic conditions. The new Roberto Huembes Market offers a fundamentally different panorama. Rather than simply spreading through the streets, it is (or was until the last few years) almost exclusively contained in one large open building with different areas dedicated to different sorts of products. It is surrounded by parking areas and is adjacent to a major bus center.

Nevertheless, for numerous reasons many buyers and sellers preferred the old market, which was much less controlled. Thus, at certain periods the government attempted to eliminate the Eastern Market by suppressing illegal sellers. This had the clear effect of producing substantial public sympathy with the sellers, who were seen as being repressed by government authorities and the police. The fact that the CDS and other base organizations were involved in supporting the official supply structures thus made them the center of resentment against government policies. Further, government admission of the existing black market clearly justified rumors, undoubtedly sometimes true, that goods were leaking from the official supply channels to the black market. This cast suspicion on those, like the CDS leaders, who were involved in parts of the system of official distribution. Though these events occurred in Managua, they could have an impact far into the countryside because of the tendency of the opposition press and radio to highlight such complaints about conditions in the city.

Similar problems arose in semi-rural areas close to Managua. For example, during one period it was forbidden for private individuals to transport large quantities of basic food supplies from rural to more urban areas. When an individual, even though basically sympathetic to the revolution, purchased fifty pounds of beans in the northern part of the country and had them confiscated when returning closer to the city, he resented not only those who stopped his vehicle, confiscating the beans, but also those in his local village who, as CDS leaders, were involved in the distribution of goods at government controlled prices. Rather than serving as an organization through which such an individual could make his complaints known to the government and the party, the local CDS came, in his view, to be a part of the administrative problem. The fact that members of his own family were actually involved in at least marginally legal transactions on a regular basis did not lead such a man to understand better why the system of providing food was necessary but, rather to the view that the CDS leaders must, themselves, somehow be involved in improper activities (personal interview, Tipitapa, 1986). Thus, those who were simply performing an important government and political function, sometimes with no remuneration or an extremely small one, were subject to criticisms that were hard to refute; as players in the game of participatory democracy they came under criticism in the presumably complementary pluralist arena.

Furthermore, in this process the CDS, as in other areas, came to play an administrative role for the state rather than serving simply as a mass organization that could be used to make demands on the state and the party, as is envisioned by pluralist theory. As the CDS also came to play a role in military mobilization and in civil defense, it once more took on a sort of administrative function. In this case the function did involve mobilization but not in a manner that could admit of anything but service to the policies laid down in the center. Although, especially in the beginning, much of what the CDS did in terms of providing "night watch" security, for example, was quite popular, it also made the CDS appear to be an agent of the state, not a group for giving expression to local concerns. As participants in administration, local CDS leaders were unable to provide effective pluralist demands on policy makers at higher levels. They did, however, make demands on citizens at the local level in response to the needs of the higher level policymakers in both the government and the party.

Given the vanguard structure of the party, local militants were selected through a rigorous process that admitted very few. Regional government and party officials were, in fact, named by the centers. This whole dynamic led to a sort of demobilizing of mass organizations. What was supposed to be participatory democracy thus became participatory administration. Here, relations between mass organizations, the FSLN as ruling party, the government, and the state as such were confused. The lowest level FSLN supporter found him or herself in the position of implementing programs while at the same time, theoretically speaking at least, constituting the base of a system of popular mobilization that could send demands up the structure.

While the processes of providing food to the local population were ongoing, or the development of local defense structures was in full bloom, this problem was not as evident as it became later. Once the administrative role was over not only was the local CDS leader likely to be the focus of any popular discontent, but the leaders themselves suffered from overwork. They could easily feel that their job was done, forgetting that political mobilization of the population, not administrative work, was the real function of the local community organization.

Setting the Limits on the Role of Unions: The Agricultural Workers Divide

A similar process occurred in the case of mass organization of both urban and rural workers but at an earlier stage and in a more complex manner. In the countryside, the original mass organization was the Association of Farm Workers (ATC). It had begun its work substantially before the revolutionary triumph, coming out of Rural Workers Committees, formed as early as 1976, as well as from the impetus of the Jesuit-sponsored Center for Agrarian Advancement (CEPA), which had begun its work in 1968 (Luciak, 1987: 41). The ATC combined substantial Christian elements, based on Delegates of the Word and CEPA (Serra, 1985: 67) with FSLN organizers from a Marxist orientation.[7] In 1977 the first clandestine conference of the new rural worker and peasant organization was held and the organization was formalized in March of 1978 (Luciak, 1987: 41).

---

[7]For a good history of the ATC and well as the development of UNAG out of the ATC, see Luciak, 1990, and for a piece specifically on the earlier period, Marvin Ortega, 1985. The latter is especially interesting in making sense of the role of different organizations on both the left and the right of the FSLN.

The founders of the ATC recognized that the farm workers consisted of three large groups. Out of a total of 260,000 workers who participated at the peak of the harvest, ATC calculated that only some 60,000 were permanent agricultural workers. Of the remainder, some subsisted for the rest of the year on small parcels of land, especially in coffee- and tobacco-growing regions where agriculture had not yet become totally capitalist and small holdings continued. In the dead season other seasonal workers, as Edgardo Garcia, one of the founders of the ATC, put it, "were converted into sellers of chewing gum, of sweet drinks, of snow cones (*raspados*) in the cities; living in the suburbs of the cities, in little villages and others in the marginal zones of the rich fertile lands" (CIERA, 1989, 6: 56). The most explosive situations existed in the western Pacific zones where cotton had come to dominate agriculture, pushing all small-holders either to the agricultural frontier further toward the interior, or to urban areas. Garcia described conditions in this area:

> But in the cotton-growing zone where, because the land was the richest in the country, or at least the richest in the Pacific area, and because of the technology utilized, the expropriation by means of arms and all other arbitrary measures was savage. There the millionaires totally flattened, and the military totally monopolized, the land, only leaving small encampments for the workers between hacienda and hacienda. They only left a place where one could sit down and in this cotton-growing zone neither the man of the country nor his domestic animals could propagate themselves (*criarse*) because the fumigation had finished off the fish in the rivers, done away with the birds, had eliminated the cattle, done away with some animals like cows that the *campesinos* could have raised; the hens had been done away with as well as the hogs, and even the dog that had always been the home companion of the countryside was gone. (CIERA, 1989, 6: 56)

Prior to the revolutionary triumph, the ATC organized the workers and peasants in these regions in a clandestine manner because "to mention the word union was a crime" (Garcia, CIERA,

1989, 6: 57). Such organizing was partially an educational task, partially an attempt to provide support for guerilla fighters, and partially an attempt to organize the farm workers to take over the task of production as the victory neared. In at least some areas there was a long tradition of struggle against rich landlords, especially through land occupations (Gould, 1990).

In the months immediately prior to the revolutionary triumph in 1979, those who occupied land in liberated areas began to cultivate both food crops and export crops, not knowing of course that the triumph would come as soon as it did but conscious of the need for agricultural work to go forward. Approximately fifty Sandinista Agricultural Communes (CAS), as they were called, were formed to undertake various agricultural tasks as the rains began to fall in June, making it essential to begin preparations for later harvests. The CAS were located mostly in the liberated areas around Léon in the fertile Pacific coast region. The members of the CAS included substantial numbers of permanent and seasonal farm workers as well as some small-holding peasants. They worked on land seized from Somoza and his close allies.

Rather than breaking up the land into small parcels, it was decided to work it collectively. A substantial influence in this was the memory of the cooperatives that Sandino had formed and that had been destroyed by the National Guard soon after his execution. Another important influence was the fact that a large number of the people involved were of indigenous descent, especially in Subtiava, a community close to León. These people "were able to synthesize in a revolutionary way the old indigenous forms of community production with the most modern form of the cooperative move-ment" (Nuñez in CIERA, 1989, 6: 65).[8] Marvin Ortega described

---

[8] It is important to note that the materials included in CIERA, 1989, often consist of items written much earlier, including "Testimonies of the Agrarian Reform," prepared by CIERA in 1981. Here I have identified material "taken from the testimony of Edgardo Garcia, Secretary General of ATC" as "Garcia in CIERA". It is important to note that this material represents what Garcia thought in 1981. Similarly, material cited from an earlier article by Orlando Nuñez Soto, director general of CIERA, is cited as Nuñez, CIERA. The "Introduction" to the ten volume work was written by Jaime Wheelock, minister of Agrarian Reform and member of the FSLN National Directorate; it is cited as "Wheelock, CIERA."

the organization of the production units as follows:

> The organization of these worker-controlled enterprises
> normally started with a general assembly composed of
> all of the workers, the members of the local guerrilla
> columns, and the peasants living on the property.
> Decisions were made by majority consensus. In these
> assemblies the decisions dealt with how to obtain the
> inputs required for cultivation, the planting of food
> crops, the organization of the labor process, the living
> conditions of the workers, the distribution of land
> among the peasants in the zone, and the defense of the
> liberated territory. (1985: 70)

These units also made all basic decisions about what was to happen
in the community, including granting travel permits and administering justice.

It was undoubtedly assumed by many people that this form of
organization—in which agricultural workers directly controlled
production where there was an integration of food and export
crops—was to be the model for Nicaragua's future. Over 20 percent
of arable Nicaraguan land was confiscated from Somoza and his
close allies in accordance with decree number 3, issued the day after
the triumph, July 20, 1979, and the associated decree number 38 of
August 8 of the same year. Nevertheless, a final decision about the
character of the agrarian reform and how it would be organized was
not made until August of 1981 with the establishment of decree
number 782, "The Agrarian Reform Law" (Luciak, 1987a: 117). By
this time it was clear that the model established by ATC
organization of the communes before July 19 was not to be followed.

What occurred in the period from the founding of the ATC in
1978 until the founding of UNAG in 1981 (which took the small
peasant and seasonal workers from ATC) basically altered the
character of farm-worker organizing. It is important to understand
the process that led to this situation in order to make sense of the

---

CIERA materials often do not identify the authors, apparently preferring
the notion that they are a collective product.

later roles of the ATC and UNAG in the development of the Nicaraguan model of guided pluralism.

The ATC was the major Sandinista affiliated labor organization in the country during this period. Thus, what happened with the ATC is of great consequence in making sense of the role of organized labor as such in the first few years of the revolutionary government. Creating and making clear the rules of the game in the countryside was a process that saw the fundamental transformation of the ATC as an organization. From an organization that mobilized those who worked in the rural area, whether permanent wage laborers, seasonal laborers, renters of land, or small landholders in creating a system of direct worker ownership, the ATC was transformed into a representative largely of workers on state farms and some large private farms. Its new role still involved some degree of mobilization, but it now functioned more like a trade union which had a substantial role in self-management than like an organization for direct worker ownership and control. Mobilization had ceased to be against the employer, whether state or private, as one normally assumes unions will work, and came to be more mobilization for production and an attempt to prevent decapitalization of private agricultural concerns. The transition period was marked by substantial struggle, however.

As the state and the FSLN began to consolidate power, the basic rule for peasants and farm workers was altered. It had always been a major aspect of peasant and farm worker revolutionary activity to take land from large landowners, especially land that was not in full use. It would have seemed that the triumph would be the time to dramatically increase these actions. Instead, the government seized Somoza's property and the FSLN began to resist further land seizures by peasants or farm workers. This was most significant with respect to those who had no land and had no permanent employment on large farms, many of which were now state farms. Yet government decrees could not control all of the action in the countryside. Of course it was possible to distinguish politically between Somoza and other large landholders. But for the farm worker or small sharecropper or renter the land looked the same, and so did many of the landowners. Few large or medium landowners had been perfectly just to their employees, tenants, or smallholding neighbors, thus making the distinction between Somocista bosses and landlords seem arbitrary. Furthermore, even some

135

landowners who were FSLN sympathizers found themselves under attack by *campesino* groups with a long history of struggle (Gould, 1990: 290). It was, in addition, difficult to see in the Historic Program of the FSLN a distinction between Somoza's land and that of other large landholders.

As summarized by Jaime Wheelock, who was in charge of agrarian reform, the Historic Program had four central points in relation to agrarian reform:

1.   Capitalist and feudal *latifundia* will be liquidated.
2.   The land will be delivered without cost to the *campesinos* in accordance with the principle that the land should belong to those who work it.
3.   A plan of agricultural development will be directed toward the diversification and increased productivity of this sector.
4.   The *campesinos* will be encouraged to organize into cooperatives, to the effect that they will themselves take in hand their own destiny and participate directly in the development of the country. (Wheelock, CIERA, 1989, 1: 17)

Here there is no distinction between Somoza as a capitalist who controls *latifundia* and other capitalists who do the same; there is no mention of state farms.

Perhaps the rural workers saw the program too simplistically, but one year after the triumph they, especially seasonal workers, had occupied twelve thousand *manzanas* (or about twenty thousand acres) of land newly in the state sector and about sixteen thousand *manzanas* from the private sector (CIERA, 1989, 6: 75). Often poor *campesinos* took land before the new Agrarian Reform Institute (INRA) could formalize the confiscations. As CIERA put it: "The most notable cases took place in the zones where there were the largest concentrations of poor *campesinos*. The workers and *campesinos* that had aided the guerrillas in the northern zone (San Ramón, Sisle, Estelí) joined in this demand. The indigenous communities of Matiquas, Muy-Muy and others demanded the return of their lands" (CIERA, 1989, 6: 75).

All of this presented problems for the FSLN and the new government. As Wheelock understands it, looking back from the perspective of ten years, there were both political and socioeconomic conditions involved in the "reality of the Nicaraguan revolutionary process" that ultimately shaped the agrarian reform. The political conditions had two elements. First, the FSLN strategy in the struggle that led up to the triumph had been based on the isolation of Somoza in order to unify the population, including large landholders, against the regime. Secondly, medium and large landowners, especially in the interior part of the country, "were not only historical collaborators of Sandino, but also cooperated actively with the FSLN in the new stage of the struggle. Any plan for redistribution would necessarily have to take this circumstance into account" (Wheelock, CIERA, 1989, 1: 21). Thus politically, the effort at national unity in the first year of the new government had to take precedence over rural demands for confiscations beyond the properties owned by Somoza and his close allies. Occupations of other lands were to be discouraged.

The first relevant socioeconomic condition was the agro-export character of the Nicaraguan economy, which meant that, as Wheelock put it:

> the development of capitalism in agriculture had constituted a pole principally of agro-exporting organized on the base of more or less modern plantations that had succeeded in articulating a broad contingent of salaried farm workers—coffee, sugar, bananas, tobacco, intensive cattle raising, etc.—, where what was found, of course, was not the demand for land, but the characteristic interests of the agrarian working class. (CIERA, 1989, 1: 21)

The second socioeconomic condition was a large group of small- and medium-sized family producers, especially in the interior of the country, that, even if they did not own much land were, by nature, integrated into a capitalist conception of agricultural landholding. These people would resist ideas like "nationalization," state expropriation of land, or establishing limits on the amount of land any one individual could own. Furthermore, an additional limit on the possibilities of what could be done in the way of reform was that the lands confiscated from Somoza "were organized under the form of plantations where tens of thousands of agricultural laborers work and therefore are not susceptible of being parcelled out to *campesinos* without land" (Wheelock, CIERA, 1989, 1: 21-22).

Although this may have been the scene from the point of view of large-scale analysis, it was not what some ATC members and other militant *campesinos* apparently saw. ATC was the fundamental organization available to promote the organization of rural workers and *campesinos* until early 1981. In its second national assembly, ATC, having abandoned the organization of rural people in local groupings to the CDS, formed itself into three sections. The Union Sector was to represent workers on large farms, especially state farms. The members of Collectives of Seasonal Workers demanded land to plant crops for self-subsistence, and those in the unit called Collectives and Cooperatives sought to meet the interests of poor *campesinos* through demands for land, credit, and agricultural inputs. ATC officers were now chosen on a municipal, regional, and national basis, not from the more communal and community-based groups from whom representation was sought during the insurrection itself (CIERA, 1989, 6: 76–77).

While the FSLN and the government had attempted to discourage occupation of land other than that seized by the state from the Somozas and their allies, rural people had taken matters into their own hands, as has been noted above. The ATC had the choice of simply attempting to follow national policy or of responding to its own bases. In February of 1980 fifty thousand agricultural workers converged on the Plaza of the Revolution in Managua, under ATC leadership. Their demands were clear:

> No to the return of even an inch of confiscated land!
> Vacant land for working hands! and
> Condemnation of peasant debt!

The FSLN was presented with the choice of responding further to the large landowners in order to promote national unity and losing its rural base as a consequence or of threatening national unity by responding to the base itself. It chose the base with respect to past practices and sought to reassure large landowners by refusing to support further land occupations. The major ATC demands were met, including substantially lowering the maximum rent on land, creating a minimum agricultural wage, and authorizing the new Ministry of Agrarian Reform to take over unused private lands and lease them out. At the same time it was made clear to the ATC that there were to be no new land seizures (Deere, 1986: 126). State farmlands were included among those granted to occupiers of unused land.

In an important sense this marks the high-water mark of the ATC. From here on the ATC was to organize for production in newly created state farms, at least sometimes replacing the old Sandinista Agricultural Communes. The creation of state farms, however, was not a response to problems of either seasonal agricultural workers or small-holding peasants who could provide for a substantial part of their basic needs through their own production. It was thought that the interests of agricultural workers and of *campesinos* who owned small or medium plots of lands were different. For the former, good wages and working conditions and some degree of control over the productive process were considered to be the basic demands; they were in an important sense a rural proletariat after all. For the latter, the primary questions were seen as access to land, credit, seeds, fertilizer, and a good and reliable system through which to market their products. Of course, many of the small-to-medium peasant holders also hired agricultural workers, both seasonal and permanent, and thus had an objective interest in low wages for their employees.

In the early developments of the agricultural situation the FSLN and the ATC were not alone. There were other organizations also active in the countryside, many connected with COSEP. In early 1979, COSEP had formed the Union of Agricultural Producers of Nicaragua (UPANIC), whose leader Jorge Salazar was later killed as described above. There were also attempts on the part of the private sector, probably with U.S. aid, to form cooperatives that would work with small rural producers as "farmers" rather than as peasants, emphasizing the concept of private land ownership that they had in common with large producers.

The FSLN saw these developments as an attempt to organize a large segment of the rural population against it. Using its connections with historical collaborators among rural producers, the FSLN was able to help organize a large group of small-to-medium agricultural producers that broke with the COSEP-related coffee cooperative. They convoked assemblies of small-to-medium producers throughout the country. With the aid of some of the elements of the ATC, this led to the development of the National

Union of Farmers and Ranchers (UNAG) at an assembly held in April of 1981 (CIERA, 1989, 6: 80–82). UNAG thus came into existence for two related reasons: 1) ATC could not, apparently, unite the two fundamentally different elements of salaried farm workers and small holders and, 2) the FSLN saw a need to create an organization that could compete with those led by the bourgeoisie for the loyalty of small and medium landholders (Vilas, 1986: 171).

The original CAS had been taken over by the state as state farms, thus changing their character from worker-owned to state-owned production units. The acronym CAS was henceforth applied to cooperatives, probably not only incidentally, as this deemphasized the elimination of the old spontaneous form of the commune and the creation of cooperatives on a different model. Organization in the countryside was thus divided between the ATC, which organized rural workers on a class basis and UNAG, which organized *campesinos* on a non-class basis. UNAG emphasized organization of all agricultural producers, "independently of their class situation, assuming the character of a national, broad, multi-class, independent organization" (CIERA, 1989, 6: 81). ATC came to exclusively represent workers on large state and private farms, while UNAG fundamentally came to represent newly formed cooperatives and some individual landholders.

There were early frictions between the two organizations, especially over the question of who was to organize seasonal workers. As paid farm workers they were, in an important sense, united with other salaried workers. As individuals who often rented or otherwise occupied small parcels on a precarious basis from which they managed to obtain part of their subsistence, they were united with small-holders. ATC originally argued that UNAG consisted of "bourgeois employers" insofar as they hired agricultural laborers. Thus they argued that the seasonal workers, or "semi-proletariat," should be organized in Seasonal Workers Collectives under ATC (CIERA, 1986, 6: 116). This position was retracted in a formal meeting of the two organizations in 1981, when the ATC agreed to work together with UNAG in a "worker-*campesino* alliance" and to cease attempting to organize seasonal workers. The seasonal workers, often the poorest elements among agricultural workers, were consequently left without a clear organizational representative. The only real response to their interests was that the types of cooperatives UNAG later organized were those already planned by the ATC. Thus the semi-proletariat was to have a strong influence in the most collectivized form of cooperative, the Sandinista Agricultural Cooperatives (CAS, the same initials as the early communes as noted above).

In 1980 ATC's plan of struggle called for the formation of four basic cooperative groups. Two of these were considered appropriate to *campesinos* without land, the semi-proletariat. They were the Sandinista Agricultural Cooperatives (CAS) and the Work Collectives (CT). The other two were for *campesinos* with land. They were the Credit and Service Cooperatives (CCS) and the National League of Small Producers. All of these entities ultimately came under the jurisdiction of UNAG so that the organization united seasonal workers with small and medium landholders. UNAG attempted to organize the latter into cooperatives until 1984.

UNAG was to become a fundamentally dynamic force during the period of FSLN government. It was more able to play the pluralist game than was ATC because it united various forces in one organization. By 1984 even large producers were admitted to UNAG. Its then president Daniel Nuñez (a medium-to-large holder who had given up much of his land), commented that "We aspire to unite all the producers of this country. . . . We want large producers, because the more we produce the more wealth the country will have" (quoted in Ruchwarger, 1987: 244). Thus, in dealing with UNAG the FSLN was relating itself not only to an organization generally sympathetic to its own agenda but also to a group that united substantial economic forces outside the basic class base of the FSLN. It therefore could not simply respond to UNAG demands by asking its members to give their continued backing to the revolution; at least some of them had other options for their alignments! Much of the later tragedy of the counterrevolutionary war was a result of some of these groups either joining or passively cooperating with *contra* forces.

When the FSLN dealt with the ATC it was dealing with a group that organized, at least in theory, the fundamental working-class base of the FSLN. Here the union, the party, and the government were all seen as having the same ends—they all promoted the interests of workers in the long-run. The ATC represented a genuinely proletarianized working force. It could be expected to, and did in fact, work to mobilize and educate workers in the interests of the system as a whole. From this perspective the ATC was not seen as another interest group to be dealt with; it was a working-class organization that could be counted on to support the revolution without reserve. Its members really had no organizational option. Its function became, in large measure, to attempt to increase production and to aid in mobilization for the war effort.

Increasing production meant two fundamental things: preventing decapitalization on the part of private agricultural producers and increasing the productivity of labor. In the latter task, ATC's function was to aid in the discipline of the labor force. A serious problem for the ATC was to attempt to increase the length of the working day. Clearly the two-to-three-hour period which had become common after the triumph as workers came to think of the enterprise as their own (and that thus there were no bosses) was far too little to sustain production. But when the function of the "workers'" organization was to get workers to work harder, the organization was serving the interests of the state in mobilization, not mobilizing in the direct and perceived interest of the workers. Thus, here, and even more importantly in organizing workers for national defense, the ATC came to play a role almost the reverse of what interest groups are expected to play in a pluralist system.

The ATC also played a substantial role in developing a system of worker participation in management of the state farms. Every basic decision involving production had to be made in consultations between the ATC and the management of the state farm. Here the workers could play a direct role in assemblies where basic rules were discussed. Yet two important problems arose. One was that workers, even though they elected their ATC leadership, were represented by their leaders. In this sense it was easy to see the ATC leadership as simply another bureaucracy that dealt with the farm management. In fact, as time went on many workers resisted participating in meetings in addition to working. It may have been the workers' right to participate but sometimes people prefer not to exercise this right. By 1985, the ATC would fundamentally reorganize itself because of concerns that it had become too bureaucratic and out of touch with the workers themselves. Pluralist interest group representation had substantially replaced participatory democracy.

UNAG, on the other hand, was to flourish as an interest group. It was formed partially as an attempt to capture small and medium producers for the revolutionary cause from groups formed by non-revolutionary interests. Thus it was not possible, even if some UNAG leaders had desired to do so, to subordinate demands of UNAG members to revolutionary goals. It was essential, if the organization was to serve its purpose, for it to take an independent line and to promote the demands of its members even against government policies and FSLN desires. The nature of the demands of the organization, especially for access to credit, for good prices for crops, for road improvements, and so forth, are typical demands made by interest groups within pluralist systems.

Here a fundamental problem in the notion of combining pluralism with participatory democracy to make revolution becomes clear. Groups such as ATC, which clearly have an interest in revolutionary transformation against the interests of the large and medium private producers, tend in this dynamic to be demobilized as agents of change, shifting their emphasis to mobilization to maintain gains already accomplished. Groups such as UNAG, many of whose members have much more direct interests in private property, even within the context of credit and service cooperatives, may have less interest in revolutionary transformation but they can be mobilized to make their demands clearly. Here it was essential to deal with the direct threat of an alternative hegemony that could appeal to small and medium producers, namely large and medium producers organized through COSEP. The trend of agrarian reform towards offering titles to individual producers after 1985 clearly recognized that many small-holders were attracted to the alternative hegemony represented by the *contras*.

In this whole dynamic the problems of a guided revolutionary pluralism become clear, especially in terms of the relation between the most revolutionary popular organizations and the vanguard. The vanguard, paradoxically, is inclined to demobilize the forces that most represent revolutionary change and to mobilize forces that can appear to make inroads in capturing social sectors from among the most conservative. It was considered more essential to respond to the interests of those who did not already support revolutionary transformation than to encourage further development on the part of the most revolutionary forces. The agrarian worker linked to the agrarian small bourgeoisie is favored over the rural proletariat as such. In this sense it is important to note that the base of the ATC was converted into unionized workers in state farms, while the largest group of rural workers, seasonal workers, was pushed toward organization as landowners, however small. Clearly the idea was for cooperatives to emphasize non-bourgeois community work styles and thus to ultimately reduce the rural petty bourgeoisie, but it is not clear that this dynamic was ever to prevail.

In the end, after the defeat of the FSLN government, the workers on state farms found themselves even more vulnerable than those on cooperatives. From owners of the land who submitted to state control in return for the right to participate in decisions they came to be workers demanding partial ownership at best of entities that were to revert to private ownership and control. A similar dynamic occurred with urban workers.

Urban Unions, Incomplete Consolidation; Controlling the "Left"

The major unions prior to 1979, though small in size, were not affiliated with the FSLN; they were peasant-based and centered in indigenous communities from the northern part of the country (CIERA, 1989 6: 73). There were two major groupings, one to the left of the FSLN and one to the right, though the strategies of both groupings in the first two years of the new government were similar. At this time the PSN-affiliated central union, the General Confederation of Workers—Independent (CGT-I), was the major union ally of the newly formed pro-FSLN CST. On the left was the Center of Union Action and Unity (CAUS) affiliated with the Nicaraguan Communist Party (PCN) and the Workers' Front (FO), associated with the Movement of Popular Action (MAP), a Maoist-oriented group that had split from the FSLN several years before the triumph (Black, 1981: 276).[9]

For a period of over a year after the triumph the actions of the non-FSLN unions consisted of organizing a large number of strikes, demanding immediate pay raises, often of over 100 percent. Their demands were consistently of a rather traditional trade-union

---

[9]For a concise list of unions and their partisan and international affiliations see CIERA, 1989, 6: 374–79.

type (assuming a necessary contradiction between owners and management, whether state or private, on the one hand, and workers on the other). The unions to the left of the FSLN saw the FSLN as the vanguard of the fight against Somoza, but not as the vanguard of the working class or of the continued revolution. They saw all FSLN demands for moderation as simply concessions to the bourgeoisie or as the demands of a new state boss that was interested in further exploitation of the worker. The unions to the right of the FSLN also followed the course of demanding wage increases and other traditional workers' benefits, in this case as a result of their own traditions, shared by many trade unions throughout the world.

The FSLN, through the ATC and the newly formed CST, called for moderation and stressed the necessity of national reconstruction and the promotion of production. Although they also called for some wage increases, they stressed the importance of the "social wage" whereby workers' lives would be improved through better education, improved health care, and policies to make goods available at reasonable prices. They urged workers to consider the inflationary consequences of massive wage increases (Black, 1981: 292). They further urged a program of vigilance against decapitalization by factory and farm owners as an essential element of worker action.

In 1979 and early 1980 it was not at all clear that the CST could obtain leadership in the newly developing union movement. The more radical groups took militant actions. CAUS alone was able to paralyze nineteen industrial businesses in February of 1980 (Molero, 1988: 64). Carlos Vilas described the situation as follows:

> In this way the last months of 1979 and the beginning of 1980 showed an increase in political tensions within the workers' movement. Stoppages, factory and farm takeovers, mobilizations, and strikes expressed these struggles for political control of the rapidly growing unions. In these conditions, each participant put a strain on all its forces and employed all its resources; the FSLN used the prestige it had won in the struggle against the dictatorship, its deep roots with the masses, and the power of the revolutionary state. (1986: 181)

Ultimately the FSLN and its affiliates won the battle. According to Luis Serra there were 27,020 members of unions in July of 1979, by 1983 there were 207,391 union members, of which 88 percent belonged to unions supporting the revolution (1985: 66). The FSLN promoted the idea of unions working with the state and its governing party to continue revolutionary change involving state ownership of some property and private ownership of other property, a social wage, fair salaries, and a common effort to promote production. The alternative notion was that unions were the fundamental agent of the working class acting against the state and private employers. The former idea won out over the latter, though it did not completely eliminate it as organizations promoting this idea continued in existence. One element of this victory is undoubtedly that it became clear to all that the largest threat to workers as a whole was the closing of their places of work through decapitalization. If the owners stopped producing or allowed their plants and equipment to deteriorate without maintenance, or simply exported equipment, there would be work for no one. The FSLN unions, both rural and urban, had early begun to fight decapitalization.

It was not only ideas that won the day; government repression also played a role. The newspapers of CAUS and of the FO, *Avance* and *Pueblo* respectively, were suppressed in late February of 1980 and three of their journalists as well as approximately fifty CAUS militants were arrested. The FO, the MAP, and the PCN were thrown out of the Council of State in May of the same year (Molero, 1988: 65). At this point the FSLN, working with the CST, began to apply the carrot as well as the stick. Molero indicates that the CST was aware that "the weakening of the other organizations would not be enough to attract the worker bases." Thus, in February the CST demanded "salary increases, . . . a wage scale, reform of the Somocista labor code, and workers' participation, principally with the view to control of decapitalization. The government, for its part, in a gesture of clear political backing to the CST, promulgated a law against decapitalization in the same month, and in May decreed an increase of 125 córdobas for salaries below 1.200 córdobas" (Molero, 1988: 66).

By December of 1980 the CST, the FO, CAUS, the CGT-I, the Federation of Union Unity (CUS), the Federation of Health Workers (FETSALUD), the Journalists' Union of Nicaragua (UPN), and the teachers union (ANDEN) came together to form the Trade Union Coordinating Body of Nicaragua (CSN). This unity was a result not only of the resolution of differences as described above but also of the threat produced by Ronald Reagan's election to the office of President of the U.S. in November and the consequent movement of some property owners to support the counter-revolution. Workers hardly had the option, as an organized force, to move to Miami and join the *contras*.

The CSN included in its plans for action elements of the demands of each of its members. In the new situation it also stressed the need to unite against the counterrevolution in promoting participation in the Sandinista militias. It also recognized the need to modify salary demands that would be "obstacles to the process of economic reconstruction of the country" (CSN Plan of Struggle, quoted in Vilas, 1986: 187). The CSN recognized the right to strike but only as a last resort and "demanded a greater development of worker participation in overall economic management and the direction of each enterprise" (Vilas, 1986: 188), calling for immediate government confiscation of any enterprise involved in decapitalization.

In September of 1981 the right to strike was suspended by the Economic and Social Emergency Law. In December of the same year the Council of State modified the Labor Code, suspending the right more formally. Early in the process of creating unions competing conceptions of labor mobilization had collided. The FSLN, the ATC, and the CST argued for mobilization within the context of revolutionary consolidation and national unity. Others on both the right and the left argued for direct worker mobilization against any employer to meet the direct demands of the workers.

By 1981 the FSLN had made the rules of the game clear. Further, it was becoming clear that mobilization was most essential in developing a sufficient military force to repel external aggression and to eliminate forces of armed counterrevolution in the country. In this context it is interesting to note that the exclusion of the actions of the Nicaraguan Communist Party's labor affiliate, CAUS, and the Maoist-oriented workers' organization, FO, had been used by opponents of the regime to stress its non-pluralist character. This is ironic inasmuch as it has been seriously argued in other contexts that strong communist organizations must be excluded from

147

systems of even highly developed industrial democracies (Lippincott, 1965).

Here the threat was not abstract; armed organizations were threatening the state in a direct manner, work stoppages promoted by communists were occurring in the context of a clear need to recover from losses incurred in the insurrection and renewed military action in the countryside. A real national emergency existed of the sort that commonly produces restrictions on the right to strike even in the most advanced pluralist systems. But the rules do not appear to be the same for the FSLN. Unions must give in to their members' demands under capitalist-dominated pluralist systems in times of emergency. The Nicaraguan workers, even when communist inspired, had every right, in this view shared even by some liberal allies of the Sandinista revolution in the U.S., to act as if there were no emergency.

Fortunately, the Nicaraguan workers as a whole could see the situation more clearly. They were able to forego immediate demands and support the CST positions. Of course a significant element in this decision was the fact that a large number of new state employees were organized in unions that favored the revolution. Their jobs were dependent on the success of the new state and many were active FSLN supporters in the community as a whole. Here the logic of pluralist representation was clear. FSLN leaning unions clearly found maintaining production in their own interests. To attack the state as employer, or even to threaten fundamental instability by attacking private owners, could only threaten those whose continued existence was dependent on the state sector.

Yet for school teachers who had to survive on wages insufficient to provide a basic level of survival, for professional employees who lived at a level often lower than those who sold goods in the informal sector, some level of dissatisfaction ultimately set in. After all, if one's work was not well paid it was, in an important sense, sacrifice for the revolution. This naturally led to the notion on the part of at least some workers that they were sacrificing enough simply by continuing in their jobs, and no further participation in organizational work should be required of them. To expect more was to strain human capacities beyond their limit. As the later period was to show, efforts to limit state employment and urban salaries, combined with a real reduction of the social wage, put the union movement in the position of attempting to control its own members' demands in the interest of the nation as a whole.

In this case, alternative sources of mobilization were not entirely eliminated. Although there were several efforts at consolidation of union organizations into important coalitions, non-FSLN unions continued to exist. They continued to put pressure on the basic logic of the system through work stoppages, even if illegal. They continued to exist as an alternative to the rules of the game. While this may seem on the surface a threat to revolutionary hegemony, at a deeper level it also made it essential for the state and the party to respond to the alternative possibilities. It helped keep alive a vibrant and real union sector.

When the FSLN lost the 1990 elections, the role of alternative unions was, to some extent, reversed. The CST now became the vanguard of those mobilized in the streets and workplaces, opposing government policies in favor of worker demands. Yet the dynamic was a live one. The FSLN as well as the government was to find itself in the position of responding to real organized workers' groups that were subsidiary to no organization, not even to the FSLN.

For the moment it was clear that the FSLN had skillfully steered its way through the process of establishing rules of the pluralist game that left some real dynamism in the union sector. It had responded to worker demands by granting concessions, using the force of the state, going to the bases of some of the unions it struggled with, and promoting unity in the end, thus establishing its legitimacy as an agent of change favoring workers. The fact that the CST was never able to completely dominate the scene was probably not seen, at the time, as the advantage it would ultimately show itself to be.

5

PLURALISM AND PARTICIPATORY DEMOCRACY THROUGH THE 1984 ELECTIONS

Some Guidelines for Assessment

There are many ways to assess economic policies and performance from a political perspective. In the overall context of Latin American economies in the early 1980s, Nicaragua may be said to have done relatively well. Indeed, in many ways the first several years were marked by both substantial economic success as well as some major problems (Molero, 1988: 55; and Conroy, 1985: 226). But "relatively well" in the context of a major economic disaster can still be seen as fundamental failure among those most affected by the general downturn. It is tempting to suggest that serious analysis should isolate the economic performance of the new Sandinista government from the general economic problems of Latin America; to ask how things would have been if the general economic situation had been better. After all, the FSLN was hardly responsible for the fall in international cotton prices or the rise in oil prices. Their performance should, in this sense, be judged in relation to how well other governments, parties, and national systems fared in the international context.

However, such a move is analytically ahistorical. Success and failure always occur in some context. The goal of analyis is to understand how well actors were able to deal with the context within which they had to work. What was important to Nicaraguans was the degree to which things in their lives were better before (1979 came to be identified with this expression) or after. After all, problems with cotton did not begin with the FSLN victory in 1979. In fact the economic problems of the last several years of the dictatorship were an aspect of the success of the FSLN in the revolutionary struggle.[1] Most people, even highly sophisticated and well educated ones, do not measure the success of their government by reference to comparative statistics, they measure on the basis of their own practical experience.

Some Dangers in Success

Of course there were many successes that were visible to large numbers of people. The literacy and health campaigns received international acclaim. In fact, especially in the rural areas, a largely illiterate population learned to read and there was a substantial expansion of electrical service so that there was light to read by. People who had never known health care began to receive it on a regular basis. Few doubted, either inside or outside the country, that there were major advances in these areas. No doubt the legitimacy of the vanguard was substantially improved by these remarkable successes.

But it is also true that when people learn to read their expectations are likely to increase. Once a family knows what it is like to send everyone to school and to a medical center, any degradation of schools and health centers is seen as a loss. Further, while a literate population can more easily be reached than an illiterate one by materials meant to create hegemony such as school textbooks and newspapers supporting the revolution, it can also be reached by counter-hegemonic agents. If only a small segment of the population has access to a newspaper such as *La Prensa*, which began to publish substantial attacks on the revolution, the problem is much less serious than when most people can read the paper.[2]

---

[1]Molero says that the economic situation that the new government inherited was "disastrous," and provides some good data by which to make sense of how bad things were (1988: 49).

[2]Not long after the revolutionary triumph, *La Prensa* underwent a process of substantial internal change. A large part of the staff which had supported the revolution left to form a new daily *El Nuevo Diario*, and those remaining came to be a major source of anti-FSLN news and analysis. The paper was so clearly a counter-hegemonic source that it received substantial financial aid from the United States as well as

When there are no textbooks (because there are no schools) it is impossible to criticize their content as pro-revolutionary propaganda. Once a curriculum is developed and texts are available, they can be attacked. The Church hierarchy, among other groups, criticized the texts, for example, for not promoting proper values.

Each advance that speaks to the real interests of the poor majorities is a double-edged sword. On the one hand, it legitimizes the agent, in this case the FSLN and the government, in the eyes of those who are benefitted. Yet, on the other hand, given the fundamental poverty of Nicaragua, no advance could be sufficient. Thus each advance produces its own discontent for lack of the fulfillment of many still-existing needs. Further, any advance necessarily favors some more than others. This may create alternative interest groups and thus lead to complaints from those who feel others have unfairly benefitted. In addition to this, it is clear that those who already supported the FSLN and the government it headed would expect to be given special attention. Historical collaborators expected FSLN administrators to give them special consideration. Not to respond to such concerns led to resentment; responding led to resentment on the part of others.

Problems of Guided Pluralism

In the rules of the game of pluralism must be included the rule that "some win and some lose." It is essential that no group should always win or always lose. Furthermore, it is important that individuals sometimes win and sometimes lose without having their winnings and losses shared with all, or even most, of the other individuals with whom they share some interests. Since an individual belongs to many different interest groups, presumably he or she wins sometimes in the context of one group and loses sometimes in the context of another group. All of this assumes that there is no hegemonic group that controls the whole process. If, in fact, there is some one group that fundamentally controls the process of decision making, pluralism does not really exist. There is, at best, a sort of "guided pluralism."

---

international moral support during times when it was censored or closed. Other right-wing media included three radio stations, one owned by the Catholic hierarchy.

For guided pluralism to function there must be clear mechanisms that can distinguish the guide, the vanguard, from other interests. The vanguard is, presumably, representative of the interests of "the people" with special concern for workers and *campesinos*. It must be conceived of as too large and all-inclusive to be a part of the pluralist process or it will necessarily function simply as one among other interests. Yet it admits a bias towards some interests and against others. In the context of an attempt to engage in "national reconstruction" with the aid of private interests, this presented the FSLN with numerous fundamental problems, as has been seen especially with regard to the CDS, the ATC, and pro-Sandinista urban unions. On the one hand, the FSLN was looking out for the whole system and thus responded so as to maintain the interest of private producers in order for the system to continue to function. On the other hand, it presumably did so in order to benefit the workers and the poor, who were presumably represented by the mass-based organizations. This led the FSLN to demand the loyalty of the latter even as it acted in the clear interests of the former. For the members of mass organizations to have their interests met in the long run they were asked to sacrifice their short-term interests while the vanguard acted differentially towards private producers. The choice of mass organizations was either to demobilize their membership or to break with the vanguard. The fact that the leadership of these organizations was largely seen as a part of the vanguard itself meant that the latter option was not to be taken. The case of UNAG was quite different as it managed to continue to function in the role of mobilization of its members to make demands on the state.

The 1984 Election Strategy:
Success through Explanation

The first fundamental test of the pluralist aspects of the Nicaraguan revolutionary model was the election of 1984. As noted above, there had been an early demand on the part of some non-FSLN elements of the revolutionary coalition for much earlier elections. The response of the FSLN had been that to have an election before the new system had been in operation for a substantial period of time would simply have been to revert to the old Nicaraguan model of elections that amounted to no more than plebiscites. It was essential, in this view, to allow the process of revolutionary participatory democracy combined with pluralism to have a chance to mature before elections could be meaningfully conducted. In August of 1980 the FSLN Directorate, arguing that a period of "national reconstruction" was needed, stated its intention to hold elections in 1985 (cited in Gilbert and Block, 1990: 237). As detailed below, the election was actually to be held in 1984.

The Political Parties Law (1983) and the Electoral Law (1984) were adopted by the Council of State after substantial debate and revisions that resulted from that debate, especially because of the views expressed by the Democratic Coordinating Committee (CDN). The CDN had become the opposition voice in the Council, representing the more conservative parties and private sector groups as well as two right-leaning unions, the CUS and the CTN. Some members of the CDN did not agree that it should participate in the 1984 elections and the Liberal Independent Party (PLI) withdrew from the pro-FSLN National Patriotic Front (FPN) to run its own campaign in 1984 (Booth, 1985: 195).

While the right wing and the United States government had vociferously accused the FSLN of totalitarianism, partially as a result of its failure to hold earlier elections, they now alleged that the time for an election was not ripe. They demanded a postponement of the elections and governmental agreement to a number of concessions, including that the government open an ongoing national dialogue with the *contras*. Ultimately, the CDN candidate, Arturo Cruz, refused to participate in the elections even though the FSLN had agreed to most of the CDN demands. There can be little question that the role of the United States government in this process was of overwhelming significance. As Thomas Walker succinctly puts it:

> CIA "asset" Arturo Cruz engaged in a highly publicized cat-and-mouse game in which he went to Nicaragua, held political rallies, and set "conditions" for formal participation, but never actually registered as a candidate in spite of the fact that many of his conditions were met and the deadline for candidate registration was extended twice on his behalf.
>
> Meanwhile U.S. officials in Nicaragua were working feverishly behind the scenes to cajole, counsel, pressure,

and, reportedly bribe the candidates of the six opposition parties that were formally registered in the election to withdraw. Their efforts were not very successful. (1991a: 136)

The elections thus proceeded with six opposition parties, three to the left and three to the right of the FSLN. Few doubted that the FSLN would win; the most important questions were whether the elections would be considered legitimate enough to obtain large-scale participation and whether they would produce international legitimacy for the revolutionary government. The fact that the earlier announcement of elections for 1985 had been replaced by a decision to hold them on November 4, 1984, just two days before presidential elections in the U.S., was hardly an accident. The expected Sandinista re-election would already be a fact when Reagan was re-elected and "this would constitute one more barrier to a possible warlike escalation" (Molero, 1988: 104).

The elections were a fundamental failure insofar as they were expected to give the FSLN legitimacy within the United States, at least in the short-run. The U.S. press had been preoccupied throughout the electoral process with the government's assessment that given the presumably "totalitarian conditions" in Nicaragua the election could only be a "Soviet style farce." The report of the Latin American Studies Association delegation on the elections points out that the media were so overwhelmed with false Reagan administration "intelligence leaks" about a massive Soviet build-up of arms in Nicaragua that they even reported results of the elections (LASA in Rosset and Vandemeer, 1986: 106). While the elections, especially as reported by LASA, may have ultimately had some minor effect in aiding those in the Congress who wanted to reduce aid to the *contras*, they clearly did not have the effect anticipated by the FSLN. Even if Nicaragua was willing to jump through all the hoops and rings of fire presented by the U.S. in the electoral arena, it was not to be granted legitimacy as a pluralist democracy by the United States.

Within Nicaragua the effects of the 1984 elections were clearly more positive. The FSLN, justifiably confident of victory, used the campaign as an opportunity to directly discuss existing problems with large numbers of Nicaraguans, especially economic problems and the recently instituted military draft (SMP, or Patriotic Military

Service). Thousands of Sandinista activists from the mass organizations and from party base committees went house to house, visiting over three hundred thousand homes, thus conducting the "largest political and ideological campaign launched by the Front since the Literacy Campaign" (Molero, 1988: 110). The results were impressive, but not overwhelming given the lack of a coherent opposition. In spite of the clear view presented by the abstaining CDN that Nicaraguans should refuse to vote, 75 percent of those registered turned out to vote. Of these, only 6 percent cast null ballots, either improperly marked or left blank. In the presidential election, Daniel Ortega and Sergio Ramírez received 67 percent of votes cast, far outstripping the nearest opposition candidates. The Democratic Conservative Party candidates (PCD) received 14 percent of the vote. Virgilio Godoy and his running mate on the PLI ticket received 10 percent of the vote, even though Godoy had split the party by withdrawing shortly before the election, too late to get his name removed from the ballot. In the National Assembly races the FSLN received 64 percent of the vote and 61 of 96 seats; the PCD obtained 14 seats with 15 percent of the vote; the PLI won 9 seats with 9 percent of the vote; and the Popular Social Christian Party (PPSC) received 6 votes and 6 seats. The left-wing parties, the PCN, the PSN, and the Marxist-Leninst Popular Actions Movement (MAP-ML) each finished with 2 percent of the vote and obtained two seats each in the new National Assembly.

The election of 1984 vindicated the FSLN in its claim to represent the vast majority of the Nicaraguan population. It also instituted a new state and governmental structure. This structure produced a constitution in 1987 that created a system of electoral democracy based on a division of powers and official respect for normal "liberal" rights and political processes. The new constitution was developed through a lengthy process of consultations directly with the public and with various groups, both national and international. It strongly resembles those of Western presidential systems with proportional representation in the legislature, replacing the model in which various groups had been directly represented in the government through membership in the Council of State. Organizations, including labor unions, the women's organization (AMNLAE), and community organizations in favor of the revolution could now play no direct role in government. In general, their access to government was now simply through the FSLN or in presenting themselves before Assembly committees.

Popular Organizations and the Vanguard

These organizations in their form as of 1985 were largely the creation of the FSLN as the vanguard. They had never been really autonomous from the FSLN and they now had no official governmental role. Given the vanguard structure of the FSLN many of these groups found themselves simply responding to the direction and orientation of the FSLN. They began to provide directions to their members from the top and to have a diminished role in communicating from the bases to the leadership. This tendency was aggravated by the need to maintain unity in the ever-increasing military confrontation with counterrevolutionary armed forces and a perceived increase in the possibility of direct U.S. military intervention. As will be discussed below, this had an impact on the FSLN's lack of knowledge of its decreased electoral support at the time of the 1990 election.

Other groups, including those such as COSEP, which were not pro-FSLN, had to depend as well on representation through other political parties in the same basic manner as in other "pluralist democracies." However, their alliance with the Church hierarchy, the U.S. embassy, and an implicit (though explicitly denied) relation with the organized counterrevolutionary forces gave them strong allies in competition for hegemony within the system.

Thus an electoral model of representation had been adopted that challenged the continued viability of many elements of participatory democracy. The question was whether the FSLN, as vanguard, could continue to promote revolutionary aims and establish a truly participatory democracy. The dynamic of the first few years could no longer continue. The FSLN as a political party was still in control of the state and its base committees would play a substantial role in the implementation of policy. But, in general, the mass organizations were now in a curious position. They were close to the party but played no legal political role; indeed, they had no clear legal status as such. Only insofar as they could bring to bear a concern that many of their members would clearly "go over" to the other side, as in the case of UNAG, could they have anything but moral force within the FSLN or the government. The union

157

sectors faced the curious anomaly of dominating the whole organized labor scene but constantly being vulnerable to attacks from more "militant" organizations that often acted with the aid of the U.S. embassy. In times of substantial economic problems this was to present serious difficulties. Furthermore, the members of state employee unions, who were generally Sandinistas at least by conviction, were also subject to severe strains such as the layoffs and wage restrictions that marked later policy. In this sense, the problem was truly one of survival both for the unions and for their individual members.

Demobilization, not Dictatorship

Before proceeding to examine the period between elections, it is important to notice, especially in the context of discussions about "democracy" in the FSLN, that the problems that have been noted in this chapter are not simply a matter of the organizational structures of mass organizations or of a lack of good will on the part of the FSLN with respect to the independence of the mass organizations. While the various mass organizations have somewhat different organizational structures as a result of the peculiar character of their constituencies, they also have substantial similarities. All of the organizations are voluntary, including the unions. Most of the leadership is elected by the membership from the lowest levels to the top. None of the mass organizations are officially dominated by the FSLN, being institutionally autonomous and independent. Generally, local officials are elected and recalled at the will of the local membership and serve as delegates to more central bodies.

Each of the organizations has undergone changes in its organizational structures as it has developed, generally focusing on attempts to make leaders and organizers more responsive to the base. Several of the organizations have undergone substantial changes in those who hold leadership positions. Thus, the problem of the relation of the mass organizations to the development of the Sandinista revolution is not internal democracy or dictation from the top by the FSLN; it is a matter of substantial contradictions within the overall theory and practice of Sandinismo.[3]

Political Pluralism, Participatory Democracy and Class

To understand the problem, one must look to the fundamental relationship of the ideas of political pluralism and participatory democracy. The theory of pluralism is a theory based on interests. Everyone has interests and everyone attempts to maximize these, according to the theory. As the FSLN has dealt with groups outside of its own mass organizational base it has understood this aspect of pluralism well. To simply shut property owners out of the game of making profits would make it impossible for them to continue to play. It was always an aspect of FSLN theory and practice to recognize that it is essential that there be incentives, in terms of real interests, for the bourgeoisie to continue to produce. The private sector was always expected to respond substantially in terms of its own interests. Thus it was important to provide some guarantees that actively producing property would not be seized by the state, and it was essential to structure credit and monetary policies so as to respond to the legitimate interests of the large property owners. From the very beginning of the FSLN, even before 1979, it has been clear that it was essential to "win over" segments of the bourgeoisie to the revolution. This is not done simply by "educating" them, though this too is important; it is fundamentally a matter of appealing to their interests.

However, the dynamic is necessarily different when dealing with those conceived of as the fundamental base of the revolution, Sandinistas. A large part of the original Sandinista militants were not from the theoretically revolutionary classes (Vilas, 1986: 113ff.) and a large number of prominent members of the traditional upper classes of Nicaragua were represented in the FSLN government. Familial relations remain strong between the FSLN and the present UNO government (Vilas, 1992). Self-interest is not what makes sense of the actions of individuals from dominant classes who become revolutionaries. They often act against their own self-

---

[3]For an extensive and detailed discussion of both the internal democracy of the mass organizations and their relation to the state and the party, see Ruchwarger, 1987, chapters 5 and 6.

159

interest and that of their families and associates in their support of the revolution. People from other classes, market sellers like Fonseca's mother, workers on farms or in factories, and other members of the dominated classes also may act against their individual interests in undertaking revolutionary activity or promoting a revolutionary government. But, of course, ultimately the revolution is in the interest of their class. Thus, it is easy to understand how, even in large numbers, such people may sacrifice their lives for the revolution; after all, they have, as a class, no real alternative.

The FSLN itself is not, and never was, composed only of people from one class, nor is it sufficient to become a militant that one is interested in the revolution and comes from the proper class background. On the contrary, to be an FSLN militant or aspirant throughout the pre-triumph and the revolutionary government periods, it was essential to have acted in an exemplary manner. A militant was a person who had put his or her self-interests aside in joining the struggle, whatever the interests may have been. Some people from working-class backgrounds who devoted their newly found professional lives to work that was in support of the revolution nevertheless chose not to be FSLN militants or were rejected in their applications because they were, for example, "too interested in pursuing their own education" (interview with economic researcher from a very humble class background at INIES, Managua, 1987). It is not that such a person was considered to be deficient, merely that he or she was judged to be unwilling to forego personal concerns for the interests of the revolution, or judged to be so.

Of course, in spite of some romantic remarks, few in the FSLN believe that all workers or peasants act without regard to their personal interests. It is not because their class is so intrinsically heroic that Sandino believed that "only the worker and the *campesino* go to the end," it is because they really have, as a class, no other alternative. This clearly does not mean that individual members of these classes never act on their own interests, even against their class interests. If this were so, the extreme security measures typical of Sandinista work, both clandestine and open, would not exist. However, collective actors are rather different from individuals.

Classes may sometimes commit suicide but they cannot be expected to do so as a matter of course. Nevertheless, members of particular classes often act outside of the interests of the class as such. Indeed, members of oppressed classes typically must do this in order to survive in oppressive systems such as capitalism. With the revolution, especially since it was based—in the Nicaraguan case—on a multi-class coalition, individuals do not automatically change their behaviors. Especially among *campesinos*, education is essential so such people can come to understand the options that exist in life. That is why Fonseca advised FSLN organizers to "also teach them to read." It is at least partially this reality that led to the high priority the FSLN gave to the literacy crusade and it is not merely coincidental that the FSLN National Directorate's pronouncements on elections were read by Humberto Ortega to those who had just completed their work in the literacy brigades. Marxism and liberation theology alike clearly work on the basic assumption that the poor can discover the road to justice through education.

The FSLN on the Place of Mass Organizations

The practice of the FSLN revealed its underlying conception of how the interests of members of mass organizations were to be handled in the development of the revolutionary program. Just as members of classes come to understand their true interests through education and instruction, members of mass organizations are expected to learn their role in the revolutionary process by understanding the logic of that process itself. While farm workers may seize land from Somocistas and other large landholders alike, they were expected to understand that to threaten all landowners would be, objectively, to threaten the revolution itself. For workers to demand higher wages and better working conditions is under-standable but in the revolutionary context they were expected to recognize that such gains are only possible with strong labor discipline and that it is essential to put off some gains until production increases. It is not enough for neighborhood groups to demand services; they were expected to learn to work together to provide them through communal action. Feminists were expected to understand that to demand legal abortion is to threaten the revolution itself, given the realities of the aggression and the strong role of the Church. Youth were expected to sacrifice their studies to work in volunteer brigades and to participate in military service.

One of the primary functions of the mass organizations was thus to make clear the higher interests of the masses, even to their members. The problem is not that the FSLN was unable to make members of mass organizations aware of their own real interests and their need to participate in the common work. In fact, it is incredible how far it was possible to do so. Farm workers supported the ATC, urban workers supported the CST, women supported AMNLAE, youth supported the Juventud Sandinista, people were active in the CDS in their neighborhoods to a high degree, and members of each group obviously made many sacrifices in the interests of the revolution and did so willingly and knowingly. Hundreds of thousands of people, probably at times a majority of the Nicaraguan population, participated in some manner or another in the various organizations and the activities they promoted.

Yet, in the logic of the revolution itself, it is clear that the mass organizations are created to promote the revolution. To do so without supporting its vanguard, the FSLN, would be quite peculiar. For any of the mass organizations to act so as to put their own perceived interests ahead of national unity, especially in the context of possible foreign invasion and an actual counterrevolutionary war supported from outside, would be inconsistent with the basic purpose of the organization itself.[4] It is not necessary to enforce

---

[4]In this context it is interesting to note that in a speech to a UNAG regional assembly meeting Victor Tirado López pointed out that it is not revolutionary simply to demand solutions to practical problems. It was, on the contrary, essential for them to understand the whole revolutionary context. He said for a cooperative that produces an "excess of 100, 200 or 300 thousand cordobas, and distributes to other cooperatives in order that they can develop themselves, this is called revolution; because what we are dealing with here is the accumulation of excesses for social, not individual, reproduction not only for the cooperative or for the firm" (Tirado, 1986: 181). It would, of course, be absurd to make the same argument to a group of profit-making producers. Here Tirado López is clearly asking UNAG to function as a mass organization promoting the common revolutionary process rather than as an interest group in a pluralist system. He is attempting to demobilize them as an agent to make demands on the system in order to mobilize them as revolutionary agents

this conception with sanctions or to control the mass organizations from outside; their own internal dynamic is sufficient to prevent them, under most circumstances, from coming into direct confrontation with the government or the FSLN or even from vociferously expressing views counter to those of the vanguard. The function of the leadership of the FSLN in this context is to "instruct" those with whom they are working, not to respond to demands from an interest group.

Insofar as the conception of the relationship between the masses and the vanguard through the operation of mass organizations produced successful results, it created a context in which the leadership and the masses shared a common language and a common understanding of the sacrifices that were necessary for everyone to make if the revolution was to succeed in meeting the ultimate interests of the majority of the population. The ethic of sacrifice was promoted by the leadership. In fact, many in leadership positions undoubtedly made major sacrifices especially in terms of lost opportunities to benefit themselves through using their skills in pursuits that would promote their self interest. As a group, members of the vanguard were able to make sense of their sacrifice of alternative paths of personal development.

Critique of the FSLN Position

Yet for individuals, even those activists who may support the revolution and the FSLN in their actions as well as in theory, the same logic does not hold. It is difficult to continue to sacrifice and to give of one's own time and energy as the objective situation gets worse. When the salaries for public employees doing professional level work become lower than the profits to be made by participating in the informal sector by selling soda on the streets, it is difficult for many people to maintain their jobs and watch their families suffer, much less to continue to work in the union and the community organizations. It is not unreasonable for such individuals to feel that they have done enough simply by continuing to sacrifice their own personal interests by maintaining a poorly-paid job. Thus individuals may become demobilized by degrees. This is a special

---

in the productive process.

163

problem for women, who often work the "double shift" of housework and income earning activity. To demand a continual "third shift" of work in a mass organization is to ask more than many women can give on a sustained basis. In fact, most individuals face the same problem to some degree as they are likely to be members or potential members of more than one mass organization. A young woman who is a farm worker and lives (as everyone does), in a community, could be an activist in AMNLAE, ATC, Juventud Sandinista, and a CDS. Such overlapping membership may lead to organizational exhaustion and ultimate demobilization. If someone else should be willing to take care of any one of these responsibilities, the woman would surely not complain. This is not to say, however, that she would necessarily always agree with what that other participant does. Nevertheless, it is unlikely that any complaint on her part would be expressed so that higher level decision makers could become aware of them. As she becomes less active she becomes less effective and more prone to see at least some decisions as coming from the top down.

As individuals become demobilized in this manner the mass organizations begin to suffer from lack of full participation. Those who remain active come to feel that their particular sacrifices are greater than those made by others and are inclined to adopt less democratic and participatory relations with nominal members of the groups. They are also more likely to look for guidance from those, such as FSLN militants, who demonstrate a high degree of revolutionary sacrifice, rather than from the sporadically active or passive members of their own groups. At the same time, confidence levels in the highest ranking authorities, the president and the members of the National Directorate, may remain high while complaints against intermediary officials multiply. Thus the whole chain of information becomes restricted at numerous points so that those at the highest levels are cut off, unintentionally, from those at the lowest levels.

When high level officials attempt to deal with this problem by direct contact with "the grassroots," as various Sandinista leaders have done, this may have negative as well as positive effects. When a *commandante* comes into the neighborhood and actually solves some problems, this grants greater prestige to the FSLN as a whole but diminishes the role of intermediary Front activists, who may be blamed for the fact that the problem became so serious that it could only be handled by the top. Intermediate mass organizational and Front officials thus lose prestige and are not likely to be made aware of local problems. Furthermore, the contrast between the "modest" four-wheel drive vehicle in which the leader comes and goes (however necessary for mobility in the context of very real physical dangers) and the lack of even very basic public transport for those at the bottom only increases the legitimacy of those who complain that the leadership is really getting rich.[5]

While there is a natural logic of demobilization inherent in participatory democracy based on mass organizations, there is a countervailing logic in pluralist response to the claims of major interest groups in a revolutionary context. Those groups, especially the "patriotic bourgeoisie," who agree to go along with the revolutionary project, even though it is not in their large scale class interest, are easily mobilized to make demands on the system. When they make strong demands they are likely to obtain a response. Of course, one possible response is repression and this sometimes occurred in Nicaragua when the FSLN and the government thought such demands could credibly be called subversive of the revolutionary order itself. However, the maintenance of pluralism and the mixed economy and the clear alternative of increased external response against the revolutionary Nicaraguan state made this option a very dangerous one that the FSLN was seldom willing to adopt. Even when it did so it often added a palliative measure to attempt to maintain the loyalty of at least some sectors of the opposition, invariably one that appealed to their interests, not their revolutionary pride, as in the case of the mass organizations.

The normal response of the FSLN to demands from interest groups on the right was to attempt to appeal to their interests, often in a directly financial way. The maintenance of parallel exchange rates for large producers was one example of such a policy. The agrarian reform seldom involved confiscation of the property of active producers and a good deal of land distribution to individuals and to cooperatives came from the state farms. Fundamentally,

---

[5]Interviews with people who have complaints about the "verticalism" in the functioning of the FSLN show that they usually are complaining about intermediate officials. They often believe that these are the people who prevent the top leadership from knowing about their problems.

large producers were always guaranteed access to credit and to a nearly guaranteed profit rate. When their property was taken for the agrarian reform they were compensated for it. While many of these policies also favored the state farms and small-to-medium producers, they were clearly a part of the large scale effort to maintain the loyalty of "patriotic producers." The very large percentage of private holdings always maintained in the Nicaraguan mixed economy (with about 60 percent of production in the hands of private producers in most sectors) made this an extremely important aspect of the dynamic of the political economy.

Here though, a positive response did not lead to demobilization, it led to more demands. COSEP and other large scale economic groups continuously threatened decapitalization on the one hand and cooperation with the United States and the *contras* on the other. The game was such that those who continually threatened to quit had a substantial advantage over those who calmly or resignedly continued to play. Any minor defeat for important private actors led to denunciations of "totalitarianism" on the part of the U.S. embassy. This was even true for those labor organizations that did not constitute part of the mass organizations that supported the FSLN. For representatives of the same U.S. administration that destroyed the air traffic controllers union to accuse the Nicaraguan government of being totalitarian for outlawing strikes in a time of emergency was a major historical irony. The large number of actors who simply went over to the side of the counterrevolutionary forces, including some leading ex-Sandinistas, and the clear U.S. aid available to those who did so made the threat (even if not explicit) by others something to be taken seriously.

In pluralist theory the government is a neutral referee, not a participant. The role of government in a participatory democracy is to facilitate participation and decision-making on the part of those involved in practical activities. In this case, the government is not neutral, it values participation by those most involved in any particular activity. Thus, abstractly, it might appear that the combination of the two theories would incline the government to defer to those in groups such as the Nicaraguan mass organizations. But in practice the reverse occurred, at least in the process of day-to-day policymaking.

In participatory democracy, the party and the government arise from the actions of organized groups, they are not separate agents. In fact they may have to facilitate cooperation among groups to reach a common consensus about the common good but they always remain fundamentally linked with the base. In pluralist theory, the party is the result of an aggregation of different, though not fundamentally hostile, interests and controls government in order to maintain a stable social structure through appropriate response to interest-group demands. When a party or government sees its relation to some groups as interest groups whose demands must be met to maintain stability and others as its own fundamental base, the former groups, paradoxically, are likely to be more effective in making demands on the government than the latter. Of course, this is supposed to be balanced out by the fact that, ultimately, the whole system is based on the popular majorities and their interests in the system as a whole.

In the first period of FSLN control of the Nicaraguan state and government, the basic organization of the system was sufficient to fulfill the needs of the population, both material and non-material, so that it could receive support from the "vast majorities." Nevertheless problems that arose from both theoretical and practical contradictions between the logic of pluralism and that of participatory democracy were beginning to surface. These problems were continously exacerbated by the pressures brought to bear on the revolutionary regime by the United States, both in terms of the *contra* war and external economic pressures.

In the latter period, as the contradictions of the model became evident, more and more demobilized ex-participants (or those who had participated willingly in the past and now were forced to participate through the military services) came to think of their relation to the FSLN as involving their interests, not their participation. The following chapters will detail how this dynamic developed. At this point it is clear that the first five years of Sandinista governance had led to substantial advances in Nicaraguan society. Transition from a backwards dictatorship towards a just and responsive political order was well on its way. Many foreign observers found the new Nicaragua an inspiration even as some of the contradictions of the new model were beginning to put substantial strains on policy-makers and political actors. Only its declared enemies could fail to see the progress that Nicaragua had

167

made under the leadership of the FSLN.   Yet changes were essential to respond to growing problems.   The revolutionary triumph had been accomplished, the revolution was well on its way to consolidation. The question was whether it could survive in the face of mounting opposition from the colossus of the North and from powerful internal forces that drew sustenance from several sectors in the United States, including most of the U.S. government.

6

THE REVOLUTION IN SURVIVAL MODE:
REWARDING ENEMIES AND LOSING FRIENDS

Priorities Shift: City-Country,
Social-Private Producers

It was clear to the FSLN even before the 1984 election results that fundamental policy shifts were in order. By 1985 a number of basically new policies had begun to function that would mark the logic of the second period of FSLN governance. These new policies were the result of three basic problems that the FSLN perceived: 1) continued and increasing aggression, both military and economic, from the United States, with the aim of overturning the Sandinista regime; 2) lack of sufficient support for the FSLN among the small-to-medium peasantry as evidenced by lower than expected electoral support, especially in the northern and interior area of the country from Matagalpa to the north; and 3) fundamental economic crisis, especially at the macroeconomic level.

In the period examined in the previous chapter the FSLN had prioritized national liberation, attempting to utilize a mixed economy to begin the process of social transformation while maintaining the support of, or at least minimizing opposition from, what were known as "patriotic producers." At the same time there was an effort to socialize production in the sense of creating a substantial state sector in both agriculture and industry and giving priority to production cooperatives in the countryside. Furthermore, through most of the early period agrarian reform was largely limited to providing land to production cooperatives and members of credit and service cooperatives rather than to individuals. Land was not added to state farms after the first confiscation of Somoza holdings. In fact, titles to land on state farms was, in some cases, given to cooperatives and precarious small-holders occupying state lands.

In the city as well as in the countryside the FSLN and the government emphasized the concept of the social wage in providing free public education, aid in housing construction, health centers available to all, and other social services as well as a system of supply of food and other basic necessities at highly subsidized prices. At the same time there was an attempt to manage the economy through control of banking and credit, foreign commerce, and a large part of domestic commerce, especially in foodstuffs. Thus, though there was a mixed economy, a substantial degree of central planning also existed.

In the second period, a fundamentally new set of priorities and policies was to be adopted. Although, especially in the area of economic policy, drastically new measures were adopted as late as 1988, the new set of principles began to be clear shortly after the election of 1984. The basic goal of promoting social revolution in the context of pluralism and participatory democracy was shifted to simply keeping the revolutionary system alive; maintaining minimal stability took the place of manipulating instabilities to make social revolution. It was not now a question of obtaining hegemony but of using whatever hegemony there was to prevent the external or internal decomposition of the revolution as a whole.

Facing Down the Colossus of the North

A large part of the problem was the war that had been nourished and promoted by the United States and the threat of direct U.S. military intervention. By 1985, substantial damage had been done to the Nicaraguan economy and to the basic social fabric of the country by the *contra* war. The economic gains of the first few years of the revolutionary government were being seriously eroded and mobilization for the war effort had affected the society in a multitude of ways. The counterrevolutionary forces had been unable to pose a genuine strategic threat, never even being able to occupy small towns for a sufficient period to claim any territory. Nevertheless, they had created a condition of terror in the countryside, magnifying the problem of rural-urban migration. Teachers, medical personnel, and members of cooperatives were priority targets of *contra* forces, threatening rural social programs.

Two days after the Nicaraguan elections, Ronald Reagan was re-elected to the Presidency of the United States and, on the same day, claimed that Nicaragua was planning to import MIG aircraft from the Soviet Union. He threatened direct military action against Nicaragua. Within three more days U.S. military aircraft had begun flying over Nicaraguan territory and the Nicaraguan government declared a national military alert shortly thereafter. Thus to the very real military action that produced civilian deaths day by day in the countryside was added a much heightened fear of direct U.S. military intervention. When trenches and bomb shelters were being constructed throughout the country, including in Managua itself, it was hardly to be expected that the newly inaugurated government could launch a bold new program for transition to socialism.

Ultimately the *contra* war would be more or less resolved through the process begun with the Esquipulas agreements of 1987, culminating in direct negotiations between the Nicaraguan government and contra leaders at Sapoá in 1988, though the *contras* continued as something of an active force, still financed by the United States until 1991. It had been a consistent theme of the FSLN in its mobilization campaigns that it would never negotiate with the *contras*, only directly with the United States. Yet by the time of the elections of 1990 it had not only done so but had made substantial concessions to them.

The U.S. Sets the Economic Part of the Trap: Nicaragua Refuses to Enter

Not satisfied with providing aid, both covert and overt, to the *contras* and making explicit threats of direct military intervention, the Reagan administration also dramatically increased economic measures against Nicaragua. It not only announced an economic embargo against the country in 1985 but also put overwhelming pressure on both international agencies and particular governments to deny any form of aid to Nicaragua, following the same basic strategy that had been used against Salvador Allende's government in Chile.

It may well have been expected by the United States that the new and heightened military and economic pressures would be enough to drive the Nicaraguan government not only into more dependent relations with the Soviet Union and Eastern Europe but also into adopting "totalitarian" measures that would fundamentally de-legitimize it both within Nicaragua and internationally. The

European Parliament in 1985 stated that U.S. policy was a "conscious attempt to push a country into dictatorship" and that unfortunately this had made it necessary for Nicaragua "to limit political and union freedoms" (Martínez Cuenca, 1992: 131). The right had always claimed that Nicaragua was "another Cuba," in spite of the fundamental differences between the two systems. Now it appeared that the policies of the United States were attempting to make this claim true. Curiously enough it appears that U.S. policy was intended to erase the pluralist elements of FSLN policy as far as possible. If Nicaragua responded to the embargo and to increased military and diplomatic pressure by increasing central control and moving away from an electoral system, perhaps support in the U.S. for increased action against Nicaragua could be increased, especially if a basic split within Nicaragua could be created. Furthermore, if Nicaragua were to accommodate itself more and more to the Soviet Union as a result of a cutoff of all Western aid it could be isolated in the international arena and its supporters in the U.S. could be labelled simply extremist communist fringe groups.[1]

Nicaragua was not to fall into this trap. As Eduardo Baumeister put it, the Sandinista revolution broke "with a principal tradition of previous revolutionary processes: the association between increments of war against counterrevolutionary forces and 'Jacobinization' (radicalization), as seen in a majority of revolutions over the past two centuries" (1991: 235). Although it was necessary to increase security measures and to request greater assistance from the Soviet Union and Eastern Europe, Nicaragua continued to seek good relations with Western Europe, with Latin America, and even with its Central American neighbors. Nicaragua was able to make

---

[1]By late 1985 the FSLN had clearly decided that it needed support in the United States from "mainline" groups such as churches and liberal citizens' groups, not from more extreme left groups. The present author was explicitly informed of this by a Nicaraguan who had been extremely active in organizing "solidarity" groups in the U.S. since before the triumph of 1979, and who had recently returned to Nicaragua. It was clear that this represented something of a change of strategy when he named several people and groups that had been active in the solidarity movement as those to whom it had been decided to devote less attention.

up for lost exports without a substantial increase in exports to the Soviet Union and Eastern Europe (Ricciardi, 1991: 259).

In the domestic arena FSLN policy sought, sometimes with little success, accommodation with the private sector and a policy that moved away from central planning to the use of market mechanisms, surely to the consternation of those who wished to see it become more "totalitarian." Once more pluralism was to serve as a fundamental element of FSLN theory as well as practice. Further socialization of production was not to be the order of the day; austerity and giving priority to winning-over the presumed social base of the counterrevolutionary forces predominated. While many basic policy shifts were to mark the period the same fundamental theory was to prevail throughout. With respect to those who opposed, or even potentially opposed, the revolutionary project there was to be a policy of accommodation; their complaints were to be treated as demands in a pluralist system that required a response that would keep such people from actively seeking the overthrow of the regime. With respect to the fundamental class base of the revolution its members were to be asked to continue to make the sacrifices necessary to the survival of the revolutionary project itself.

An analysis of the basic elements of agrarian reform and economic policy can show how this is the case and also make clear a fundamental problem that surfaced in the first period but came to have its fullest expression in the second period. The problem is that the FSLN worked from the beginning with a conception of class that assumed that the "advanced" proletariat, whether urban or rural, would consistently support the revolutionary project, even to the extent of accepting substantial sacrifices. On the other hand, the less advanced members of the mass of workers, especially the small and medium *campesino* producers, had to be won over to the revolutionary project by appealing to their interests.

In the first period, prior to 1985, this took the form of attempting to bring such producers into cooperative arrangements where they would gradually lose their "backward" characteristics through participation in social production. The more advanced workers were organized on the large farms, especially state enterprises, by the ATC; they were isolated in organizational terms from the less advanced small and medium producers who were organized in UNAG. In the second period, from 1985 to 1990, the plan was to give "priority to the countryside" and thus to win over the small-to-medium producer by granting individual land titles. This had the unintentional consequence of even further isolating farm workers in the ATC from the small and medium producers in UNAG. It was hoped that giving *campesinos* title to a parcel of land and a rifle would make it clear that their interests were with the revolution and thus that they would know that they should point their guns at the counterrevolutionary forces.

The basic problem with this analysis is that the working class as such tended to disintegrate. Many of its members joined the informal sector, especially in the cities. Along with those who stayed on state farms or cooperatives they came to think, at least as individuals, that they suffered as much or more than others from the war and from economic austerity but that they had not received the same benefits that others had. The *campesinos* as a group were not dramatically won over to the FSLN, even if they were neutralized to some extent as active *contra* supporters. As a class they do not seem to have shifted towards thinking of themselves as workers but to have maintained connections with the ideas of larger landholders. Their demands were seen simply as those of owners, not of workers who needed land upon which to work. The FSLN came to respond to their demands on this basis, considering them to be small producers who had the same interest in land ownership as did medium and large producers. But it was not difficult for many of them to see UNO as the better option; after all, it claimed to represent the principal of private property ownership and could credibly claim to end the *contra* war for good, which would shift U.S. opposition and hostility to support and aid to those who owned private property. In large numbers the *campesinos* knew how to aim their ballots in their own interest; they aimed them against the FSLN.

Participatory democracy gave way to pluralism as participation came to mean sacrificing for the revolution. Pluralism meant that benefits could be obtained by those who made continued demands on the system and threatened to quit the game. When the electoral option of choosing a new government within the existing state was presented to Nicaraguans, they voted in large numbers on the basis of their perceived interests, not on the basis of class solidarity with the revolutionary project. The FSLN as state and party was unable to maintain the loyalty of a majority of the population, even though it was able to continue to function as the single largest political party. These developments were not simply a matter of ill will on the part of some leaders or of a conscious betrayal of the working classes by the FSLN. They were a result of the practical struggle to promote revolution given a particular set of theoretical assumptions about class relationships, pluralism, and participatory democracy. An examination in some detail of the practical struggles is essential to make sense of possible theoretical lessons that can be learned from this experience. It is not possible to change the past but refusing to examine it makes it impossible to act practically in the future.

The Owl of Minerva

Retrospectively it is impossible to judge what might have happened if the FSLN had chosen a different course; for it to have done so, conditions would have had to be different from what they were. Had conditions been different all that we can say with any degree of certainty is that they would have been different. As Hegel says about the idea that philosophy can reshape the world: "The owl of Minerva spreads its wings only with the falling of the dusk" (Hegel, 1952: 13).

Political Successes in the 1985–1990 Period

One of the most substantial advances made during the second period was the defeat of the counterrevolutionary war. Counter-revolutionary forces continued to be a problem after 1987, yet it was clear that they could not succeed militarily in destroying the revolution. Especially on the Atlantic coast, the FSLN was able to turn what had been a serious military problem into a political one, with the process of autonomy receiving sufficient legitimacy that it was the focus of attention even among the indigenous groups and the Moravian Church. What had begun as a serious military challenge by indigenous people, armed and promoted by the U.S., was skillfully handled through processes of negotiation that, while they did not satisfy everyone, shifted attention to peaceful processes of change and away from massive armed resistance. Evidence of the continued development of this dynamic is that after regional elections in 1994, the FSLN and its previously armed adversary, Yatama, formed a coalition to govern in the Northern Atlantic

Autonomous Regional Assembly, thus frustrating the hopes of Arnaldo Alemán and his party to control the government of the whole Atlantic region.

No U.S. invasion took place. This was at least in part a result of the legitimacy the FSLN had been able to obtain for the Nicaraguan government within influential U.S. political circles. The large numbers of North Americans who visited Nicaragua and were positively impressed with achievements there made a substantial difference in the U.S. Congress. The clear costs that direct U.S. military intervention would have entailed within the domestic politics of the United States, including massive resistance on the part of those committed to such action among the American left, clearly played a role in avoiding an invasion. For many of those in the "solidarity movement" in the United States it was important that the FSLN followed fundamentally liberal politics, maximizing pluralism and civil liberties as well as social programs and participatory democracy.

There were obvious successes in the general arena of international politics as well, especially due to a reluctance to become overly dependent on the Soviet Union. It is doubtful, given the nature of developments in the Soviet Union and Eastern Europe as well as in relations between the United States and the Soviet Union, that it would have been possible for Nicaragua to have obtained greater aid than it did from the Soviet Union and Eastern Europe. Even if it had been possible to do so by following different domestic and foreign policies it is certainly obvious in retrospect that this would not have been a better policy than the one Nicaragua followed. After all, having had good relations with the Soviet Union and following policies typical of the Soviet Union and Eastern Europe was of little positive value anywhere in the world by 1990, much less in Central America. While Cuba is struggling with great difficulty to deal with the new realities of international politics it is clear that the much smaller, poorer, and less powerful Nicaragua would have been unable to survive changes in Eastern Europe at all if it had developed such close relations as Cuba did with the Soviet Union.

Nicaragua's relations with some Western European countries, including Western Germany, France, and several Scandinavian countries, as well as with many Latin American countries, would have become difficult to maintain if it had adopted more hard-line domestic policies or aligned itself more closely with the Soviet Union. These relationships were essential in maintaining some support for social programs within Nicaragua. Western states that continued to support the Nicaraguan revolution were subjected to substantial stress because of pressures from the United States, even given the policies that Nicaragua followed. Yet the relatively liberal route the country actually pursued reduced the effectiveness of U.S. pressures.

Maintaining relatively good relations with other Latin American countries, even with other Central American countries, was also essential to the ultimate resolution of the counter-revolutionary war and would have been more difficult with a further shift toward alignment with the Soviet Union. The long-standing aid of the Contadora countries, a group of Latin American countries that had worked for peaceful resolution of Central American problems, and development of the Arias peace plan were extremely important and were undoubtedly dependent on the relatively benign domestic and foreign policies that Nicaragua followed in response to U.S. threats. The Bolivarist aspects that had always been an important part of the thought of Sandino and of Sandinista practice served Nicaragua well in this respect.

Some Paths Not Followed

Yet, of course, things might have been done differently. Perhaps Nicaragua could have succeeded in annihilating the *contras*, including eliminating their base camps in Honduras with a more aggressive policy, and the United States might not have intervened. The *contras* had, after all, been dealt a strategic defeat in 1985–86 (Baumeister, 1991: 235). A more harsh policy with *contra* collaborators might have produced better results than were obtained with attempts to win away their potential social base. Perhaps this would have consolidated FSLN support in the country and provided it with at least as much international legitimacy as the policies that were actually followed. Economic problems within Nicaragua could have been handled in a fundamentally different, and perhaps more satisfactory, manner.[2] Surely the FSLN would not have lost government control in the same manner if elections had not been held or if they had been held at a different time or in a different manner.

But to consider these possibilities is to engage in pure speculation, not serious theoretical analysis. What Hegel said about philosophy is applicable to the present theoretical task: philosophy is the "apprehension of the present and the actual, not the erection of a beyond, supposed to exist, God knows where, or rather which exists, and we can perfectly well say where, namely in the error of a one-sided, empty, ratiocination" (1952: 10). Many today would like to discuss what the FSLN "ought to have done" or are content to say that the FSLN did what it did because, for example, of its "bourgeois" character. Little can come from such an analysis. Yet it remains important to understand that what happened in Nicaragua was a result of conscious decisions that were made as they were partially because the FSLN worked with particular theoretical understandings of the situation they confronted. It is important to examine the extent to which events subsequent to the 1990 defeat cast doubt on some elements of these theoretical conceptions if we are to be able to further develop theory as a guide to our own future practice.

It is clear that the combination of pluralist theory and the idea of participatory democracy played some role in the developments that took place and that these developments have significance for making sense of the degree to which these core concepts can co-exist in practical revolutionary theory directed by socialist conceptions. It is also important to note that much of what happened in this context was related to the underlying class analysis that directed FSLN guidance of the process in terms of understanding how to use pluralist responses to pressures from some groups and how to count on participatory democracy in making sense of how to deal with other groups.

---

[2]In a sophisticated and intelligent manner, Carlos Vilas discusses the issue of alternative economic policies that might have been taken (1990b: 35–36).

Pluralism and Economic Analysis

In this context it is clear that the second period of FSLN governance was to move more and more towards a pluralist model and away from participatory democracy and that there is a clear theoretical logic to explain why this happened, based on the FSLN's underlying assumptions about class relationships. It is also clear that the dynamic of this development further demobilized revolutionary forces and decreased support for the FSLN as the vanguard of the revolutionary process. In general, the theoretical discourse in this period, at least in public speeches and official interviews, "emphasized the connection to Sandino and downplayed the role of Marxism" (Prevost, 1991: 101); it emphasized national development and solidarity with Latin America, not a transition to socialism. From an emphasis on the development of a new and different economic system based on its own model, Nicaraguan economic policy and discourse came to emphasize traditional economic analysis.

Beginning in 1985, a series of austerity measures was introduced which consistently reduced price controls, eliminated subsidies for basic food and other supplies, tightened credit for the smallest and least efficient producers, economically favored large exporters in the rates of exchange, held down wages, and reduced public expenditures in education, health, and housing. Finally, in 1988 the Nicaraguan government began to apply economic measures quite similar to those usually required as a condition for loans from the World Bank and the International Monetary Fund. There were massive cuts in public employment and social services, some privatization took place, and costs such as those for public transportation rose dramatically for individual citizens, as did unemployment. Public investment in agriculture as a percentage of domestic agricultural product fell from 24 to 12 percent (CIERA, 1989, 9: 366), thus bringing to an end the attempt to create large-scale projects to alter the role of Nicaragua in the international market. The only major difference between the programs adopted by Nicaragua and those required in other cases by the IMF and the World Bank was that these measures were not accompanied by any promise of external aid in the Nicaraguan case, only the hope that they would be "like keys that would open the doors to Western European hard currency" (Vilas, 1990a: 38).

In the agrarian reform the emphasis shifted from promoting state farms and producers' cooperatives to supporting credit and service cooperatives and, even more strongly, to providing land titles to individual producers with no requirement that they join cooperatives. Restrictions on marketing and transportation of food crops were eliminated early in 1986 (Baumeister, 1991: 234).

Losing the Election

At the end of the second period of FSLN governance the military draft still existed, the *contras* remained at least a potential threat, safely in sanctuaries in Honduras and still supported by U.S. "humanitarian aid"; economic conditions were worse in many ways than before the revolutionary triumph of 1979 and showed few signs of improvement. Most of the economic and social gains that had been realized in the earlier period had been reversed. For individuals prices were higher, jobs were fewer, guaranteed access to basic food supplies had been dramatically reduced, and health care services were on the decline. The U.S. embargo continued to have a dramatic effect on daily life. Changes in the policies of the Soviet Union and Eastern Europe were beginning to have a substantial impact on the extent to which Nicaragua could count on their aid to counterbalance U.S. pressures. It was in this context that the FSLN went to the elections of 1990 and was surprised to lose to the UNO coalition.

It is the surprise more than the loss that needs to be explained.[3] After all, the basic economic crisis of the 1980s in Latin America led to the defeat of the incumbent party in virtually every election held in the region, including those in El Salvador and

---

[3] One of the few documented doubts about the FSLN's chances in the 1990 elections expressed by scholars sympathetic to the revolution is contained in a study of women in the revolution. There, Collinson says that "despite widespread predictions that the FSLN would gain a sound victory over the U.S.-backed UNO coalition, it was clear to the authors of this study that support among women for the Sandinistas was far from unanimous" (1990: 188). It is significant that a close study of one of the groups presumably mobilized by a major mass organization should have yielded this observation while public opinion polls generally produced an opposite result.

Guatemala, where military control and election fraud were old realities only partially ameliorated by international attention. Just as Nicaragua's electorate chose a government to the right of the FSLN, the Salvadorans and the Guatemalans chose governments to the right of the ruling Christian Democrats. Economic austerity measures played some role in each of these defeats. Many commentators have suggested that even in Mexico the Party of the Institutional Revolution (PRI) candidate won only because of fraud and manipulation. None of these developments seem to have come as major surprises; they were politics as usual in a continent that had suffered massive economic crisis over a ten-year period. Why should the defeat of the FSLN have come as a surprise to its friends and enemies alike?

The answer is that it was assumed, even by its enemies, that the FSLN, continuing with the legitimacy it had gained in 1979, was the clear hegemonic force in the ongoing revolution, and would thus obtain an electoral majority. The right wing and the U.S. could attribute the assumed victory of the FSLN to its "totalitarian" practices, including brainwashing, propaganda, and police-state tactics. The FSLN and its allies and sympathizers could attribute its assumed hegemonic position to the fact that it continued to have the confidence of the vast majorities it claimed to represent in each of its actions as well as in its general theory and practice. The actual results show that both of these views were in error. The former was based on a simple denial of the basic facts, the latter on a misunderstanding of the contradiction that had developed between participatory democracy and pluralist theory, given the FSLN's class analysis. As suggested in the first chapter above, although the revolution was to continue, the vanguard role of the FSLN was called into question by the election results.

A close examination of two basic lines of policy developed after 1985 is useful in elaborating these developments. They are: 1) giving priority to individual producers in the country, rather than to those on state farms and production cooperatives and to those in the city; and 2) development of economic austerity programs as a means for survival and reconstruction.

181

Priority to the Country

Distinguishing the Countryside from the City

There had always been two sides to the Sandinista revolution. On the one hand, it had been based on the development of small military forces in the most remote regions of the country which developed close relations with the peasantry, especially in the northern interior; on the other hand, the development of urban insurrection was essential to the ultimate success of the FSLN. The pre-triumph division of the FSLN had been based on the two aspects of this analysis. The GPP emphasized the guerilla in the mountains of the interior and the need for a prolonged struggle and the Proletarian Tendency based in the urban areas emphasized the importance of action in the cities.

At first sight this might simply appear to be a matter of rural agrarian organizing and urban industrial organizing. In fact much of the "urban" aspects of the Front's work had been in what would be considered "rural" and agricultural regions in most parts of the world. In addition to the actual industrial and commercial center of Managua, the "urban" area includes much of the agricultural center of the country along the Pacific Coast. León, Chinandega, and Masaya are considered urban in this sense and yet their economic base is agriculture. In these areas agriculture was modernized and mechanized, the rural workers were largely wage workers or "semi-proletarians," that is to say seasonal workers who survived the rest of the year by cultivating small parcels or in the urban informal economy. These are the areas in which the state farms and many of the early production cooperatives were formed. To give priority to these areas is to focus, in an important sense, on the city, not the countryside. That is, the city is the whole Pacific coastal region, the "countryside" is the remainder of the country, especially the mountainous regions of the north.

The counterrevolutionary forces never had substantial support in the agricultural areas of the "urban" Pacific. Their strength was originally in the Atlantic coast and in the northern interior regions, the mountains. The fundamental base of the FSLN was in the Pacific area, even though the original guerilla forces were located in the mountains. Thus, when the agrarian reform began in the Pacific region with the development of the state farms there was a sense in

182

which this was giving priority to the city, not the country; it was a response to the rural workers as proletarians, not *campesinos*. The latter came to constitute the social base of the counterrevolutionary forces in the countryside. An analysis of this fact is essential to making sense of some of the problems with the agrarian reform policies.

Loss of Base in the Countryside

With the election of 1984 it became clear that there was substantially reduced support in "the country," that is, among the traditional *campesinos*. Despite the substantial victory of the FSLN in all areas there were differences in the degree of support that came from different groups of rural workers. Molero reports that in *municipios* (rural governmental units roughly corresponding to counties in the U.S.) where agricultural workers predominated, the FSLN received more than its average vote in twenty-two of thirty-one voting units; where the commercial *campesinado* dominated (mostly in the southwestern part of the country), the FSLN received greater than an average vote in only seven of twenty-one *municipios*, and obtained a similar result in only twenty-four of fifty-eight areas dominated by the "traditional" *campesinos* (1988: 129). Combined with other factors, most notably the fact that it was apparent that the counterrevolution was able to recruit most successfully from the same sectors where the FSLN victory margin was less than average, it became obvious that the FSLN had a problem in maintaining support among some important sectors of the rural population—those who had not benefitted from the agrarian reform either on state farms or in cooperatives appeared to be less satisfied than others. The logic of pluralism suggested that this sector should be prioritized. Doing so required both a shift in emphasis away from the state farms and from those actually living in the cities, especially wage workers. As the policy developed, the *campesinado* was to be newly favored through the distribution of land titles on an individual basis. UNAG was the primary representative of these forces.

How the City Had Been the Priority

It might appear that the early years of Sandinista governance had already granted priority to the countryside. After all, the agrarian reform was the principal policy of the period. The literacy campaign, as well as much of the health campaign, had been directed at the countryside in large measure, with urban youth and urban workers volunteering in massive numbers to serve even the most remote rural population centers. Electrification of the rural areas was also a high priority of early economic programs. Certainly the basic plan of investment was to create capital in the rural areas, most especially with development of transportation infrastructure and irrigation projects. Credit had been made widely available in the countryside. But to view it this way is to forget the extent to which much of the Pacific coast is considered, as discussed above, more urban than rural. Orlando Nuñez Soto says about this subject:

> Nevertheless there are three factors that determined that there would be a greater benefit to the city in detriment to the workers in the countryside:
> a)   The power, the infrastructure and the investments were concentrated in the cities of the Pacific for several reasons. The center of all of the powers of the state was in Managua, the capital of the country, and the immense majority of civil, political and military functionaries are of urban origin and live in Managua. The largest part of the social and economic investments were concentrated in the Pacific, which is where the majority of the population of the country is located. A demonstration of this reality is that 76 percent of the investments in state farms of the agrarian reform were in the Pacific, 22 percent in the central region and 2 percent in the Atlantic.
> b)   The social and political weight of the urban sectors. The majority of the population is urban; a third of the population lives in Managua alone, which is one of the Latin American capitals with the largest relative urban populations. In addition, the urban sectors are more and better organized than the rural sectors; we can also affirm that they are more politicized and exercised more pressure in favor of their immediate social interests than the remainder of the rural sectors.
> c)   The war of aggression in the countryside. If the insurrection took place in the cities, the war of aggres-

sion and counterrevolution developed fundamentally in the countryside, which made economic activities enormously difficult, in production as well as in investment. This made it so that the revolution retreated in the first moment to the cities of the Pacific, leaving many rural sectors more like a battlefield than anything else.

One of the results of this contradiction is the unleashing of a struggle for the surpluses through commerce and speculation that manifests itself in the differentiation of prices between the countryside and the city. (1987: 187)

Furthermore, according to Nuñez Soto the subsidized prices paid to the rural producers did not keep pace with the real consumer prices in the black market to which many rural people found it necessary to resort in order to purchase consumption goods. They thus were paid in official prices but were forced to buy at higher black market prices.

Campesino Unhappiness with Losing Old Intermediaries

One of the problems that had become clear in this area of the country was that traditional *campesinos* in some areas of the country were quite unhappy with a fundamental element of the FSLN program that supported the "social wage" through government control of the market in basic grains and a corresponding system of price controls for basic food products in the cities. The idea had been that before the revolutionary triumph merchant "intermediaries" had been involved in exploiting *campesinos* through unreasonable rates of credit, low prices for the goods they purchased from the direct producers, and high prices for the inputs they sold to them. As noted above (see chapter 4), the revolutionary government created ENABAS to purchase grains from the producer which were then sold at subsidized prices to urban consumers. It also created credit mechanisms that were to respond to the needs of the *campesinos* in a more rational manner than the intermediaries had used. For various reasons there had been resistance to this system from the beginning. Laura Enríquez wrote that "although the traditional intermediaries usually exploited the dependency of the *campesino* population in the functions they performed, the system worked. In contrast, the course leading through the new state system, composed of multiple bureaucracies, was laden with potential for bottlenecks" (1991: 100).

However unjust the old system might have been in its large-scale class terms, it had been very personalized. Individuals with a problem had someone to go to whom they knew and to whom they were related by a complex web of social interrelations. Those responsible for the new system could, perhaps, see the large-scale injustice in the old system and could attempt to replace it with one that is more fair. They could not, however, function in terms of the same set of familial networks that their predecessors had. Often those responsible for the actual policies were seen by individual *campesinos* as strangers from the city who responded not only to local situations but to policymakers and administrators from outside the local community. Thus, even insofar as the work was done efficiently and fairly it was often perceived as impersonal and arbitrary. While FSLN administrators saw things in terms of large-scale divisions in which some sets of people were the exploited and others the exploiters, local people often had connections with one another that crossed these barriers. Thus it often happened that the "outsiders" from the city actually increased divisions between the rural and urban populations through their very efforts to reconstruct rural relationships on a basis that was seen as promoting social justice. Government officials often met with some degree of resistance, especially passive resistance, as they implemented policies meant to build solidarity between urban workers and rural populations.

It had been possible for ENABAS to monopolize the purchase of basic grains. However, it was noticeable in 1985 that there was substantial resistance to the process, centered in the interior mountainous regions where the traditional *campesino* dominated production. The resistance was made clear by the failure of ENABAS to purchase the amounts of corn it had been able to obtain even in 1984 in later years.

New Directions for Agrarian Reform

It was clear that an alternative basic policy would be required with respect to the agrarian reform. A textbook on agrarian reform published in 1990 by the Center for Rural and Social Promotion, Research, and Development concludes a section on the period from

1980–84 entitled "The Reaction of the *Campesinado* Towards the Transformation and State Policies," as follows:

> In conclusion, the result of the policies of the state toward the countryside is that the majority of the *campesinado* has still not been attended to because they were not organized into cooperatives. At the end of 1984 no explicit policy existed to pay attention to this sector, even those organized in CCS [Credit and Service Cooperatives]. In this period they were not considered either a social or an economic force of the country. It was as if the *campesinado* had ceased to exist. In November of 1984 the FSLN won the elections but the results of the voting in the countryside were not very favorable for the FSLN. (Matus Lazo, Capietto, and Cerrato, 1990: 152)

The same analysis notes that there had also been problems within existing cooperatives, including the CAS. Here the major response had been demonstrated through "passive resistance" such as individuals ceasing to participate in the militia, in educational programs, and so forth. More active resistance had been marked by some "association with opposition sectors (in particular with reactionary sectors of the Church)" (Matus Lazo, Capietto, and Cerrato, 1990: 150).

The Move Toward Individual Production

The response of the FSLN to these problems, as well as to some cases of massive peasant-led rallies demanding land, was to distribute individual titles and let beneficiaries determine their own mode of organization, to create "peasant stores," and, in 1986, to free the internal market to allow access by the rural producers to the market. This constituted a re-orientation of priorities away from socialized relations of production in the countryside towards reinforcing individual and family production. The freeing of markets for basic commodities was to lead to an elimination of price subsidies on basic foodstuffs, giving an advantage to rural dwellers who could produce some of their own food; there was an official policy of "prioritizing the countryside." But as these and other

187

economic policies developed, urban workers saw their wages fall in relation to prices and, as will be seen below, unemployment rose dramatically.

Giving priority to the countryside has a fundamental logic in a country that is so clearly dependent on agriculture. The point of new policies adopted in 1985 was, apparently, that earlier policies had had the effect of prioritizing urban dwellers. Production in an agricultural country such as Nicaragua was seen as fundamentally occurring in the countryside; in the city much of the activity (outside of industrial production) was "unproductive," consisting of commerce, of various service functions, of government activity, and of an "informal sector" that did not produce goods. Foreign earnings were almost exclusively from the export of products produced in the countryside. A CIERA document had stated as early as 1981 that the urban industrial sector was "a bottomless pit of social consumption" (1989 1: 145). Thus to have prioritized the city in practice was seen by 1985 as having inadvertently made the error of emphasizing unproductive labor at the expense of productive labor.

The Worker-*Campesino* Alliance before 1985

In the countryside, production occurred in two fundamental sectors: the large mechanized farms of the Pacific and the dispersed less-mechanized farms of the remainder of the country. The first sector, from a revolutionary point of view, was the center of organized workers, represented by the ATC. This clearly advanced working class constituted a fundamental base for the revolution. In the early period the "worker-*campesino* alliance" that was fundamental to the FSLN was understood as an alliance fundamentally of the members of ATC and the members of cooperatives that were organized by UNAG. In this sense both groups constituted the productive backbone of the revolutionary coalition. The analysis seemed to be that workers, including agricultural workers paid in wages, were one class that was in alliance with another class, fundamentally represented at this point by UNAG and its membership in the cooperatives. Both groups were intrinsically revolutionary. The proletarianized wage workers were by definition the working class as understood in traditional Marxist analysis. The cooperative members were those who were learning the virtues of social production and could be expected to develop in a revolutionary direction. Thus the two groups in alliance constituted the fundamental base of the FSLN in the countryside.

Rethinking the Worker-*Campesino* Alliance

As a result of analysis of the loss of support for the FSLN among rural producers as discussed above the strengthening of the "worker-*campesino* alliance" was seen as requiring a greater response to the *campesinado*, seen as individual producers, including small, medium, and even large landowners, rather than to those working in, or willing to form, cooperatives. The *campesinos* were now fundamentally defined as all rural producers other than those on state farms. The worker-*campesino* alliance was to become a cross-class alliance in a new sense; while some peasants were workers, at least some of the time, others were the "petty bourgeoisie" or even the "patriotic bourgeoisie" itself. The point was no longer to see *campesinos* as workers but to understand them as *allies* of the workers. That which would benefit landowners would now be understood as benefitting peasants as well. It was essential for workers, both urban and rural to understand the need for property on the part of their allies and to sacrifice their own interests where necessary.

With the change in analysis came a change in UNAG. As noted in the previous chapter, in 1984 UNAG had started a campaign to attract rural producers who were not organized in cooperatives. In 1984 at its Second Ordinary Assembly UNAG stated as one of its goals: "To promote the affiliation of all producers without distinction of creed, color or size, especially individual medium and large producers and those in the declared priority regions 1, 5, 6 with the objective of strengthening the unity of all producers with respect to the tasks of production and defense" (CIERA, 1989, 6: 136). In 1986, UNAG held the first "national *campesino* congress." Rather than continuing to prioritize cooperative organization in the countryside UNAG decided that it should "have as a principal priority the small producers, the poor *campesinos*." This implied, as Victor Tirado López put it, that "if UNAG is an organization that fights to improve the conditions of the life of the *campesinos*, it should fight, in the first place, for the solution to the principal problem, the land" (quoted in Matus Lazo, Capietto, and Cerrato, 1990: 155).

From this time forward, land distributed in the agrarian reform would include substantial portions given to individuals. In the period from 1981 to 1984 land distributed to individuals had only exceeded 10 percent of the total land distributed in one year, with an average of slightly less than 10 percent per year over that early period. From 1985 to 1988 the average was nearly 20 percent of all land distributed, with the high being 35 percent in 1986 (Enríquez, 1991: 92). From 1985 until 1990 highly publicized events at which land titles were distributed to individuals were common. These documents either secured precarious or non-existent titles that people already held or granted them new lands from the agrarian reform's program of land redistribution. The 1986 law on agrarian reform had appeared to make it possible for the state to take land from a broader sector of private holders, eliminating a restriction on the taking of unused land from farms smaller than five hundred *manzanas* in the Pacific and one thousand *manzanas* in the rest of the country. But in fact relatively little private land was seized during this period,[4] constituting only 16 percent of total confiscations since 1979 (Baumeister, 1991: 238–39). Most of the re-distribution during this period was taken from state farms. By 1988 state farms were reduced by 43 percent from their maximum size in 1983 (CIERA, 1989, 1: 300). Here we see that not only did a change in the character of the conception of the worker-*campesino* alliance grant a greater role to the *campesino* as individual producer, it also implied the restriction of the land dedicated to the most clear form of working-class production, state farms.

---

[4]The most highly publicized exception to this was the seizure of relatively small properties from COSEP leaders Jaime Caudra, Nicolás Bolaños, and Arnoldo Alemán on June 22 of 1989. This action was not, however, based as much on the need for land for the agrarian reform as it was a direct political challenge to these people, who had an "open attitude of confrontation . . . against the process of economic *concertación* which the government is carrying out with the producers" (Martínez Cuenca, 1992: 149). This was an attempt to isolate the COSEP leadership from other, more cooperative, producers.

Giving Priority to the Individual *Campesino* Producer

At least one FSLN analysis of its lack of support among the *campesinado* and the base it provided for the counterrevolutionary forces depends upon the notion that the FSLN itself had held an inappropriate image of the *campesino* in the early years. This analysis notes that the early emphasis on state farms and cooperatives was based on the notion that the *campesinado* was a symbol of the backwardness and lack of development of Nicaragua. As such it had to be eliminated in its present form in the process of development. The proletarian character of advanced agricultural work represented a higher stage of development of the worker. It was essential to "'liberate' the 'confused' *campesino*" in order to overcome the backwardness of the country (Bendaña, 1991: 42). This was why the first stage of the agrarian reform established state farms and promoted cooperatives in the assigning of land to peasants. It is also why the "intermediaries" in rural commerce had been eliminated. This analysis points out that the original agrarian reform had assumed that the private productive sector would be gradually diminished in size as the revolution proceeded (Bendaña, 1991: 42–43). In fact this would suggest that as Nicaragua reached its new level of development the traditional *campesino* would eventually disappear as a significant element of the society.

It is clear that by 1985 the FSLN saw this early view as a fundamental mistake. The original overestimate of the size of Somoza's holdings, shared alike by Jaime Wheelock and relatively conservative analysts such as Ralph Lee Woodard, had obscured the role of small and medium producers that had been characteristic of the pre-Somoza agrarian structure (Baumeister, 1991: 230 n. 5, 244). Bendaña points out that the complex structure of *campesino* life in the interior of the country linked *campesinos* who had marginal land holdings with those who had middle-size and large holdings in a series of relationships. In the context of the development of the counterrevolutionary forces in this area there were a number of problems for the revolution that arose from these structures of relationships. In addition to problems that arose from errors and abuses in dealing with suspected counterrevolutionaries and the taking of land, crops, and animals in ways unauthorized by official policies, the FSLN had to face the reality that even owners of extremely small plots feared that their land would be confiscated.

After all, it had happened to people that the small-holders knew and were intimately linked with in a variety of ways—their neighbors who were distinguished from them only by being more successful. Why wasn't it reasonable to expect that it might happen to the small-holder himself? Given this reality of life in the countryside many people had joined with the counterrevolutionary forces. The lack of support for the FSLN in this area was, thus, at least partially a result of Sandinista errors in understanding the *campesinado* (Bendaña, 1991: 43–51). Clearly there had been cases of substantial confrontations between security forces and *campesinos*. While many in the rural population were avid supporters of the revolution others found themselves allied for many reasons with those who felt damaged by government counterinsurgency actions.[5]

Policies adopted after 1984 were a clear response to the new understanding of how to deal with individual producers. At the time of its formation, UNAG had a strategic role in attempting to bring small and medium producers over to the revolution and to break their alliances with the larger producers, especially those organized by COSEP. The earlier idea had been to bring them together in cooperatives, especially credit and service cooperatives, and thus to break their links with the larger producers. The new plan was to attempt to organize producers of all sizes and to obtain

---

[5]Much has been made of a mass grave found in the northern mountains, alleged by some to be the result of a systematic set of violations of human rights by security forces. While evidence is not clear about this particular case some deaths undoubtedly occurred. There were problems with security forces acting too harshly towards peasants whom they saw as supporting *contra* forces. There were mutual communications barriers between some basically urban military personnel and the peasants with whom they came into contact.

On the other hand, some individual peasants were willing to at the same time cooperate with counterrevolutionary military groups and complain that they had been unjustly disturbed by security forces. One old man in the northern mountains described to a group of U.S. visitors how he had both sold and given food to the "commandos" and how the military and police had, in his view, unjustly detained his sons for questioning about their connections with the counterrevolutionary forces. He did not seem to understand that providing supplies to the *contras* was grounds for suspecting that he had aided them!

the loyalty of small and medium producers by the delivery of individual land titles. If the large patriotic producers could be used as the allies of the small-to-medium producers perhaps the drainage of support could be ended. Some relatively large producers had been Sandinista collaborators in the insurrectionary period prior to 1979. Perhaps they could now be used to build a unity with small producers in favor of the revolution. Attempts to ally the small producers with the "advanced" farm workers had failed in some cases, it might make better sense to ally them with other producers rather than other workers.

There had been a persistent demand for distribution of land to individual small-holders since the beginning of the revolutionary period. As was noted in the preceding chapter this had been discouraged in favor of creating state farms and cooperatives. A mobilization of *campesinos* in Masaya was used by the government to make the new policy clear. Matus López and his colleagues describe the situation as follows:

> In the middle of 1985, when the economic crisis had arrived at an intolerable point, the fourth mobilization of the *campesinado* broke out in Masaya. The popular mobilization, unlike the last one in 1981 was backed by, even promoted by, the FSLN. Many of these *campesinos* came from the same strata that took lands in 1979 but they had not obtained a response from the revolutionary state at that time. Now, in response to this mobilization, in June of the same year the first delivery of land to the *campesino* took place in which he was able to choose the organizational form he considered most appropriate. (1990: 154)

UNAG was clearly to be a pressure group to make the demands of its members clear to the government. In this respect a new institution was created through which UNAG members could have direct interaction with government and party officials where they could make their demands clear. This practice was ultimately extended to the national level, involving virtually all groups in the country in meetings that were often televised. They were known as *cara al pueblo* (face to the people). This sort of plebiscitary participation is quite distinct from genuine participatory democracy.

It is much more like a forum in which the leadership responds to demands, as in a pluralist model, than like a council that deliberates or makes decisions.

The shift that occurred with the new model of agrarian reform and the new orientation of UNAG was fundamental in class terms. When the FSLN discouraged land seizures after 1979 and altered communal forms of landholding that had been created by the farm workers themselves, they in fact drove a wedge between the presumably "advanced" proletarian agricultural workers and less advanced semi-proletarian agricultural workers who might have, in the past, held small parcels of land. The clearly proletarian worker who came to be represented by ATC was to work in "modern" conditions with mechanized farms. The ultimate plan was for the modern farms to produce export crops in the wet season and food crops in the dry season, once large-scale irrigation projects were completed. Further food processing was to take place in relation to this modern farming that would allow the re-insertion of Nicaragua into the international market at a higher level. In the meantime, those in producer cooperatives and the even more "backward" individual producers, who were given strong incentives to join credit and service cooperatives, were to be relied upon to produce consumption crops. Of course, there was also a remaining large-scale private production as well.

Agricultural workers in all of these sectors were to become alike, as modern production eventually replaced traditional production in the older analysis. Now this idea was seen as presenting serious problems in practice. The response was to diminish state farms, to continue to promote cooperatives but, most importantly, to offer incentives to small and medium producers. A large part of the problem was that modern mechanized farming required substantial inputs of imported capital, not only in terms of machinery but also in the use of petroleum products, insecticides, and fertilizers. More traditional farming was able to survive better in the context of the U.S. embargo, the rising price and diminishing availability of petroleum, and a growing imbalance of trade. By 1987 the original project of massive investments to produce "double cropping" and other more modern farming techniques had been substantially abandoned for lack of availability of capital.[6]

The continued fall of the price of cotton and other export crops in relation to the price of imported goods that were necessary as agricultural inputs played a large role in this dynamic as well. Maintaining the loyalty of "patriotic producers" required a continued subsidy to their operations in the face of these realities, especially as large producers continued to resist the use of their own capital in production.

All of these factors, in addition to the loss of support from small producers described above, put overwhelming pressures on the original project that was to lead to a sort of "withering away" of small and medium producers. The delivery of land to individual producers had always been resisted, in part, because of problems with the supply of harvest labor. These problems increased as individual producers were able to survive without leaving their own land to participate in the intensive seasonal harvest of export crops.[7] In fact the new policies were to require putting a renewed emphasis on less modern agriculture. In this context the agricultural proletariat was more likely to "wither away" than was the traditional rural producer. But both of these sectors were damaged by their disproportionate mobilization in the war effort and the disproportionate losses inflicted on cooperatives and state farms by the *contra* war. In this context, the fundamental class base for transformation toward socialism, centered in the state farms, and to a lesser extent in production cooperatives, was put under substantial objective attack. The new policies were to favor the sectors that had always been less enthusiastic about the revolutionary project.

---

[6]Some of these large projects came to fruition, including the vegetable growing and packing plant at Sebáco and the *Victoria de Julio* sugar project. Enríquez reports that the *"Plan Contingente"* involving the use of irrigation to produce food crops also had some success (1991: 171). It is ironic that discussions of privatizing these ventures included the mention of selling the Sebáco plant to Taiwanese interests, since it was constructed with aid from Bulgaria.

[7]For a thorough and insightful analysis of problems related to the agrarian reform and harvest labor supply, see Enriquez, 1991.

Yet the change in focus was incomplete. It seems that there was little real consideration given to the possibility that the problem was not merely conjunctural, to be dealt with by short-term measures. The alternative would have been to recognize the fundamental failure in the earlier analysis to deal with the question of productive relations in agriculture itself. On the world scale it has become clear that few workers in the countryside ever benefit from the development of "modern" agricultural techniques that make a factory of the countryside. In the very country where the use of intensive chemical farming had destroyed not only the social structures that made rural life valuable but also the very land and water itself, it is curious that insufficient attention was paid to the large-scale development of alternative farming methods that could make use of large amounts of intensive labor to produce a variety of crops rather than the increased use of mechanization, which requires massive use of expensive inputs. The question is how to develop new forms of farming that can unite workers with each other and with a concern for the soil, the very foundation of the "backwards" peasants' interest in land ownership. Although there was some effort to develop alternative experiments in agriculture and to enforce rules for environmental safety, these were never sufficiently developed to replace a number of assumptions about the meaning of modernization in agriculture.

Part of the problem is undoubtedly a result of the world-wide phenomenon of division between those, like Marxists, who emphasize class relationships in agriculture, and ecologists and environmental activists who emphasize the need to consider alternative models of agricultural development. The irony here is two-fold. On the one hand, Karl Marx himself emphasized the massively destructive character of capitalist farming techniques, issuing what comes close to an environmentalist's manifesto:

> In modern agriculture, as in the urban industries, the increased productiveness and quantity of the labour set in motion are bought at the cost of laying waste and consuming by disease labour-power itself. Moveover, all progress in capitalistic agriculture is a progress in the art, not only of robbing the labourer, but of robbing the soil; all progress in increasing the fertility of the soil for a given time, is a progress towards ruining the lasting

196

sources of that fertility. The more a country starts its development on the foundation of modern industry, like the United States, for example, the more rapid is this process of destruction. Capitalist production, therefore, develops technology, and the combining together of various processes into a social whole, only by sapping the original sources of all wealth—the soil and the labourer. (Marx, 1967: 506–7)

On the other hand, actual developments in the Soviet Union and elsewhere have reaped the dismal results of this reality. Thus Marxist theory and Marxist practice seem radically distinct in relation to the logic of developing capitalist techniques in agriculture as an element of transformation to a socialist system.

Yet the FSLN was by no means an orthodox Marxist organization. It is odd that its leaders should not have seen, especially after the experience of the first five years, that the model of factory agriculture could never succeed without even greater devastation of the Nicaraguan agricultural potential than had been seen under Somoza. Nevertheless, the second aspect of the irony is the apparent unwillingness of the FSLN to pay attention to newly developing ideas throughout the world that might have made a truly unique experiment possible in Nicaragua. It was never rational to believe that even more intensive mechanized agriculture and the consequent system of double-cropping could avoid the problems discussed here or could succeed without massive investments. It was irrational to divide workers on the "advanced" state farms from their cousins rather than attempting to put them together to make sense of new possibilities of agriculture that would combine some traditional techniques of mixed agricultural farming with new models of land tenure. Oddly, the FSLN adopted an agricultural model too close to that of the Soviet Union, whose theory it criticized in substantial ways in other areas, and too far from the vision of Marx himself. Yet by 1985 the options had already been limited. The most creative elements of the practices of the workers who originally seized land in the Pacific region had been frustrated and state farms had been created to maintain an industrial model. These did not constitute an attractive model for other people who worked the land.

197

There was little that could be done under these circumstances to meet the objective needs of the FSLN's own fundamental class base. Very early in the revolutionary process the FSLN had disaggregated farm workers by the division between ATC and UNAG. Those organized in ATC were intentionally separated from those organized in UNAG. The communal farms where farm workers had attempted to create agricultural units that combined food production with export production had been based on the notion that modern techniques required specialization of production. One person involved in implementing the early agrarian reform programs reports that this went so far that high officials required the removal of citrus trees that had served as fences and their replacement by concrete fences. The citrus fences had produced sufficient income to pay the wages of the workers on the farm, leaving the rest of production as a source of profit. Nevertheless the idea of modernization required their destruction on orders from "high in the ministry" (interview, Managua, 1992).[8] By the later period it had become clear that these sorts of programs were counterproductive and new programs were developed to produce food crops even on the most highly mechanized state farms. Cooperatives were also encouraged to produce export products (Enriquez, 1991: 170–72).

The policies of the later period had the potential to reunite those who worked in agriculture on a class basis. Given sufficient time this might have allowed the development of more ecologically rational farming techniques. But the process had gone too far. FSLN policies had divided one large segment of agricultural producers, the "proletarian farm workers," from their potential allies, "small producers," and put the latter in alliance with those less likely to support the revolutionary project. Thus, giving "priority" to the countryside had, in fact, given greater political weight to those who could easily move into supporting an alternative to the project of revolutionary transformation than to those for whom that project was their only fundamental option, farm workers organized by the ATC, predominately in the Pacific region. The

---

[8]Oddly, the same person who reported this event responded to a suggestion that Nicaragua could learn much from students of alternative agriculture with derision: those "crazy" folks did not understand the real world, they were mere visionaries.

latter, as wage workers, suffered from the new economic policies as they had suffered from the costs of the war. There is little reason to believe that the smallest producers so clearly benefited by the new policies, especially given the restrictions that developed in the area of credit policies, that they would become enthusiastic supporters of the FSLN. After all, from their perspective, if the FSLN had finally recognized some of their needs, all that had happened was that they had gotten some of what they deserved all along. They had already developed a set of attitudes that made for resistance to change, not openness to new models of production.

Economic Rationality Replaces Revolutionary Logic

Reaching the Bottom of the Barrel and Costs of War

In the previous chapter it was noted that there are a number of ways of assessing economic performance in a political context. The Kissinger Commission Report of 1984 drew a fundamentally dismal picture of Nicaraguan developments but Michael Conroy, after subjecting this analysis to criticism, stated that the data for the first four years: "were distinctly better than either the Central American averages or the Latin American averages on most terms. Even if we ignore the widely documented internal social changes, advances in literacy, public health, and education, and the external military aggression to which Nicaragua has had to respond, the Nicaraguan economic record was impressive" (1985: 226). Nevertheless, only a few months after the elections of 1984, "the FSLN National Directorate became convinced that we were reaching the bottom of the barrel." As early as 1983 the same group of economists that had worked on the development of an FSLN economic plan before the triumph had begun to meet again to rethink basic economic issues (Martínez Cuenca, 1992: 65).

The war had come to be a major economic cost by 1984, having done material damage and led to losses in production of nearly $4 hundred million in 1983 and 1984 alone (over 8 percent of the gross domestic product for the two years). Defense expenditures had been over 18 percent of the total state budget in 1983 and 24 percent in 1984 and would grow through most of the second period of FSLN governance (Stahler Sholk, 1990: 58–59). The addition of the U.S. embargo in 1985 made clear that new policies would have been essential even without economic problems not directly attributable to the war.

In any case, by 1984 a number of serious problems had developed. Real wages were only 68 percent of what they had been in 1980 and inflation was over 50 percent for 1984 (Stahler Sholk, 1990: 58–59). There was a fiscal deficit of over 20 percent of the gross domestic product, a financial deficit due to negative interest rates, and a large and growing trade deficit, as well as an increasing rate of inflation and a consequently increasing decline in real wages. A black market had developed that threatened to overwhelm official and legal systems of distribution. The costs of subsidizing agro-export production by large producers through use of special exchange rates had risen in 1983–84 and were putting continual pressure on the government to issue new currency, thus increasing problems with inflation. Government expenditures exceeded tax revenues and external aid so that the fiscal deficit was nearly 30 percent of the gross domestic product in 1983 and close to 25 percent in 1984 (Samillán, 1988: 58; and Stahler Sholk, 1990: 61).

Economic Adjustments 1985–87

The 1985 economic plan was based on the assumption that there had been serious errors in the earlier plans (Martínez Cuenca, 1992: 65). Thus the Nicaraguan government began to work on a fundamentally different economic basis than it had for the first five years. The general lines of the new policies were laid out in 1985 and were maintained with some changes until the major new "shock" therapy implemented in February of 1988.

Fundamentally the effort was to increase production, support the war costs, and adopt economic measures that could deal with the macroeconomic imbalances of the earlier years through a greater emphasis on the market and less emphasis on state planning. For example, it was planned to reduce price subsidies on goods and to compensate for higher prices with regular increases in nominal salaries, eventually indexed to the price of a basic group of products. Producer prices, especially for corn and beans, were freed from state control and marketing for these products was liberalized, including eliminating roadblocks that had been used to prevent unauthorized marketing of these goods. Reduction of state services was an essential element of the plan; the government itself was put on an austerity program. There was to be no further increase in the education budget and there were cuts in spending for urban infrastructure in schools, housing, and the provision of water and electricity. There were major currency devaluations through the period and changes in various rates of exchange, especially directed at eliminating subsidies to importers and at improving the profit on exports. Credit growth was curtailed and access to credit was restricted. State enterprises were subjected to new measures to increase efficiency and productivity as well as greater financial and administrative discipline (Samillán, 1988: 59–60).

The basic logic was to maintain the support of private producers, to prioritize the countryside and productive labor, and to restrict the growth of state employment. There was also a hope that these measures, especially those concerned with elimination of controls over the marketing of basic goods and of currency exchange, would reduce the role and influence of the growing informal sector. In the informal sector it had been possible to buy goods or currency at controlled prices and sell them at unofficial prices. Workers who received part of their compensation in goods produced by their firm had also been able to introduce these goods into the black market. The informal sector accounted for 43 percent of the economically active population of Managua in 1985 (Stahler Sholk, 1990: 75).

While the 1985 measures were sufficiently successful so that the same basic lines of policy were continued with some adjustments through 1987, the economy had deteriorated so substantially that a major re-orientation of policy was to take place again in 1988. In addition to any failures in the plan itself the Nicaraguan economy was subjected to continued major losses from the war, a substantial drought, and a major drop in the international price of coffee that saw the value of the 1986–87 coffee harvest fall by one-half. The economic situation by the end of 1987 was quite serious, especially in terms of inflation, which had reached the alarming rate of 1340 percent.

With the Promise of Peace Comes Economic Austerity

The signing of the peace agreement among the Central American governments at Esquipulas, Guatemala in August of 1987 set the stage for the demobilization of the *contras*. Martínez

Cuenca, a professional economist who was to play a chief role in conceiving and implementing the new economic program, remarked: "this opened up a window to the possibility for peace and, with that, there were greater possibilities to manage the economic affairs of the country in a decisive way. With the Esquipulas Accords as a background, it was possible to have a more meaningful influence over the deteriorating economic situation, which, in my opinion, was as big a threat as the counterrevolution" (1992: 69). According to Martínez Cuenca, until 1987, policy-makers had "maintained an erroneous position of separating the political front from the economic front. The economy was seen as technical; political issues were seen as distinct" (1992: 49). As minister of Foreign Trade, he had found himself in the minority position of opposing central planning as the appropriate way to socialism. He favored a decentralized view that emphasized the role of the market while recognizing the role for the state as "director of economic policy and as an instrument to compensate for the injustices of the market" (1992: 52).

It appears that after 1987 his vision would have its chance to show the way to economic recovery and that decisions were to be based on professional economic thinking rather than considerations of how to organize the social base of the revolution, which had dominated economic policy in the earlier years (1992: 50, 52). With a new "Stabilization and Adjustment Program" that could produce economic recovery and with the end of the *contra* war in sight, the FSLN thought that it could go to the electorate having demonstrated that it could guide the country both through U.S. aggression, military as well as economic, and a time of economic crisis.

A series of measures was taken in February of 1988 to inaugurate the new program that would be continued throughout the remaining two years of FSLN governance. The first step was the issuance of a new currency that devalued the old córdoba by 3000 percent. The new policies were inaugurated by the dramatic introduction of the new currency in a surprise measure. One morning it was simply announced that all old currency would have to be exchanged for a new one. The new currency had been prepared in an operation involving an amazingly high level of secrecy so that the announcement came as a complete surprise to the whole country.

According to Martínez Cuenca, the attention of the National Directorate was diverted from economic to political questions for several months after the first measures were implemented and some time was thus lost in responding to events in that period. However, after a few months, and with the transfer of Martínez Cuenca to the Ministry of Planning and Budget, there were regular discussions of the new policies by the National Directorate.

It was necessary to convince the originally skeptical National Directorate of the need for further austerity measures in early 1989, including further reductions in public spending, even for the military. Martínez Cuenca describes the discussions as follows:

> The discussion with the National Directorate went on for almost a month, including Saturdays and Sundays, and we were attempting to convince them that what we should implement weren't measures inspired by a particular economic theory or doctrine, but that they were the only alternative given the hyperinflation that the country was experiencing. I remember that at the beginning, Ortega rejected all the ideas that were put forward. (1992: 75)

Finally, though, the economists' views prevailed. Martínez Cuenca says that there was a consensus in the National Directorate, "although everyone was fully aware of the political costs we would incur" (1992: 75). Daniel Ortega was to take full public responsibility for the new measures. He explained the program widely through numerous public appearances and the now ubiquitous *cara al pueblo*, arguing that economic austerity was essential to the country as a whole.

For the new economic program to succeed it would once again be necessary to accept substantial suffering. The problem of inflation could only be solved by a dramatic reduction in government spending, so there was to be a program of "compacting" the government. This meant not only eliminating some government ministries and increasing bureaucratic efficiencies but also laying off some fifty thousand public employees, including 20 percent of those employed by the central government. By the beginning of 1989 official levels of unemployment had reached 28 percent (Vilas, 1990a: 37). Virtually all subsidies except for transportation and social services were eliminated and all price controls were lifted in the second round of adjustments in June of 1988, even though they had been frozen for basic goods in the first adjustment, in February.

Freeing the market for nearly all commodities, combined with other measures, in fact increased the availability of many items in the markets but the loss of purchasing power was so great that, as Ricciardi put it, echoing the words of many Nicaraguans, "the real question was, who could afford to pay the new higher prices?" (1991: 264).[9] The answer is that many merchants and those with property as well as those who possessed dollars could buy them. The poor and public employees (whose wages were controlled to the extent that many were forced into the informal economy to survive) suffered extremely serious declines in their standard of living. A program was instituted for public sector employees by which they received a limited supply of basic goods—called the AFA for rice (*arroz*), beans (*frijoles*), and sugar (*azucar*)—but the quantities were insufficient to make up for losses due to inflation.[10] A limited sector of the population thrived sufficiently so that the market was maintained even at high prices. One could see new automobiles in the streets and observe construction of new luxury additions to a limited number of new homes. The poor simply made do with much less and Nicaragua once again took on the look of a typical third-world country, as more and more beggars were to be seen in the streets and prostitution once more became evident. While children on the streets had often asked for pencils from tourists in the past they now wanted money. During this period, one informant whom I had visited numerous times in the past pointed out to me that his two-year-old daughter had never tasted meat. Although his family had always been poor they had previously been accustomed to

---

[9]In visits to Nicaragua since 1985, I have consistently noted an increase in goods available in supermarkets and in more traditional markets. On each visit informants have told me that things are worse than before, including the fact that they can obtain fewer goods. When it is pointed out that the markets have more goods than before the nearly unanimous response echoes that given by Ricciardi.

[10]The total AFA for an employee for two weeks could be put in a small bundle, lifted to the head with one hand and carried away with no difficulty, as was observed in Managua in 1989. The items varied slightly according to availability.

regularly consume small quantities of beef. Now it was simply not available to his family, although ample supplies were in markets close to his home and he was regularly employed.

The government made an explicit attempt to develop better relations with large producers who could contribute to exports. The government and the FSLN launched a program of *concertación* attempting to create "conciliation" through a series of meetings with producers to reach common agreement about possible policies. In this context Jaime Wheelock announced in February of 1989 that there would be no further land confiscations except in exceptional cases, and a series of meetings was held in which the government agreed to a number of further concessions to producers of export goods. Carlos Vilas cites a particularly revealing example of the extent to which the *concertación* process offered economic concessions to large private producers but gave virtually nothing to workers. At a large meeting including workers, agricultural producers, and business people held by the Ministry of Agrarian Reform, "the cotton magnates were awarded a subsidy of one million *córdobas* [$250] per manzana of land—something they had not actually requested—while the workers' demand for a wage that would cover a minimum supply of eight basic foodstuffs was rejected" (Vilas, 1990c: 12).

Coffee producers were also granted payments (Martínez Cuenca, 1992: 77). Although credit was substantially restricted in the new measures and indexed to retail prices, private producers could still borrow sufficient funds to, in practice, cover their whole year's planting expenses. When production cooperatives complained about rates of interest that they considered would prevent them from producing crops, the Ministry of Finance "responded that unless they adjusted to the new policy, many of the cooperatives would 'irremediably disappear'" (Vilas, 1990c: 12). On the other hand, when private sector producers complained about their problems in 1989 they were granted *reliquidaciones*, or exchange rate compensations (Ricciardi, 1991: 267).

Although in early 1988 there had been substantial mobilization of the mass organizations to hold down prices, the more common pattern was mobilization against the measures. There were strikes by teachers and health workers as well as by construction and automobile workers. The response to these demands was harsh. In the case of one of the teachers' strikes, Daniel Ortega was to be heard on television lecturing the teachers that they were unproductive workers and could not expect to receive pay raises in the context of the need for common struggle to overcome the problems facing the revolution. Teachers' salaries were so low that it was impossible to live on them without additional income.

There were some positive effects of the 1988–90 economic policies. Inflation, which had reached an annual rate of 33,000 percent in 1989, fell to less than 1,700 percent in 1990. Export earnings increased by nearly 30 percent in 1990. The fiscal deficit was substantially reduced, from 25 to less than 5 percent of the gross domestic product, from 1988 to 1989 (Martínez Cuenca, 1992: 76). The latter was accomplished by the lowering of state expenditures, by abandoning the large-scale state investment projects, and by selling some state properties to the private sector. Martínez Cuenca, looking back on the 1989 economic adjustment program, said:

> Our major goals were met. To have been more success-ful would have required more international cooperation, which unfortunately did not come about. . . . With the 1989 adjustment measures, the basis was laid for the beginning of economic reactivation. Unfortunately, the insufficiency of outside resources didn't allow for a lowering of the social costs of the adjustment. This concern was a central one in the elaboration of the 1990 plan. (1992: 76)

The social costs, not the improvement of economic indicators, were what were most obvious to most Nicaraguans. Wage workers, small producers, and the poor suffered very serious losses. Real wages had been falling for some time, having become as little as 5 percent of the cost of production in some areas of industry. As Vilas put it, "Sandinismo had obtained the abolition of salaries, but in a manner quite different from that imagined by Marx" (1990a: 38).

Small and medium agricultural producers also suffered. The rise in real rates of interest and costs of production as well as new restrictions on credit meant that Nicaraguan producers were in worse conditions than in any other Central American country (Vilas,

1990a: 38). Vilas summarized the negative effects of the 1988–89 adjustment program as follows:

> The adverse effects included a severe slump in productivity, lack of liquidity, and further deterioration of social services. Nearly 35 percent of the population was unemployed or underemployed. The shrinking of consumption, the rising debt burden of the peasantry, and the plummeting of wages—all normal effects of such strategies—followed on years of negative economic developments for the poor. Real wages fell from an index of 29.2 in February 1988 (1980 = 100) to 6.5 in June 1989 and to 1 by December. During 1988, milk consumption fell by 50 percent. Sugar consumption fell from 200,000 hundredweight per month in 1988 to 124,000 at the beginning of 1989. Tuberculosis and malaria spread widely, and during the first trimester of 1989 infant mortality due to diarrhea was double that of a year earlier. . . . The illiteracy rate in Region 3 (Managua) was 30 percent among the adult population at the end of 1988. (1990c: 12)

Thus, although the economic indicators as seen by professionals in the government who were also influential FSLN leaders may have given reason for hope, for many other people things seemed to be bad and getting worse. For the first time in the revolutionary period of governance it was common for people to say, referring to economic conditions, "it's worse than in the times of Somoza."

The 1990 Election: Everything Will Be Better

Although the leadership of the state and the party were undoubtedly aware of the widespread suffering in the country they were convinced that electoral victory was inevitable. In part this was due to an interpretation of public opinion polls that indicated that the FSLN and Daniel Ortega still had the confidence of the population. However, more fundamentally, the basic FSLN understanding of the class nature of the revolutionary project convinced its leaders that the vast majority of the population still backed the revolution and understood the FSLN as the vanguard.

The complex class character of the FSLN and of the revolutionary victory has been discussed above. The FSLN was convinced that pluralism could continue to make it possible to win over the middle classes and even elements of the bourgeoisie to its side, but even more—that the working class and *campesino* base would hold firm. When asked why the workers had not reacted more forcefully to the economic measures of 1988-89 that clearly hurt them in the short run, Martínez Cuenca stated that:

> most workers were convinced that even with all the mistakes that we might have made while in government, a class project with a popular content was being promoted. This basically allowed for the political discourse to be accepted by the masses even when they didn't give it their blessing.
>
> When an adjustment program—applied with the harshness with which we applied it—is carried out by a government which has a basic conflict of interest with the popular sectors, it is a program doomed to failure. . . .
>
> In our case, the cushion wasn't just in having a certain flexibility provided by measures such as the AFA or some subsidies to basic services, but rather that there was the conviction that it was a program needed to favor the majority of the people. Besides the program was made widely known, it was explained, and there was a vast amount of dissemination of information. The cards were on the table, we were never demagogic, and we never tried to hide the severity of the measures.
>
> Furthermore, it should be recognized that the informal sector also played a cushioning role. It was smart not to hit the informal sector. (1992: 78)

That is, it was believed that the fundamental class base of the FSLN—rural and urban workers combined with the *campesinos* (who had been won over with agrarian reform policies granting individual titles)—could be counted on to vote for the FSLN if they continued to receive honest explanations of the situation. For them it would be sufficient to make clear that the economic problems were the continued result of imperialist aggression. Present suffering was a result of the war and the embargo. It would soon be over, peace agreements had been signed. With victory in an honest election observed by the whole world, including the United Nations, no one could deny the democratic character of the Nicaraguan regime. Even the Republican administration in Washington would have to recognize the reality, cease funding the *contras* and remove the embargo. As the main FSLN slogan stated: "Everything will be better."

The election campaign itself was to serve to legitimize the process. Perhaps it could win over some support among the middle classes if it was conducted in a manner that could show the fundamentally modern character of the leadership of the FSLN. A liberal campaign firm from the United States was hired to advise on campaign strategies. Polls were taken just as in the United States. Television adds showed Daniel Ortega as a media star, dressed in flashy casual clothing. "Daniel" was shown on a white horse or walking on the beach, as in music videos, presumably to appeal to the youth and their interest in popular culture. The FSLN handed out caps, shirts, and toys emblazoned with slogans and pictures of the candidates. A mass rally with hundreds of thousands of people was held at the end of the campaign, its size convincing the FSLN that victory was inevitable as much as did the polls.

Yet on election night the media went silent. It was several hours before anyone would admit, at least publicly, that the FSLN had lost the election, obtaining slightly over 40 percent of the vote more or less evenly throughout the country. As Carlos Vilas put it, when people left the FSLN rally where they had seemed so enthusiastic they returned to their homes to "face the empty rice dish, the vacant place of the son recruited into the army, the photo of the son killed by the *Contras*, or the neighbor's shiny new car" (1990c: 15).

In virtually every segment of the society, including the military, and in virtually every region of the country, nearly 60 percent of the vote went to the FSLN's opponents. The economic policy of the previous two years, the continuing U.S. embargo, and the lingering existence of the *contras*, had worn down the fundamental base of the FSLN and the new policies had not succeeded in winning over new support. It is hard to deny the accuracy of James Petras and Morris Morley's claim that: "Sandinista economic policy, played out on the terrain of the capitalist class and confirming the power of the

209

agrobusiness elites, had the effect of substantially eroding the government's support among the working and lower-class base without gaining the confidence or votes of the petty bourgeois and property-owning classes" (1992: 137). It is also important to recognize that Nicaraguan voters went to the polls "with their hands up," as one informant put it, as a result of the continued aggression of the United States.

These two views—that the FSLN was overly conciliatory and that there was overwhelming external pressure—may constitute explanations of the electoral loss as a particular event but they are of little value in terms of further development of revolutionary theory or even of making sense of later developments in Nicaragua. Nor do we get very far by simply insinuating that the problem was and continues to be the fact that the FSLN is dominated by a "bourgeois elite" (Petras and Morley, 1992: 128). Sophisticated analyses about the relationship between "elites and subalterns" or those suggesting something about the inevitable logic of bureaucracy leave us with no clear understanding of these particular events. It is also not very illuminating to conclude that, in spite of the socialist rhetoric of the FSLN, the Nicaraguan revolution "was a popular revolutionary struggle for national liberation, but not a socialist revolution" (Harris 1992: 19). The basic self-criticism offered by the FSLN that a part of the problem was "verticalism" in the FSLN itself is of substantial practical moment, as is being demonstrated day by day in post-election Nicaragua. Yet none of these critiques gets at the theoretical foundation of the errors that occurred nor is of much aid in making sense of future revolutionary practice.

What is needed is not a series of prescriptions for future revolutions such as that provided by Petras and Morley (1992: 141). Politics is not an abstract process to which we can simply apply a set of rules and formulas. The fundamental question of all revolutionary political activity is the identification of the forces that actually undertake such activity and how it is possible to work with them. In this sense there is much that can be learned from the critique of Sandinista theory and practice in terms of two fundamental questions—the identification of the class foundations of revolutionary activity, and the relation between classes, parties, and governments. The following chapter will examine these fundamental issues in an effort to contribute to future revolutionary theory and practice.

210

7

CLASS, STATE AND PARTY

Sandinista Theory and the
Rejection of "Orthodoxy"

From its inception, Sandinista theory and practice was based on the rejection of several elements of "orthodox" Marxism, especially with respect to the role of classes in revolutions in countries suffering from dependent relations on international capital. Conditions of dependency in an imperialist system were such that revolution had to take place in a situation where neither the national bourgeoisie nor the proletariat was fully formed. In many ways this was no novelty for twentieth-century socialist revolutionary practice; Leninism itself was an explanation of how revolution in the context of imperialism necessarily depended on a vanguard that could guide revolutionary practice in systems where the overwhelming majority of the population was a rural peasantry. The notion of a broad class alliance was not new to the Nicaraguan revolution, its implications had been well understood even before Mao discussed them in detail. Yet the particular understanding of the ramifications of this fact developed by Carlos Fonseca in the Nicaraguan context is peculiar to the FSLN and constituted the foundation for its notion that pluralism could be combined with participatory democracy in the context of a mixed economy as the basis for a transition to socialism. This view also led to the rejection by the FSLN of traditional Marxist-Leninist opposition to elections in which even bourgeois elements were allowed to compete for power.

As seen in chapter 2 above, Fonseca thought the peculiarity of the Nicaraguan situation was that the nascent bourgeoisie had fused itself with the dominant landlord class that had preceded it, rather than displacing it. The international situation combined with this class history meant that political power in Nicaragua was not held by the national bourgeoisie and that it was possible to move to control of the state by popular forces without going through a period of bourgeois hegemony; it was possible to have a revolution based on a united struggle against Somocismo as the agent of international capital. Such a struggle could unite various class forces under the leadership of the FSLN as the armed vanguard. Based especially on students and youth in general, the FSLN was able to forge a unity in struggle that involved both *campesinos* and urban workers.

The actual revolutionary process, as has been discussed above, was based on the common struggle of members of various classes and groups of people. In this context the FSLN saw itself as the vanguard of the people, not merely of the proletariat, as orthodox Marxist-Leninists would understand it. This did not mean, however, that the idea of a socialist revolution, ultimately based on the working class, was to be abandoned in favor of some sort of populist view of the state as rising above alternative class interests. On the contrary, the notion was that the FSLN, as vanguard, could guide the system through a long process of transition towards socialism based on the working class.

The Third Force as Social Subject of the Revolution

Orlando Nuñez Soto, director of CIERA, a graduate in sociology of the Sorbonne, director of the University of Central America (UCA) School of Sociology in the period immediately preceding the revolutionary triumph (a major center of FSLN recruitment and education), and FSLN militant, has been a major force in explicating the theoretical foundation of the Sandinista revolution. He argues that the fundamental class struggle between the bourgeoisie and the proletariat is not expressed directly as an open struggle between these two classes but

> between two contradictory and antagonistic projects, in the ranks of which all of the forces of the society align themselves (a bourgeois project and a project that can be nothing other than proletarian). The fundamental factor in this alignment is the capacity of the vanguard to unify all the classes and existing forces, independently of their class origin or class situation, especially with

212

respect to the *campesinado* and the urban petty
bourgeoisie, that are the majority forces in this society.
(1987: 15)

Thus while the fundamental character of the revolution is
proletarian and therefore socialist, many of the most significant
actors in the revolutionary process are not proletarian.

The "social subject" of the revolution is a group of people
that do not come from the proletariat in their majority. Carlos Vilas
points out that in Nicaragua as well as other dependent capitalist
countries the proletariat is a very small "fraction of the dominated
classes." As he says: "The working class is submerged in a mass of
peasants, urban and rural poor, office workers, domestic workers,
artisans, seasonal workers, people with no place under the sun, who
often are not fully differentiated from the proletariat" (1986: 15).
These were the people, along with the students who were their
children, that constituted the actual basis for the Sandinista
insurrection; they are what Nuñez Soto calls the "third force,"
which he describes as the "social subject" of the revolution (1986).

He divides this third force into three classifications: there are
"economic groups (peasants, artisans, and merchants) and
technological-ideological groups (professionals, technicians,
government officials, administrators, students, non-productive
salaried workers in general, etc.)," and "special movements." The
special movements are "youth, student, feminist, pacifist, religious,
ethnic, or cultural movements" (1986: 241). All of them together
Nuñez Soto sees as the "petty bourgeoisie" in Marx's terms. They
must be won over to the proletarian project for fear that they will
realize their potential to be its "main enemy" (1986: 242–43).

The Vanguard and Social Forces

The party as vanguard is not necessarily formed from people
with origins either in the proletariat or the third force. It consists
of those with "a strong revolutionary ideology" who are also "the
activists in participatory democracy." It is their function to organize
all of the relevant social forces in terms of the historical proletarian
project, mediating between theory and practice. Although it
organizes all of these forces it remains "a workers' party in the strict
political sense, since the ideology that cements it is proletarian

213

ideology; it represents the interests of the workers, peasants, and remaining social sectors (in that order) at the same time as it represents the interests of the movement as a whole" (Nuñez Soto, 1986: 246).

The state, once it has been seized and put in the hands of the vanguard, "lies between the party and the masses and its task is to devise policies that express the masses' immediate interests and the project's general interests" (Nuñez Soto, 1986: 247). The general interests of the project are proletarian and will lead, ultimately, to socialism in the context of pluralism and participatory democracy. But this does not mean that the immediate interests of the workers will always prevail. Indeed, the relatively small proletariat, as the fundamental historical subject, must understand that it is often essential to "subordinate its immediate needs to the interests of the project itself" (Nuñez Soto, 1986: 245). Ultimately the vanguard will guide the state in promoting policies that will unite disparate social elements in developing a set of forces of production that will lead to sufficient development that the proletariat can, as Marx predicted, transcend its own existence as a class. In eliminating itself as a class it will "eliminate the rest of the classes" (Nuñez Soto, 1986: 245).

The Too Orthodox Nature of FSLN Class Theory

What we have in Nuñez Soto's theory, and in the practice of the FSLN in its ten years in government, is a sophisticated understanding of the meaning of class analysis for political practice. Overcoming simple-minded notions of the proletariat as the leading class in both the insurrection and in ten years of development as well as the notion that the FSLN was simply the vanguard of the proletariat was, in large measure, responsible for the vitality of FSLN practice. Yet ultimately this view of class and its relation to the vanguard party and the state did not go far enough. A still-too-"orthodox" sense of class and consequent major lines of policy development played a large role in the failure of the FSLN to understand its electoral weakness in 1990 and continues to inform FSLN practice today. Overcoming the problems with the FSLN theory of class and the concomitant notions about the role of the party, the state, and the government can help make sense of the continuing revolutionary struggle in Nicaragua in which the broad mass of workers, rural as well as urban, has once more become the leading revolutionary force.

Through all of this analysis and through the practice detailed in the previous two chapters what stands out is that the FSLN at the same time succeeds in transcending a narrow sense of the proletariat as simply industrial workers, whether rural or urban, and yet continues to function in a manner that internally divides, both theoretically and practically, the broad mass of Nicaraguans who derive their living from work. The FSLN was able to understand that revolutionary practice cannot be guided by a notion of class that assumes that only industrial workers can be major participants in revolutionary development. Yet it maintained the orthodoxy that a Marxist understanding of socialist revolution must ultimately rest on the view that the "proletariat" is the historical basis of socialism. This notion contains, at least implicitly, the view that the working class must be finally understood in relation to the concept of the "proletariat" as workers in industrial settings. Thus the existing working class is not yet fully developed.

Class Complexity and the Vanguard

The FSLN position is that the class matrix in Nicaragua is complex and thus that it is essential for the political vanguard of the revolution to exploit this complexity in the development of a new social order just as it was necessary to do so in guiding the insurrection against the oppressive political structures of Somoza's political rule. This is part of what gives the vanguard its role in guiding developments in the pluralist system. It was to aid the development of a proletarian project in the context of a complicated social reality. The proletariat would eventually emerge from this complexity. In the meantime it was possible to forge a revolution based on the concept of national liberation. National liberation was not, in itself, peculiarly proletarian, but was of interest to the Nicaraguan people themselves. There were Nicaraguans, of course, who benefited from the fact that the country was not truly free, independent, or sovereign; these were the Somozas and their close allies. Uniting the "popular masses" or the "poor majorities" to struggle for national liberation and for social justice was the immediate goal of the vanguard.

It was in this context that liberation theology could play such a large role—it united the popular masses, "the people," in terms of their actual life situations. While the vanguard was to be "popular" (that is the FSLN was the "vanguard of the people"), perhaps unlike some other social forces in the country, it had the unique function of controlling developments in such a way that there would ultimately be a transition towards socialism. Guiding the popular struggle required the FSLN to continually reassess the significance of its political policies so as to produce those conditions through which "the people" had become the proletariat and class distinctions could, at last, disappear within the ruling coalition of forces. FSLN control of the state was essential to this practice. Other popular forces, including groups organized through the development of the theology of liberation, did not have to be completely under its control, but the FSLN was to be the guiding political force. This was not a position derived from merely abstract speculation, but had resulted from the practice of the FSLN in the insurrectionary period.

Carlos Vilas described the "profile" of the group that actually participated in the insurrectionary triumph as a "complex working mass of artisans, peasants, semiproletarians, sellers, tradespeople, people without trades, day workers, students, the poor of the city and the countryside from whose center the proletariat is becoming slowly differentiated; the forge from which emerged the *social subject* of the Sandinista revolution and the popular insurrection" (1986: 108). While the proletariat continued to emerge, aided by large-scale investments in mechanizing agriculture and promoting irrigation, the vanguard had to guide the social order in the interests of the emerging class of the future. The implicit developmentalist model here seems to suggest that when Nicaragua becomes "modern" it will have a political structure in place through which the proletariat can act directly. In the meantime the complex social and class reality would have to be controlled in the interest of revolutionary development. The FSLN, through its control of government and the state, would be the agency that provided appropriate control.

This view guided the revolutionary project from the early years of FSLN governance in an explicit and practical manner. It led the FSLN to count on ideological mobilization of urban youth to overcome the potentially reactionary attitudes that could arise among the urban sectors that Nuñez Soto saw as the third force. As early as 1981 CIERA pointed out that more than two-thirds of the population comprised a "secondary social stratum" that was neither proletarian nor bourgeois. People less than twenty-four years old also accounted for two-thirds of the population. The claim was that Marxism had discovered the importance of the working class to revolution, that Leninism showed the importance of the "worker peasant alliance for the taking of power," but that it was revolutions in the third world, such as in Nicaragua, that had "demonstrated the necessity of a worker-peasant-youth alliance that acted as a social force for mobilization and transformation." The youth, mobilized by the FSLN "against the culture of consumption and in favor of its insertion in productive work," would fight the "ideological reaction that grows in the petty bourgeoisie and urban middle strata" (CIERA, 1989, 1: 78).

With respect to workers and *campesinos* there would be a "policy of distribution of political and economic information from the superstructure to the bases." This, along with participatory democracy, would make it possible for workers to understand the policies determined by the FSLN (CIERA, 1989, 1: 78–79). It was recognized that policies would have to be undertaken that would be "against the immediate interests of all the popular sectors taken together." This would be necessary to avoid putting the "required political stability in danger" in the search for social and political transformations (CIERA, 1989, 1: 71).

In agriculture, just as in the urban areas, "propaganda" was to overcome the practical problems that resulted from governmental policies that went against the immediate interests of various groups in promoting the proletarian project. Here the message, "propaganda, political education and training," was to focus on "the administrators of State Production Units (UPEs) and the technicians working for *Campesino* Programs (Procampo) and the National Development Bank." These people were to be "ideologically mobilized"; otherwise "the transmission of the message to the *campesinado* and the agricultural proletariat will be confused" (CIERA, 1989, 1: 152).

What all of this suggests is that the burden of understanding the proletarian project and implementing it fell on the FSLN. Implementation of policies that the leadership of the party found necessary to guide the project to its ultimate proletarian, and thus socialist, conclusion, was the business of the government. This was made necessary by the fact that there was no substantial proletariat whose direct demands could constitute the basis of state policy. The complex class profile of Nicaraguan reality required sophisticated management of state structures and government policy that could ultimately create a revolutionary proletarian class in itself. In the meantime, each sector of the society would have to be guided by those with a better understanding of the project that would ultimately liberate it when the proletariat became the dominant class.

The Proletariat Must Suffer, Other Classes Get Preference

As we have seen above, this led to a sort of preferential pluralism for those who were least naturally allied with the proletarian project, the "patriotic" large and medium producers, who were to be compensated for their exclusion from exercising political power as a class with policies that would keep them producing. The long-term proletarian project required the mobilization of the national bourgeoisie for production and sharp limits on their political role. As this theory worked itself out in practice FSLN policy also required that the Nicaraguan state have international legitimacy, especially in the eyes of possibly supportive political sectors in the United States. This, in turn, meant that the bourgeoisie could not be simply excluded from the political process. Therefore, in order to assure UNO participation in the 1990 elections, it was essential to make concessions even to the point of allowing external financing for the bourgeois political alliance. The ultimate influence of the bourgeoisie in the process was to be limited by the fact that they were sure to lose the election. The FSLN's victory was thought to be assured both by its strong class base in the proletariat and other popular classes and the support it was to draw from its identification with the project of national liberation. The practical result of the FSLN loss in 1990 was to put the bourgeoisie in control of the government. This left the FSLN without control of the state, the fundamental instrument upon which it counted for the fulfillment of the revolutionary project.

A similar result was reached in dealing with the least proletarian elements of the agricultural work force. As it became clear that there was a substantial sector of agricultural small-holders who were dissatisfied with revolutionary developments they, like large producers, became the beneficiaries of guided pluralism. FSLN policy sought to meet the direct interests of non-cooperative small *campesinos* through land distribution. UNAG had originally had the role of attempting to create cooperatives so that the least "advanced" rural workers could learn habits of social work. Yet the larger class project required it to shift focus after 1985 to attempt to attract the new potential recipients of individual agrarian reform land titles. Thus, those who had resisted incorporation into social work as the FSLN saw it were to be rewarded. Once again this was seen as necessary to protect the long-term proletarian project, not simply as a response to rural workers' demands. There is little evidence that this, in fact, improved support for the FSLN in the electoral process.

The Third Force Must Suffer, Too

Those most ideologically allied with the revolution were members of the urban third force, especially government employees, including teachers and health workers. They were expected to understand the need for sacrifice in terms of the long-term project because of their close affiliation with the FSLN. Thus their demands for better conditions could be postponed. Furthermore, since they were not really productive workers, their immediate interests were sacrificed for the good of the proletarian project.

Workers on state farms and in industry were the most clearly proletarian force. They participated in decision-making in the administration of their units of production and could be counted on to support the revolution—after all, it was their project. It was important to maintain information about how government policies were promoting this project as a part of making clear why the individuals that constituted its base should accept necessary sacrifices. In a sense it appears that the workers and the *campesinos* were the only ones that would "go to the end" because, though the journey was difficult, they would constitute the basis of the class that ultimately would control the state. Governmental policies were to be undertaken promoting this end and were to be explained to those whom they would benefit once social and economic transformation made them the class that would be in "the overwhelming majority." Those policies themselves, however, were to be developed by the vanguard and to be implemented by the government which, since 1985, was elected. Political parties were to represent differing interests. The interests of the workers was to be represented by the FSLN. Of course unions were to play a role in this process but their role was seen more as disciplining the work force than promoting what their members might see as their immediate interests. Strikes and other direct means to make their views known were to be avoided. Thus, once more, FSLN and government policy sacrificed the immediate interests of workers in order to promote the proletarian project.

It would appear that this basic line of analysis consistently underrepresented the interests of those whose project the FSLN existed to support and overrepresented those whose project it was intended to frustrate. To understand how this is the case it is important to see how the FSLN made sense of classes as actors in the political process.

The "Forces" and the Working Class

According to Nuñez Soto, the political revolution had occurred with the triumph, its principal social subject had been the "third force," the urban masses. The "struggle against the oligarchical expression of capitalism and imperialism" was undertaken by the "agricultural workers, especially the *campesinos* (the second force)." In his view, "as the revolution advances through overcoming economic contradictions, the working class will achieve higher levels of maturity and hegemony over the process" (Nuñez Soto, 1987: 21). Once the political revolution takes power, it

> initiates changes in the most backward social relations; and finally prepares itself to establish the economic-technical conditions of development and proletarianization of the society. Only then does the social revolution become possible, the order of which is: development of the productive forces, change in the capitalist relations of production, elimination of classes through the construction of popular power and the creation of a de-alienated consciousness and behavior. (1987: 21)

220

Only at this stage has the real working class, the first force, become the real subject of the process. Apparently, at this stage the "historical subject" and the "social subject" become one.

The Party as Intermediary

In the political revolution, ideological development (presumably among the members of the third force) led to political action. The social and economic revolution proceeds from "material economic" changes to political and ideological ones (Nuñez Soto, 1987: 17–18). Thus, objective changes brought about by government policy are essential to the creation of a self-conscious proletarian force, the real historical subject of the revolution.

An intermediary between the historical subject and the social subject of real development would seem to be required. Classes do not, apparently, act for themselves. The party is this intermediary. It prepared the ideological way for the political revolution and the third force took action with the FSLN acting as military vanguard. Without the development of the FSLN as a vanguard the actions of the third force in overthrowing the dictatorship would not have been possible. The FSLN showed that it was possible to fight Somoza and the National Guard. FSLN leadership made it possible to destroy the Somocista state and to create a new one that could ultimately carry out the proletarian project through the development of participatory democracy.

Once the new state was created it was the function of the FSLN and the government to implement the material changes necessary to prepare the way for the proletariat to ultimately come into existence and transcend itself. In the meantime it must guide the process with the continuous recognition that workers and *campesinos* in their actual existence in the complex class structure of the Nicaraguan social order are not, as such, the proletarian class actor. People who make up the actual social forces must be guided in such a manner as to make sure that they understand the importance of a long-term development through which they will merge into one proletarian class. Organizations must be created that can at the same time aid them in learning new social ways of work and unite them with the revolutionary government. In this process the FSLN is to work with mass organizations in making clear to their members that particular economic policies may be necessary that are not immediately beneficial to them.

Sandinista Theory as Developmentalist Marxism: State, Class, and Party

Yet why was it necessary to wait for the ultimate revolutionary class while a revolutionary government under the leadership of a vanguard developed policies that could make it possible for that class to emerge as a real actor? Because that is what Marx taught? It would appear that, in spite of the extraordinary creativity of Sandinista theory and practice, this mechanical answer prevailed. FSLN thought was formed by those who understood a new critical Marxism, yet it retained a notion of what constitutes a "class" that misled its theory and practice. This is in large part why Sandinista practice was based on a sort of developmentalist logic that emphasized "modernization" of productive techniques. The notion that socialism depends upon the proletariat conceived of as industrial workers leads easily to the idea that until some substantial degree of industrial development occurs no working class can exist that is capable of understanding its own interests without mediation.

The state must create a revolutionary hegemony that will maintain subjective support for a vanguard party that can promote the most revolutionary project. For this project to succeed the party must control a government that can implement policies that promote and defend this project. The project requires the creation of objective developments in production that will eventually allow for the revolutionary class to develop. Especially in the context of imperialist aggression this may involve immediate losses for those who actually work in the existing social order. For Marx the revolutionary class was the industrial proletariat, therefore socialist revolution must wait for industrial development. Nevertheless Sandinista theory held that a political revolution can precede and guide such development.

Agriculture as Guided Development

In Nicaragua this was taken to mean that agriculture would have to become mechanized and that it would have to be integrated with large-scale processing of agricultural products. As was pointed out above, Jaime Wheelock translated this idea into practice with the notion of creating irrigation systems that could result in "double cropping," through which the richest agricultural zones of the country could produce both export crops and crops for domestic consumption on the same farms. This seemed to suggest that small-scale farming would gradually disappear as a major feature of the system as mechanization spread throughout the country. Thus agricultural work would become industrialized and agricultural workers would become an industrial proletariat.

This theoretical perspective led to several important problems, especially in agrarian reform. As has been shown above, the FSLN saw full-time workers on highly "developed" farms as proletarian. The creation of state farms thus seemed a natural development where the proletariat would constitute the work force. Although the already "advanced" form of agriculture had been enmeshed in a set of relations of domination, it represented technically advanced methods of production. These agricultural methods had to be preserved for the survival of the country but could ultimately be improved by even greater modernization through mechanization. The original agricultural communes that had been created by the workers were insufficient because they threatened to break down modern export agriculture. Without guidance from a vanguard, agricultural workers tended to engage in agricultural practices that would threaten the export earnings that Nicaragua required. The original communes developed in the insurrectionary period threatened to emphasize production for immediate consumption. Further, left to their own devices, the traditional attitudes of those in the countryside would lead to parcelling land out into plots that were not easily exploited by modern agricultural techniques. The basic plan was to "seize the heights of the economy" and thus to control the system as a whole. Both farming which integrated the production of direct consumption goods with export production, as existed in the original communes, and allowing rural workers to take over small plots of land threatened this strategy.

The FSLN determined that the basic strategy of national unity required that "patriotic" large landowners not suffer from expropriation of their land. Furthermore, granting small-holding titles would decrease the availability of seasonal agricultural labor for both state and private producers of export groups. Thus the demands of the workers themselves had to be resisted in the interests of the workers' long-term project.

Of course the basic plan for agriculture was to ultimately benefit the workers, but it had to be undertaken in a modern way as understood by the leaders of the new government, not directly in response to worker demands. For the workers on state farms the ultimate plan was to, indeed, produce both export and basic consumption crops. But this was to be done through the development of large-scale projects, especially involving irrigation, not through the direct initiative of those working on the state farms.

Class Division, Not Class Consolidation in Agriculture

The immediate demands of those seeking land were met through the creation of cooperatives. In this process the workers on state farms became organizationally divided from those in cooperatives through the creation of UNAG. ATC was to continue to represent the already proletarianized workers on large farms, especially state farms. UNAG represented agricultural workers, who were to be encouraged to learn social work habits and thus to develop appropriate ideas through the formation of cooperatives. The state farm proletariat was advanced, those working in cooperatives would advance as well, under the leadership of UNAG and FSLN cadre. The idea seemed to be that UNAG could gradually attract small-holding agricultural producers toward the working class. Yet this was to take place by the division of actual agricultural workers into two quite different groups, those represented by UNAG and those represented by ATC.

Many small-holders were threatened by this process and developed or maintained strong relations with larger holders. Thus these workers were drawn away from the working class and associated themselves with larger landholders, including members of the bourgeoisie. The fear that the petty bourgeois attitudes of these not yet advanced workers might prevail was realized, at least in part, because they had been divided organizationally and practically from others who worked in agriculture. They were divided from full-time wage workers by their exclusion from ATC. Many seasonal workers were organized by UNAG into cooperatives, dividing them both from wage workers and from those who continued with individual production. Small holders drew closer to medium and large producers and often came to support the *contras* in this process.

The response of the government was to begin to grant land titles to individual workers. UNAG moved to organize those demanding land and, in the process, incorporated more large and medium producers into its ranks. In this process UNAG and its membership was not becoming "proletarianized" as the large-scale plan suggested it should; if anything, it was becoming "bourgeoisified." The process came to take on an appearance of inevitability as it developed. Those who were least proletarian in orientation were able to obtain a response by threatening to oppose the state itself through allying with its armed enemies. The pro-revolutionary UNAG moved continually away from a proletarian line as it attempted to accommodate social sectors that had resisted the revolution. The more it did so the less proletarian it became.

At the same time, the most proletarian agricultural work force was inadvertently demobilized as a social force as it was mobilized to support government policies and the revolution itself. Farm workers and members of cooperatives were required to take up arms to defend the state and were under substantial pressure to increase production without obtaining greater compensation. Government policies, even when they were directed to giving priority to the countryside, demanded greater and greater sacrifices from this sector as it granted land titles to those outside it. The more a group of workers supported the revolution through sacrifice the more it was asked to do so. The more a group resisted the revolution, even going so far as to support the counterrevolution, the more policies were adopted that favored that group.

This was thought to be a revolutionary policy because it advanced the long-term proletarian project. Ultimately, as the material changes in production that were planned came to fruition, it was assumed that social structures would change. Yet there was little in the character of day-to-day life for those who most resembled the proletariat to make this clear. What was to fill the breach was political education and the fulfillment that was to come from participating in the revolutionary project. Yet the level of actual participation did not extend to the making of large-scale policy; that was the function of the vanguard, which had a larger view. Government policies were to be explained to the base, they were not to come from it because the base could not, for objective reasons, be sufficiently mature to make sense of what was required to protect the class project itself.

Throughout the period of FSLN governance there was a reluctance to respond to immediate demands of the proletarian base in the countryside and an emphasis on promotion of productive efficiency. Promotion of large-scale projects was a consistent element of FSLN policy until the last two or three years, when economic reality required postponing many of the projects. Some had come online but it was far from true that they had solved the problems of agricultural workers or reinserted Nicaragua at a new level in the international economy. Perhaps more time would have shown how this could be done but by the election of 1990 there was little evidence that the large projects could improve the lives of those in the countryside.

The Economics of Large Scale Agriculture

The economic reality of large-scale mechanized agriculture had become more clear by 1990. A continual fall in the price of most export products, especially cotton, had made it so that even greater production in terms of quantities of goods could not maintain real agricultural income. The high price of inputs, including fertilizers, pesticides, and herbicides also made large production less possible. The ecological costs of such farming had also become clear as soil and water quality deteriorated, just as they do in "modern" agriculture in all other parts of the world. Though there had been substantial projects in alternative agricultural practices the emphasis on the factory model of agriculture meant that they had played little essential role in altering basic productive relations in agriculture. Labor supply problems continued even as did migration to urban areas. Though some plans had been made to attempt to bring urban workers back to the farm, they had had relatively little success by the time of the 1990 elections. State farms, and those who worked on them, were no longer a major priority and it was clear that they had not succeeded in seizing the agricultural initiative, much less "the heights of the economy." In fact, the state farms were being used as a source of land for distribution to individuals and to cooperatives. After the electoral defeat of the FSLN the basic demand of rural dwellers was the same as it had been for years: "land to those who work it." The formation of a new *campesino* organization uniting UNAG, demobilized *contras*, and demobilized members of the Sandinista army was evidence that there could be objective unity where disunity had prevailed.

In the private sector little had been gained in terms of production by the "patriotic" producers, who still showed a remarkable distaste for investing their own capital in production. There is little evidence that the small-to-medium producers had been won over to the extent of supporting the FSLN in its long-term plans. Even those who may have turned their guns in the right direction often turned their ballots away from the FSLN and towards those who spoke more to their interests as owners than as workers. UNAG, which had been founded with the hope of promoting social production had moved closer to the promotion of individual land ownership than to the further promotion of cooperative labor.

The Urban Dynamic

For urban workers, especially government employees, the dynamic was even more damaging. Their objective position deteriorated and yet they were supposed to continue to support the revolutionary project. The fact that they were not a key element of production for export meant that their work was not "productive" in many cases. Therefore they "had to understand" that they could not receive priority in social and economic policy.

While youth were to be counted on as the ideological base, objective conditions for young people declined both in terms of availability of educational and career opportunities. At the same time they were counted on to protect the revolution by participating in the military and to be the source of inspiration for others in the city. Here, there was no long-term in which it was to get much better. After all, proletarianization was to take place in the countryside, not the city. As the youth that had constituted the fighting element of the revolutionary third force aged they hoped for better possibilities. A person who was sixteen at the time of the triumph was twenty-seven by the time of the 1990 election. Sixteen-year-olds who obtained the right to vote in 1990 had been five years old at the time of the triumph. The preceding two or three years of their lives had not been lived in the exhilaration of overthrowing a hated dictator, they had been years of severe economic hardship. Then, for a young man, the immediate future was military service. The theory of the revolution held that he would eventually become proletarian; his daily life told him only that he was poor and there was little hope for things getting better. For many young women things were no better. They were sometimes incorporated into the work force but often found themselves, like their mothers, forced into the informal economy. They were also likely to lose their jobs when young men came back from the war. Although AMNLAE had struggled for opening discussion of abortion rights the FSLN had resisted making this or birth control major issues for fear of giving ammunition to the right-wing elements of the Church. Young mothers were concerned that their children would be drafted in the future.

Thus, in the country as a whole there had been little advance either for the proletariat or for proletarianization. Division of interests among workers in different sectors had not been notably diminished, but seem to have increased since 1984. Class unity was not the actual result of the attempt to apply the theory through which the FSLN could mediate between the long-term interests of the proletarian project and the short-term needs of the members of the second and third forces. This was not a result of bad will, it was to some extent the result of strategic misjudgment of the facts and of the external pressures that were brought to bear on the revolutionary project. But it was also, at least in part, a failure to understand the real class forces in the country.

The FSLN was not waiting for the proletariat, it was attempting to create conditions such that it could arise as a conscious agent. Theory made clear what a social system would ultimately have to be in order for the universal class that Marx had envisioned to come into existence, the class that would transcend itself and, therefore, all class relations.

Marx on Class

Yet what did Marx actually have to say about the nature of the revolutionary class? Several serious scholars have shown that Marx actually had no clear and consistent notion of the precise character of classes and emphasize that for Marx the notion of a class as an actor is better developed in his explicitly political discussions of contemporary events than in his more abstract theoretical works. He did not have a theoretical model that he then applied to political reality; rather, he developed his conceptions of class relations from observing political events (Draper, 1978; Munck, 1984: 82ff.; and Poulantzas, 1975 and 1978).

What was clearly essential to Marx's basic understanding of the revolutionary possibilities of the proletariat was that it constituted the "immense majority" of the social systems with which he was familiar. He wrote in *The Communist Manifesto*: "All previous historical movements were movements of minorities. The proletarian movement is the self-conscious, independent movement of the immense majority, in the interest of the immense majority. The proletariat, the lowest stratum of our present society, cannot stir, cannot raise itself up, without the whole superincumbent strata of official society being sprung into the air" (Marx, 1976: 495).

The Immense Majorities as the Working Class in Nicaragua

In Nicaragua the immense majority had risen in 1979 as a self-conscious actor that threw the old system as a whole into the air. Nothing prevents an understanding of this majority as the revolutionary class except old theoretical formulas based on Marx's observations of nineteenth-century European industrial societies.

It was evident to the FSLN and all serious observers that there really was no substantial industrial proletariat in Nicaragua. Instead of therefore seeing the overwhelming majority *as* the working class that Marx understood as the ultimately revolutionary force, the FSLN set out to create conditions for the formation of a class that did not exist. There is really no existing social system in which the proletariat, conceived of as the industrial working class, or even of "productive workers," constitutes the vast majority of the system. Marxian students of the most advanced social formations, such as Erick Wright and Nicos Poulantzas, attempt to develop proletarian class analyses of advanced capitalist systems. They recognize that the industrial proletariat constitutes a minority of active classes in these systems. Students of Latin America such as Alejandro Portes and Ronaldo Munck see the proletariat, traditionally defined, as a minority as well. Somehow each of these authors attempts to explain these facts away in their analyses. They attempt to retain the old definitions but to show that they do not really apply in the particular cases they examine. It is as if the students of each particular social formation think that the real working class, the proletariat, exists as the major force somewhere other than in the formation that student knows best. The proletariat appears to be a sort of ghost that exists nowhere but explains what is real everywhere.[1]

For the FSLN this analysis was not merely an academic matter, it constituted one basic element of their practical strategy. The Nicaraguan proletariat existed only in the future. The actual workers, whether urban or rural, were to be measured against this model of the future and, by definition, were inferior to the model. Problems that resulted from this analysis should lead us to re-examine how to make sense of class in the revolutionary context. Two basic strategies are available. The first is to simply give up on the concept, replacing it with the notion of "grassroots movements" or "popular movements." The second is to refocus our understanding of what constitutes the working class.

Can Grassroots Movements Replace Class?

The first strategy has led some political activists and scholars to suggest that contemporary revolutions are not based on class struggle but on the development of "grassroots movements" that cross class lines. Feminist groups, Christian base communities,

---

[1] I attempted to deal with these matters explicitly in an earlier piece with which I remain in partial agreement. See Bruce E. Wright, 1989 ("Class and Revolutionary Actors in Latin America," *Review of Latin American Studies* 1, no. 2: 65–80).

neighborhood organizations, environmental groups, and ethnic groups in this view are the essential subjects of revolution.[2]

No serious observer of contemporary reality can deny that such groups play a substantial role in progressive organizing in many parts of the world. Yet to notice that such groups exist is not the same as to develop a large-scale theoretical understanding of their significance. To develop such an analysis is far beyond the limits of the present work. If one were to attempt to develop a theory based on the role of grassroots movements as the foundation for revolution it would be necessary to explain why certain movements are able to have a political impact and in what conjunctures of social and economic circumstances they are able to do so. It would, further, be essential to show that the actions of various organizations of oppressed or dispossessed peoples constitute a unified force that can produce generalized social change in one or more social formations. Oddly enough, this is what the concept of class was able to do for the FSLN—it presumed to show how various movements constituted a coherent whole in revolutionary terms.

The complexity of FSLN class analysis is, in large measure, dependent on practical efforts to give some unity to diverse struggles. In this sense the grassroots movements of the FSLN period of government were the mass organizations. Class analysis was an attempt to give them direction. It will not do to simply take these movements, including AMNLAE, as fully autonomous developments. Their actual development was based on assumptions about their relation to the concept of a working class, ultimately of the proletariat.

The Vast Majority as the Working Class in Nicaragua

What has occurred in Nicaragua since the electoral defeat of the FSLN suggests that the better strategy is to broaden our conception of class. The vast majorities did not vote for the FSLN; in this sense the working class abandoned the FSLN as vanguard. Yet as attempts have been made to dismantle fundamental elements

---

[2]There are numerous individual works that examine the significance of particular groups in various systems, including Nicaragua, that seem to depend on some such analysis. For an explicit examination of the idea that we should focus on these groups, see Hogan, 1987.

of the FSLN project, substantial forces have arisen, based at least partially on the existing mass organizations, to oppose the new, clearly bourgeois, project. Furthermore, in substantial measure they have protected the most fundamental gains of the Nicaraguan revolution, as was shown in chapter 1 above. The FSLN is neither leading nor guiding the popular forces that have faced down the new government. It is fundamentally responding to them. All of those who work, whether salaried farm workers, *campesinos*, industrial workers, government employees, teachers, health workers, or truck and taxi drivers, have taken effective actions to continue the revolution, or at least to protect gains that it has made. They have shown that it is not only a vanguard that can act in a revolutionary manner, though it can sometimes lead revolutionary actions. They are demonstrating that they constitute the class of workers that really exists and can act in it own interests without mediation at every historical step. It is to the mass of workers, the vast majorities, that the revolutionary task is entrusted. They need no vision of a future class different from themselves. The struggle for revolutionary hegemony continues, its subject is the working class.

Reducing Differences among Workers as a Class

To understand the working class simply as those who work to live, whether they work in industry, in the government, on large farms or on small plots, is to make sense of what really happens in all social systems. To attempt to impose an abstract notion of "productive labor" or of "social relations" of work that divides workers into those who are really workers in an advanced, proletarian sense and those who are a "third force," is to raise theory above practice.

To see work—not degree of industrialization, method of payment, or production of goods for sale through the addition of labor (thus producing surplus value through "productive" labor)—as the fundamental characteristic of those who form the working class is to reduce differences among different forms of labor and to highlight differences between fundamentally different ways of living. Individuals often, in fact, engage in more than one form of work. The clearest example of this is women who work to maintain a household and rear children and also work to obtain a monetary

income. Yet this phenomenon is not restricted to women. Many
people, men and women alike, engage in one kind of activity part of
the day or part of the year and another type of activity during the
other.   This is especially true in areas where agriculture is a
predominant activity. Many people work for others and are paid a
wage or in kind part of the time and produce goods for consumption
and for sale another part of the time. Some people work most of
the time for a wage and still engage in small-scale agricultural
production.[3] Many people change their type of labor over time in
every social system.   This is not always a matter of "upward
mobility." Industrial workers can become small producers, small
producers can become small merchants, government employees can
become workers or merchants for many different reasons.

   While individuals are thus not capable of being clearly defined
as members of one or another class, it is even more difficult to sort
out people when we pay attention to the fact that individuals
typically live in groups, especially families, that have a complex
profile. Most economic units contain people who work in quite
disparate activities.   Within a domestic unit often a woman
undertakes domestic work both at home and for others and a man
works in a factory, for example. Members of the same unit may also
be merchants or even farm workers or work in the "informal
sector." Indeed it is by following a conscious strategy of diversified
employment within the same domestic unit that many people have
survived the dramatically shifting economic fortunes of revolutionary
Nicaragua. In a state where a high level government employee
brings home an income inferior to that of someone who sells soft
drinks on a neighborhood corner, such diversity can be essential for
survival. Office workers who sell small food items in the streets
after office work hours are not uncommon in Managua. Such a
person is a worker in both activities, just as those who live in family
units where different individuals work in different ways are from
working class families.

---

[3]Those familiar with rural life in the United States should not be
surprised by this mode of activity. Many small farmers work part of the
time in small or medium towns while they also produce crops. Some
teachers are also farmers. People who work in cities often participate in
the harvest of crops either regularly or sporadically.

Thus, people may have little real sense of themselves as members of one segment of the working class rather than another.[4] They simply see themselves as workers. While there may be some consciousness of differences among different workers, especially based on differential incomes and privileges, there is little sense of a class difference among such people. Indeed they may well resent attempts to suggest that such differences exist.[5] There is, in fact, a substantial cultural reality shared by those who work for a living. While an individual worker may not be able to identify the exact occupation of another simply by interacting with him or her, s/he is able, in general, to identify a person as a worker or a member of the "popular sector." There are many cultural markers that make this possible, including styles of dress, manners of speaking, and basic attitudes that are quickly identified in even a brief interaction. In

---

[4]One long-time informant has told me quite different things about his own class identification over time, even though his basic work has not changed. At one point I asked this man, who lives in a small village close to Managua, what class he belonged to. Although his formal education is minimal he owns and reads books involving class theory, including the works of Jaime Wheelock. He answered at this time that he had done a lot of different things, he had worked in construction, he had done some factory labor, he had worked as a salaried agricultural worker, had planted crops of his own, and was most recently employed as a mechanic's helper in a large sugar refinery. But, he said, "I live in the country, I have mostly worked in agriculture, and I like the countryside, therefore I am a *campesino*." A few years later he simply said that he is "proletarian," and was surprised when he was reminded of the earlier conversation. Ultimately he said, "really, it's all the same." He is a member of a labor union, an FSLN militant, and a leader of the communal movement in his village.

[5]In the United States this fact has been used to label, at least in popular discourse and political rhetoric, the large group of people who work as "middle class." The lower class is not seen as workers but as those who live from public assistance or from crime. This labeling has been quite successful in maintaining a fundamentally non-revolutionary stability in the United States. On the left, arguments that real "productive workers" are different from "petty bourgeois non-productive workers" has had little success except in further marginalizing those who make such arguments.

234

this sense the working or popular class is an objective phenomenon. For theory to fail to identify the phenomenon is for it to fail in developing genuinely revolutionary practice.[6]

Other people are basically employers and administrators who guide the work of others. This is true in the urban setting as well as in rural areas. Large landowners may participate in some aspects of agriculture, especially in cattle ranching, on a sporadic basis. Nevertheless, their fundamental activity, just as that of high level administrators, is organizing the work of others. Of course, some people simply derive their living from the profits that ensue from ownership. These people have a fundamentally different class interest from those who derive their income from their own work.

Thinking of classes as divided between those in the vast majority who work and those in the small minorities who administer the work of others can sharpen genuinely clashing interests and minimize differences among those whose interests are fundamentally the same. At one level, Sandinista discourse has taken advantage of this in alleging that the FSLN is the "vanguard of the people." Yet, at a deeper level, thinking of the proletariat as the ultimate development of the working class has had the opposite effect.

In the countryside the FSLN has, as we have seen, consistently followed policies based on drawing distinctions between classes of agricultural workers. This created a problem that is most serious with respect to *campesinos* who hold, or wish to hold, small plots of land. Differences do exist among agricultural workers. It is true that small landowners both work the land and hire others to do so. It is also true that they may think of themselves as more like larger landowners than like seasonal workers when they consider the possibility of expropriation of their land. Even here, however, the reality is that the large landowner will continue with his or her existing lifestyle largely intact after expropriation, at least on the scale experienced in Nicaragua; for small landholders expropriation would mean a fundamental change of lifestyle such that they would in fact be likely to become seasonal workers or members of the urban or rural informal economy. Uniting small landholders with medium and large ones while dividing them objectively in

---

[6]For the cultural dimension of this analysis I am indebted to Roger N. Lancaster.

organizational terms from those—sometimes their own family members—who own no land, exacerbates the problem, it does not resolve it. Most fundamentally, thinking about these people as "backward" small producers who will eventually be eliminated by modernization of agriculture fails to see the potential for genuinely progressive change in agriculture. It is essential to develop a reality in which small landholders and other agricultural workers can see the possibility of a new future in which they are united, not to make small-holders think that they can be united with large factory farmers.

As was noted in the previous chapter, many progressive students of agriculture today have come to agree with Karl Marx that "all progress in capitalistic agriculture is a progress in the art, not only of robbing the labourer, but of robbing the soil; all progress in increasing the fertility of the soil for a given time, is a progress towards ruining the lasting sources of that fertility" (Marx, 1967: 506). Yet the FSLN, in the development of state farms out of the original agricultural communes, insisted on promoting such agricultural forms. In class terms this was seen as promoting the proletarianization of agriculture. The farm workers themselves originally seemed to be setting out on a path of alternative agriculture. This development was foiled as state farms were created that operated largely as had the private farms they replaced in terms of production. Eventually agricultural workers were divided on presumed class grounds into quite different organizations. A less narrow conception of class might have led to an attempt to draw farm workers together and to think of themselves as different from large landlords. To have done so would have given a fundamentally different dynamic to agricultural policy than that which actually developed. The FSLN would have had to respond to the actual demands of those who worked in agriculture rather than attempt to bring these demands (especially for more land) in line with the presumed "proletarian project."

New Opportunities since the Electoral Loss

Nevertheless, developments since the election, especially in relation to the formation of the National Peasant Coordination, which unite former *contras*, army, and Ministry of the Interior troops, and UNAG in a new organization, may produce a new opportunity for the FSLN.[7] A more sophisticated understanding of class and of the possibilities of agricultural development could make it possible for the FSLN to once more become the vanguard of a genuine class movement. It is time to rethink the past and to move to a model of agricultural development that takes advantage of the sometimes extremely advanced concepts of actual farm workers. Privatization of state farms "to the workers" could lead to a new unity of the real rural workers with a new vision of development as state farms become the property of those who work them.[8] Furthermore, taking these actually united forces as a class can distinguish between these agricultural workers and the agricultural bourgeoisie. For the former, less highly specialized, less mechanized, and more diversified agriculture is a real possibility. To take only one example, small producers can take ready advantage of the use of animal manure as a fertilizer and mulch in restoring land damaged by heavy chemical use. Agriculture for the true rural bourgeoisie is much more clearly a matter of developing further dependence on the very techniques that lead to further degradation of the productive environment. The former process can absorb more labor, the latter can only contribute to the unemployment that already plagues the rural areas, especially in the old cotton-producing zones.

In the cities, a similar problem resulted from a narrow concept of class. Here urban workers, especially government employees and the very large numbers of people who worked in the lower levels of the "informal sector" as day laborers and small merchants, were seen as "unproductive workers" throughout the FSLN period of government. They were not considered "proletarian." As noted above, the informal sector was made the object of substantial negative policy in the early years of FSLN governance. In the last two years of FSLN rule, as Martínez Cuenca noted, the informal sector was left alone to play "a cushioning role" to help counteract

---

[7]For an early discussion of this experience, see Luciak, 1992, whose examination of a number of elements of the UNAG experience in the countryside is extremely valuable.

[8]For a plan for agricultural development that takes some of these elements into consideration, see Central American Historical Institute. 1992.

the effects of the government's economic austerity measures (1992: 78). But the informal sector had been subject to FSLN disfavor, if not contempt, for a large part of the period since 1979. They were not seen as proletarian, they were a regressive force that was to be minimized, just as were the supposedly backward peasants. When elections came these very real workers voted for the vanguard that promoted the proletarian project in minimal numbers. They saw themselves as people who worked but they could not, ultimately, be counted on to wait for a project that would make them into proletarians. Many of them, like rural workers, have been at the barricades in the continuing revolutionary process since 1990. The FSLN will continue to see them as something other than members of the working class, at its own peril.

Since the "prioritizing of the country" in 1985, "unproductive" urban workers, especially government employees, suffered the brunt of government stabilization programs. With the austerity measures of 1988–90 they suffered massive layoffs and dramatic loss of real income. Yet since these members of the third force had always been close supporters of the FSLN it was assumed that they would vote for it in the 1990 elections in the overwhelming numbers of the past. Here, once more, real people who worked could not put off their very real interests in survival and many voted for UNO in spite of their fine revolutionary credentials. They have nonetheless been the urban vanguard in resisting counterrevolution through election. They have shown that they cannot be controlled by the FSLN, but the party must understand that it can never return to power without their support.

Conclusion

The above analysis should make clear that political organizations, whether the party, the government, or the state, cannot automatically be assumed to act in the interests of any particular class. To believe that the FSLN simply represents the long-term interests of the proletariat—even when it demands substantial sacrifices from actual workers and grants subsidies to capitalist producers—is as erroneous as it was to assume that Somoza always acted in the objective interests of the bourgeoisie, even when his actions damaged some of its members.

A political group must continually demonstrate that it represents workers' interests, it will not do to define an abstract proletariat and argue that its long-term interests demand sacrifices from real groups of workers. To believe that the "real base" of the revolutionary party and government will respond in terms of their "real" interests is illusory and dangerous. A vanguard of the workers must be more than the vanguard of the proletariat, or it will inevitably be less than a vanguard of the people.

The bourgeoisie and some elements of the petty bourgeoisie (large merchants, some professionals, and managers), that is, part of the people, has an objective conflict of interest with workers as a whole. It will not do for the workers' vanguard to ignore this genuine reality. When that vanguard becomes the government, however, it must adapt its policies in some measure to this class if it is not to immediately eliminate large-scale private property ownership. But it cannot begin to sacrifice its own working-class constituency by excessive compromise with these elements either. It is essential to continue to draw distinctions in policy as well as rhetoric between the real bourgeoisie and the working class as a whole if the governing party is to maintain legitimacy with that class. In the Nicaraguan case this was not successful. Whether the FSLN can regain its vanguard role out of government will depend on the extent to which it can regain that legitimacy.

In large measure the FSLN depended for the maintenance of its vanguard role on the image that its members, unlike those of traditional political parties, did not use their position for personal gain. Yet, in failing to understand that its own members and their closest allies were themselves government workers, it ultimately ran into a serious contradiction that continues to manifest itself in discourse within the party and in the general public.

The FSLN's failure to deal with government workers and many others who were committed to it in an objective and serious manner resulted, as well, in the disaster of what has come to be known as *la piñata*. Many workers in government, in quasi-independent organizations, and in the party itself had worked for very meager salaries and had received some aid in terms of housing, transportation, and other support structures that were never legally regularized. Some elements even of the agrarian reform had not been legalized in terms of formally granting titles to those who benefitted from it. As the transition between governments occurred there was an attempt to take care of these failures by granting property titles both to real estate and other property (such as automobiles) to those who had long enjoyed their use. This, probably combined with some cases where individuals simply received property for no very good reason, gave rise to the argument that members of the FSLN, especially its leadership, simply took advantage of the transition to enrich themselves. Whatever the extent to which these actions involved corruption, there can be little doubt that this experience served to de-legitimize members of the FSLN as a genuine vanguard acting in the interests of the revolution itself. The sorry spectacle in which many people found themselves having to defend what should have been rightly theirs has damaged the FSLN and some of its individual leaders to a substantial extent.

The extent to which corruption actually took place has undoubtedly been magnified in the public eye as a result of some of these errors. Divisions among FSLN members and supporters have been opened by complaints, whether justified or not, that some individuals have profited from the final settlement of accounts in numerous organizations. Yet much of this problem might have been avoided by treating government workers and those in non-profit organizations more as regular workers all along, rather than seeing them as heroic individuals who were willing to sacrifice their own good for that of the whole. It was unreasonable not to regularize compensation for these people. It was a serious mistake not to have distinguished between the government, the party, and non-profit organizations, and their employees, seeing many of the latter as people who could legitimately receive substantial compensation for their work rather than as heroic actors who could appropriately be granted special favors. Had this been done regularly throughout the period of FSLN governance it would be easier now to distinguish between actual corruption and a legitimate settling of accounts.[9]

---

[9]Once the genie had been let out of the bottle, division among former comrades became rife within the FSLN. Charges of misappropriation and of overly verticalist leadership are now easily made and very difficult to disprove. In at least some cases individuals have had to suffer from organizational problems that arose at least partially from a failure to see that even those in charge of major government or quasi-official agencies had rights as employees.

To think that the vanguard can remain incorruptible, can teach the real proletarian base, and guide it to understand its real interest is to depend on abstract formulas where real theory is required. To neglect the fact that mass organizations are becoming demobilized and even diminishing in size while insisting that public opinion polls and large rallies prove that the ruling party will be returned to control of the government is to believe that participation in low level administration can substitute for genuine mobilization in the interests of the revolution. Yet all of this was done in Nicaragua as a result of an overly abstract conception of the nature of the working class, and of the role of the party, the government, and the state in relation to that class.

In the present context the FSLN is most prominent as a political party in the government. It has so far been able to mediate, at least part of the time, between the active forces in the streets and the countryside and the government, aiding in the prevention of massive violence. Yet many who still see themselves as Sandinistas have resorted to such violence both as individuals and as well-organized groups, as in the case of the occupation of Estelí by Sandinista army veterans or the taking of major UNO leaders hostage in response to the seizure of hostages by *contra* forces. While debate continues in the party itself about what to do, despair grows in the countryside and the city. The extent to which the FSLN can constitute itself as a viable alternative to this despair remains uncertain. That there should be strenuous debate within the FSLN as occurred at the second session of the FSLN Congress is a healthy sign that these questions are at least under serious consideration.

The FSLN has been able to play an important role in the National Assembly in protecting many elements of the policies that, in fact, produced some measure of social justice in the countryside. In protecting the fundamental revolutionary state it has worked with the existing government to attempt to promote some measure of national reconstruction and to obtain the economic aid that is necessary for any further development. It has acted as an opposition party within an established state, responding to various interests and attempting to regain support from those that have always constituted the base of the revolution. The FSLN has succeeded in promoting divisions within UNO to such an extent that it was able to become, in alliance with a small number of legislators known as "the Center," the major force in the National Assembly during 1993. These are appropriate actions for any political party. It is hardly surprising that, in this context, it has joined the Socialist International; the FSLN is a social democratic party in practice.

During its governance, the FSLN consciously created a pluralist political system with elements of participatory democracy. As a political party it continues to play a substantial role in the pluralist structures and within rules of the game that it largely created. It can hardly be expected to violate those basic rules so long as the system as such is not fundamentally broken. Its goal is clearly to once again become the governing party as the system it created matures, not to start all over with insurrection. Yet the question remains whether the FSLN can be more than a traditional party in a bourgeois government. For it to regain its actual position as vanguard of the popular masses it must learn not only to respond to demands from the organized workers but to once more lead them in a creative alternative to the politics of elections and political manuever. Those who would threaten to violate the basic rules of the game, clarified through transition agreements and through a formal protocol of *concertatión*, can expect the FSLN to respond to calls to destabilize the narrowly political order as it has done on some occasions, even if mostly in a verbal manner. Those who would engage in further acts such as the desecration of Fonseca's tomb do so at their own peril and that of the stability of the Nicaraguan state.

Attempts to fundamentally alter the structure of state power by breaking those agreements in order to create a new police and military force that would recreate a "repressive police and guard" can be expected to be met by a strong response. Daniel Ortega's statement that the Sandinistas would meet such a threat by taking up arms once again is not merely an idle threat. It is, as Victor Hugo Tinoco said, a "process of logical reasoning" that leads to these remarks, not a mere unconsidered or intemperate remark *(La Opinion*, July 10, 1992: 3A). Nevertheless, many substantial changes have been made in the police force and there are serious debates about what will happen with the army. The FSLN clearly maintains the flexibility that has been its (perhaps unfortunate) hallmark. Flexibility must, however, be tempered with the recognition that not all change is possible. The point is that threats to fundamentally alter the pluralist order in order to impose an alternative hegemony that would create irreversible movement towards a bourgeois project can only be met with counter-threats to destabilize the political system. Recent events suggest that any such changes would meet with massive public resistance to which the FSLN could remain aloof only at its peril. It is in this context that the FSLN's agreement to negotiate changes in the constitution only through the established process and not through the constituent assembly that UNO has demanded must be understood. The FSLN seems to be taking the view that change is not only desirable but essential and that such change cannot come from a simple dismantling of the state that was created and led to its own electoral defeat.

The FSLN thus remains an important political actor. It is responding now, as perhaps never before, to the actions of the real working-class base of the revolution. If it is to hope to once again control the government in the revolutionary Sandinista state, or even to remain an important actor within it, it must respond to the real class that is in action, now freed from the restraints imposed upon it by the FSLN itself. It cannot assume, however, that it is the vanguard of the working class, nor even its representative. If it wishes to play this role it must prove its capacity to do so in future practice. It cannot depend on its image from the past or on abstract formulae.

It is difficult to exaggerate the extent of misery that exists in the country. For most people the present situation is one in which abstraction is impossible. The question is not how to organize a political party, but how to survive. Many remain committed to the FSLN, even more to the notion of Sandinismo, yet for the broad majorities it is a struggle merely to exist. As one correspondent, himself still a committed FSLN supporter, put it: "There's a lot of illness, a whole lot of malnourished children; fathers are robbing because they don't have work, mothers are selling their bodies to maintain their children" (personal letter, September 9, 1993). In the midst of such misery, abstractions of political thought may appear out of place. Yet it is only political thought backed by political action that produced the Nicaraguan revolution in the first place. Numerous events make clear that the workers in Nicaragua continue to believe in their capacity for action, at least to prevent some government policies. Whether their actions can be directed with a strategic line of action remains a question that must be answered if the FSLN is to once more achieve the political capacity to move the Nicaraguan revolution forward.

Success in this endeavor is by no means assured. There are forces of disintegration and of stagnation that act on and within the FSLN. There are divisions within it and the circumstances are undeniably difficult. After all, if the present government should somehow miraculously turn things around, the FSLN will have been the opposition that opposed the miracle-makers. If the situation further deteriorates or remains the same the FSLN will be asked to share in the blame as the group that cooperated with the failed administration. Only the creative practical and theoretical energy that the FSLN has shown at crucial moments in the past can make its future as a revolutionary actor possible.

Whatever happens in Nicaragua, revolution will continue in the world. Those who support such action should learn from the Nicaraguan experience, among other things, that no abstract class actor, represented by a party or government, can take precedence over the vast working majority. Only this real class can determine events. One of the fundamental lessons of the twentieth century is that parties or governments that presume to rule in the long-term interests of an ideal class, rejecting the demands of the very real class of those who work, cannot expect to maintain their power except by force. No theory that ignores this reality can guide genuinely revolutionary practice.

REFERENCES

Amador, Armando.
   1987. *El exilio y las banderas de Nicaragua.* Mexico:
   Federación Editorial Mexicana.
   1990. *Un siglo de lucha de los trabajadores en Nicaragua
   (1880–1979).* Managua: CIRA.

Ambursley, Fitzroy, and Robin Cohen.
   1983. *Crisis in the Caribbean.* New York: Monthly Review.

Arce Castaño, Bayard.
   1985. *Política de la revolucion Sandinista: Una respuesta ante la
   política agresiva de la Administración Reagan.* Managua: Centro
   de Communicación Internacional.

Arias, Pilar.
   1981. *Nicaragua: Revolución: relatos de combantientes del frente
   sandinisita.* Mexico: Siglo XXI.

Arnove, Robert F.
   1986. *Education and Revolution in Nicaragua.* New York:
   Praeger.

Balcarcel, José Luis.
   1980. "El Sandinismo, ideología de la Revolución
   nicaragüense." *Nicaráuac* 1 (July and August): 112–19.

Barahona, Amaru.
   1989. *Estudio sobre la historia de Nicaragua: Del auge cafetalero
   al triunfo de la revolución.* Managua: INIES.

Barry, Tom, and Kent Norsworthy.
1991. "Nicaragua." In Tom Barry, *Central America Inside and Out*. New York: Grove Weidenfeld.

Baumeister, Eduardo.
1991. "Agrarian Reform." In Walker, 1991: 229–46.

Baumeister, Eduardo, and Niera Caudra.
1986. "The Making of a Mixed Economy: Class Struggle and State Policy in the Nicaraguan Transition." In Fagen, Deere, and Coraggio: 171–91.

Belausteguigoita, Ramón de.
1985. *Con Sandino en Nicaragua*. Managua: Nueva Nicaragua.

Bell, Belden, ed.
1978. *Nicaragua: An Ally Under Seige*. Washington, DC: Council on American Affairs.

Belli, Humberto.
1985. *Breaking Faith: The Sandinista Revolution and Its Impact on Freedom and Faith in Nicaragua*. Garden City, MI: The Puebla Institute.

Bendaña, Alejandro.
1991. *Una Tragedia Campesina: Testimonios de la Resistencia*. Managua: Edit-Arte, CEI.

Bermudez-Onofre Guevara, Carlos Pérez.
1985. *El movimiento obrero en Nicaragua*. Managua: El Amanecer.

Bilbo E. Jon Ander.
1988. *Migration, War, and Agrarian Reform*. Washington DC: Center for Immigration Policy and Refugee Assistance, Georgetown University.

Biondi-Morra, Brizio N.
1990. *Revolución y política alimentaria: Un análisis crítico de Nicaragua*. Mexico: Siglo Vientiuno.

Black, George.
    1981. *Triumph of the People: The Sandinista Revolution in Nicaragua*. London: Zed Books.

Booth, John.
    1985. *The End and the Beginning: The Nicaraguan Revolution*. Boulder: Westview Press.

Borge, Tómas.
    1981. *Los Primeros Pasos. La Revolución Sandinista*. Mexico: Siglo Vientiuno.
    1984. *El axioma de la esperanza*. Henao, Spain: Desclee de Bouwer.
    1984a. *Carlos: te seguimos viviendo*. Managua: Ministry of the Interior.
    1989. *La Paciente Impacienca*. Managua: Editorial Vandguardia.

Brockett, Charles D.
    1990. *Land, Power, and Poverty: Agrarian Transformation and Political Conflict in Central America*. Rev. Ed. Boulder: Westview.

Brown, Doug.
    1990. "Sandinismo and the Problem of Democratic Hegemony." *Latin American Perspectives* 17 (Spring): 39–61.

Bugajski, Janusz.
    1990. *Sandinista Communism and Rural Nicaragua*. New York: Praeger.

Burns, E. Bradford.
    1987. *At War in Nicaragua: The Reagan Doctrine and the Politics of Nostalgia*. New York: Harper and Row.

Bye, Vegard.
    1991. *La paz prohibida: el laberinto centroamericano en la década de los ochenta*. San Jose, Costa Rica: D.E.I.

Cabestrero, Teófilo.
    1985. *Nicaragua: Cronica de una sangre inocente*. Mexico:
    Katùn.

Camejo. Pedro, and Fred Murphy, eds.
    1979. *The Nicaraguan Revolution*. New York: Pathfinder.

Central American Historical Institute.
    1990. *Envío* (July).
    1991. *Envío* (June).
    1991a. "My Enemy's Enemies Are Not My Friends." *Envío*
    (August): 7–8.
    1992. "The 'Revueltos': Just the Tip of the Iceberg," *Envio*
    (English-language edition) 11, no. 131 (June): 27–38.

Cerdas, Rodolfo.
    nd. *Sandino, el APRA y la internácional comunista*. Lima: El
    Centro de Investigación y Adiestramiento Político
    Administrativo.

Chamorro, Edgar.
    1987. *Packaging the Contras: A Case of CIA Disinformation*.
    New York: Insitute for Media Analysis.

Chamorro, Pedro Joaquín.
    1981. *La Patria de Pedro: el pensamiento nicaragüense de Pedro
    Joaquín Chamorro*. Managua: La Prensa.

Chamorro Cardenal, Jaime.
    1988. *La Prensa: The Republic of Paper*. New York: Freedom
    House.
    1990. *Diario político*. Managua: Nueva Nicaragua.

Chavez, Roberto.
    1988. "Urban Planning in Nicaragua: The First Five Years."
    Latin American Perspectives 14 (Spring): 226–37.

Christian, Shirley.
    1985. *Nicaragua: Revolution in the Family*. New York:
    Random House.

CIERA (Centro de Investigación y Estudios de la Reforam Agraria).
1989. *La Reforma Agraria en Nicaragua, 1979-1989*. Managua: CIERA. Ten volumes, entitled as follows:
1. *Estrategia y Politicas*
2. *Sistema Alimentario*
3. *Formación y Capacitación*
4. *Economía Campesina*
5. *Movimento Cooperativo en el Sector Agropecuario*
6. *Organización y Participación en el Campo*
7. *Mujer y Transformación de la Vida Rural*
8. *Marco Jurídico de la Reforma Agraria*
9. *Cifras y Referencias Documentales*
10. *Imágenes de la Reforma Agraria*

Clemens, Harry.
1991. "El modelo agroexportador renovado." *Revista de Economía Agrícola*, no. 2 (June-August): 3-9.

Close, David.
1988. *Nicaragua: Politics, Economics and Society*. London: Pinter.

Cochrane, Augustus III, and Catherine Scott.
1992. "Class, State and Popular Organizations in Mozambique and Nicaragua." *Latin American Perspectives* 19 (Spring): 105-24.

Colburn, Forrest D.
1986. *Post-Revolutionary Nicaragua: State, Class and Dilemmas of Agrarian Policy*. Berkeley: University of California.

Collado, Carmen.
1988. *Nicaragua*. Mexico: Nueva Imagen.

Collins, Joseph, with Francis Moore Lappé, Nick Allen, and Paul Rice.
1985. *Nicaragua: What Difference Could a Revolution Make? Food and Farming in the New Nicaragua*. San Francisco: Institute for Food and Development Policy.

Collinson, Helen.
1990. *Women and Revolution in Nicaragua*. London: Zed.

Conrad, Robert Edgar, trans. and ed.
1990. *Sandino: The Testimony of a Nicaraguan Patriot, 1921–1934*. Princeton NJ: Princeton University Press.

Conroy, Michael.
1985. "Economic Legacy and Policies: Performance and Critique." In Walker, 1985: 219–44.
1985a. "External Dependence, External Aggression and Economic Aggression against Nicaragua." *Latin American Perspectives* 12 (Spring): 39–68.

Córdova Rivas, Rafael.
1983. *Contribución a la revolución*. Managua: Centro de Publicaciones de Avanzada.

Corragio, Jose Luis.
1985. *Nicaragua: Revolución y democracia*. Mexico: Editorial Linea.

Corragio, Jose Luis and George Irvin.
1985. "Revolution and Democracy in Nicaragua." *Latin American Perspectives* 12 (Spring): 23–38.

Cortázar, Julio.
1984. *Nicaragua tan violentamente dulce*. Mexico: Katún.

Cortés Domingo, Guillermo.
1990. *La lucha por el poder*. Managua: Vanguardia.

Craven, David.
1990. "The State of Cultural Democracy in Cuba and Nicaragua During the 1980s." *Latin American Perspectives* 17 (Summer): 100–19.

Dahl, Robert A.
1956. *A Preface to Democratic Theory*. Chicago: University of Chicago Press.

1961. *Who Governs?* New Haven: Yale University Press.

Deere, Carmen Dianna.
1986. "Agrarian Reform, Peasant and Rural Production." In Fagen, Deere, and Coraggio, 1986: 97–142.

de la Selva, Salomón.
1985. *La guerra de Sandino o pueblo desnudo.* Managua: Nueva Nicaragua.

Diaz, Maria Aminta.
1990. "La promesa de los cien (100) días 'Magicos'." *Critica* (August): 1.

Diaz Castillo, Roberto.
1985. "Tres aportes fundamentales de la revolución popular Sandinista." *Mimeo* (May 2).

Dodson, Michael, and Laura Nuzzi O'Shaughnessy.
1990. *Nicaragua's Other Revolution: Religious Faith and Political Struggle.* Chapel Hill: University of North Carolina Press.

Draper, Hal.
1978. *Karl Marx's Theory of Revolution: Volume 2 The Politics of Social Classes.* New York: Monthly Review.

Eich, Dieter, and Carlos Rincón.
1984. *The Contras: Interviews with Anti-Sandinistas.* San Francisco: Synthesis.

Enríquez, Laura.
1987. "Half a Decade of Sandinista Policy-Making: Recent Publications on Revolutionary Nicaragua." *Latin American Research Review* 22, no. 3: 209–22.
1991. *Harvesting Change: Labor and Agrarian Reform in Nicaragua, 1979-1990.* Chapel Hill: University of North Carolina Press.

Fagen, Richard, Carmen Deere, and José Luis Corragio, eds.
1986. *Transition and Development: Problems of Third World Socialism*. New York: Monthly Review Press.

Ferrari, Sergio.
1990. "A Once Años: ¿Una Revolución Vigente." *Critica* (July): 7–9.

Fitzgerald, E. V. K., and Rob Vos.
1989. *Financing Economic Development: A Structural Approach to Monetary Policy*. Aldershot, The Netherlands: Gower.

Fitzgerald, Valpy.
1989. "*Estado y economía en Nicaragua*." In Raul Ruben and Jan P. de Groot, 1989: 25–46.

Fonseca, Carlos.
1984. *Vive Sandino*. Managua: Departmento de Propagande et Education.
1985. *Obras*. Vol. 1, *Bajo la bandera del sandinismo*. Managua: Nueva Nicaragua.
1985a. *Obras*. Vol. 2, *Viva Sandino*. Managua: Nueva Nicaragua.

Fonseca, Carlos, Oscar Turcios, and Ricardo Morales.
1980. *Que es un Sandinista?* Managua: Secretaria Nacional de Propaganda del F.S.L.N.

Gilbert, Dennis, and David Block.
1990. *Sandinistas: Key Documents*. Ithaca, NY: Latin American Studies Program, Cornell University.

Girardi, Giulio.
1987. *Sandinismo, Marxismo, Cristianismo: la Confluencia*. Managua: Centro Ecumenical Antonio Valdivisieso.

González Casanova, Pablo.
1984. *La hegemonía del pueblo y la lucha centroamericana*. San Jose, Costa Rica: EDUCA.

Gould, Jeffrey L.
1990. *To Lead as Equals: Rural Protest and Political Consciousness in Chinandega, Nicaragua, 1912–1979.* Chapel Hill: University of North Carolina Press.

Gramsci, Antonio.
1957. *The Modern Prince and Other Writings.* New York: International Publishers.

Gutierrez, Alejandro Mayorga.
1988. *Municipalidades y Revolución.* Managua: CINASE and Fundación Friedrich-Ebert Stiftung.

Hamilton, Nora, Jeffry A. Frieden, Linda Fuller, and Manuel Pastor, Jr.
1988. *Crisis in Central America: Regional Dynamics and U.S. Policy in the 1980s.* Boulder: Westview.

Harris, Richard.
1985. "The Revolutionary Process in Nicaragua." *Latin American Perspectives* 12 (Spring): 3–22.
1987. "The Revolutionary Transformation in Nicaragua." *Latin American Perspectives* 14 (Winter): 3–18.
1988. "Marxism and the Transition to Socialism in Latin America." *Latin American Perspectives* 15 (Winter): 7–54.
1992. *Marxism, Socialism, and Democracy.* Boulder: Westview.

Harris, Richard, and Carlos Vilas, eds.
1985. *Nicaragua: A Revolution Under Seige.* London: Zed.

Haynes, Keith A.
1988. "Mass Participation and the Transition to Socialism: A Critique of Petras and Fitzgerald." *Latin American Perspectives* 15 (Winter): 112.

Hegel, G. W. F.
1952. *Hegel's Philosophy of Right.* Translated by T. M. Knox. London: Oxford University Press.

Heyck, Denis Lynn Daly, ed.
1989. *Life Stories of the Nicaraguan Revolution*. New York: Routledge.

Hodges, Donald C.
1986. *Intellectual Foundations of the Nicaraguan Revolution*. Austin: University of Texas Press.

Hogan, Mary Jane.
1987. "Grassroots Women's Movements and the Crisis in Central America." Paper presented at the annual meeting of the Western Political Science Association, Anaheim, California.

Hurtado de Vigil, María, ed.
1986. *La Ecónomia Mixta en Nicaragua: Proyecto o Realidad (una visión de academicos y politicos nacionales)*. Managua: Centro de Investigación y Asesoria Socio-Economic and Fundación Ebert-Stiftung.

INIES (Instituto Nicaragüense de Investigaciones Económicas y Sociales).
1987. *Plan Económico 1987*. Managua: INIES.
1988. *Nicaragua: Cambios estructurales y políticas económicas, 1979-1987*. Managua: INIES.

Instituto de Estudio del Sandinismo, ed.
1985. *El sandinismo: documentos básicos*. Managua: Nueva Nicaragua.

Instituto de Estudios Nicaragüenses.
1991. "El gobierno y la oposición a un año del cambio de gobierno en Nicaragua." *Cauderno de Sociologia* 14 (January-August): 64-65.

Invernizzi, Gabriele, Francis Pisani, and Jesus Ceberio.
1986. *Sandinistas: Entrevistas a Humberto Ortega Saavedra, Jaime Wheelock Román y Bayardo Arce*. Managua: Editorial Vanguardia.

Jonas, Susanne, and Nancy Stein.
1990. "The Construction of Democracy in Nicaragua." *Latin American Perspectives* 17 (Summer): 10–37.

Judson, Fred.
1987. "Sandinista Revolutionary Morale." *Latin American Perspectives* 14 (Winter): 19–42.

Kaunt, Elia María, and Trish O'Kane.
1990. *Nicaragua: Political Parties and Elections 1990*. CRIES Working Paper. Managua: CRIES.

Kornbluh, Peter.
1991. "The U.S. Role in the Counterrevolution." In Walker, 1991: 323–50.

Lake, Anthony.
1989. *Somoza Falling: A Case Study of Washington at Work*. Amherst: University of Massachusetts Press.

Lancaster, Roger N.
1988. *Thanks to God and the Revolution*. New York: Columbia University Press.
1992. *Life Is Hard*. Berkeley: University of California Press.

Latin American Studies Association.
1984. *The Electoral Process in Nicaragua: Domestic and International Influences*. Austin, TX: The Latin American Studies Association.

Lenin, Vladimir.
1939. *Imperialism: The Highest Stage of Capitalism*. New York: International Publishers.
1968. *State and Revolution*. New York: International Publishers.

Lippincott, Benjamin.
1965. *Democracy's Dilemma: The Totalitarian Party in a Free Society*. New York: The Ronald Press Company.

López, Francisco.
    1988. "¿Economía de mercado vs. economía planificada?"
    Boletín Socioeconómico 8 (June-July): 2–4.
    1989. "Democracia en la revolución." *Boletín Socioeconómico*
    14 (July-August): 1–2.
    1990. "Nicaragua: El proceso de Transición y la Economía
    Mixta" *Critica* 1, no. 2.
    1990a. "¿Reconciliación o lucha de clases?" *Critica* 1, no. 2:
    66–68.

López, Mario.
    1991. "Los productos agrícolas no tradicionales en Nicaragua:
    un perfíl del productor melonero." *Revista de Economía*
    Agrícola 2 (June-August): 30–38.

Lozano, Lucrecia.
    1985. *De Sandino al triunfo de la revolución.* Mexico: Siglo
    Veintiuno.

Luciak, Ilja A.
    1987. "Popular Democracy in the New Nicaragua."
    Comparative Politics 20 (October): 30–55.
    1987a. "National Unity and Popular Hegemony: The
    Dialectics of Sandinista Agrarian Reform Policies,
    1979–1986." *Journal of Latin American Studies* (19): 113–40.
    1990. "Democracy in the Nicaraguan Countryside: A
    Comparative Analysis of Sandinista Grassroots Movements."
    Latin American Perspectives 17 (Summer): 55–75.
    1992. "The Political Economy of Reconciliation in Nicaragua:
    Contras and *Compas* in a Quest for Peace and Land." Paper
    presented at the 17th International Congress of the Latin
    American Studies Association, Los Angeles, CA, September
    24–27.

Macauley, Neill.
    1985. *The Sandino Affair.* Durham, NC: Duke University
    Press.

Marchetti, Peter.
    1986. "War and Popular Participation." In Fagen, Deere and Coraggio, 1986: 303–30.

Marcus, Bruce, ed.
    1982. *Sandinistas Speak.* New York: Pathfinder.
    1985. *Nicaragua: The Sandinista People's Revolution: Speeches by Sandinista Leaders.* New York: Pathfinder.

Martínez Cuenca, Alejandro.
    1992. *Sandinista Economics in Practice: An Insider's Critical Reflection.* Boston: South End Press.

Marx, Karl.
    1967. *Capital, Vol. 1.* New York: International Publishers.
    1976. *The Communist Manifesto.* In *Collected Works.* New York: International Publishers.

Masuhr, Dieter.
    1984. *Los ojos de los guerrilleros.* Managua: Nueva Nicaragua.

Mathéy, Kosta.
    1990. "An Appraisal of Sandinista Housing Policies." *Latin American Perspectives* 17 (Summer): 76–99.

Matus Lazo, Javier, Francois Capietto, and Marisol Cerrato.
    1990. *El cooperativismo agropecuaria en Nicaragua.* Managua: Centro para la Promoción y del Desarrollo Rural y Social.

Medal Mendieta, José Luis.
    1988. *Nicaragua: crisis, cambio social y política economía.* Managua: CINASE.

Meister, Robert.
    1990. *Political Identity: Thinking Through Marx.* Cambridge: Basil Blackwell.

Mendoza, Orlando.
1991. "Teodor Adorno, Hegel, Marx y otras cosas: como no fiarse de la historia." *Revista de Economía Agrícola* 2 (June-August): 39–44.

Molero, Maria.
1988. *Nicaragua Sandinista: del sueño a la realididadt.* Managua: CRIES.

Mondragon, Rafael, and Carlos Decker Molina.
1986. *Participación popular en Nicaragua.* Mexico: Claves Latinoamericanas.

Moore, John Norton.
1987. *The Secret War in Central America: Sandinista Assault on World Order.* Frederick, MD: University Publications of America.

Morales Avilés, Ricardo.
1983. *Obras: No pararemos de andar jamás.* Managua: Nueva Nicaragua.

Morley, Morris, and James Petras.
1987. *The Reagan Administration and Nicaragua: How Washington Constructs Its Case for Counterrevolution in Central America.* New York: Institute for Media Analysis.

Munck, Ronaldo.
1984. *Politics and Dependency in the Third World: The Case of Latin America.* London: Zed Books.

Nolan, David.
1984. *The Ideology of the Sandinistas and the Nicaraguan Revolution.* Coral Gables, FL: Institute of Interamerican Studies.

Norsworthy, Kent, and Tom Barry.
1990. *Nicaragua: A Country Guide.* 2d Edition. Albuquerque: Interhemispheric Education Resource Center.

Nuñez de Escorcia, Vilma.
   1990. *Independencia del Poder Judicial.* Managua: Editorial Ciencias Sociales.

Nuñez Soto, Orlando.
   1986. "Ideology and Revolutionary Politics in Transitional Societies." In Fagen, Deere, and Coraggio, 1986: 231–48.
   1987. *Transición y lucha de clases en Nicaragua, 1979–86.* Mexico: Siglo Veintiuno.
   1988. *La insurrección de la conciencia.* Coleccion Monografías No. 1. Managua: Escuela de Sociología, University of Central America.

Nuñez Soto, Orlando, and Burbach, Roger.
   1986. *Democracia y revolución en las Americas (Agenda para un debate).* Managua: Vanguardia.
   1987. *Fire in the Americas: Forging a Revolutionary Agenda.* London: Verso.

Nuñez Soto, Orlando, et al.
   1987. *La transción difícil: La autodeterminación de los pequeños países periféricos.* Managua: Vanguardia.

O'Kane, Trish.
   1990. "The New Old Order." *NACLA Report on the Americas* 24 (June): 28–35.

Ortega, Daniel.
   1984. *Discurso.* . . . Managua: Departmento de Agitación y Propaganda del F.S.L.N.
   1988. *Combatiendo por la paz.* Mexico: Siglo Veintiuno.

Ortega, Humberto.
   1980. "La Insurrección Nacional." *Nicaráuac* (May-June): 25–57.

Ortega, Marvin.
   1985. "Workers' Participation in the Management of the Agro-Enterprises of the APP." *Latin American Perspectives* 12 (Spring): 69–83.

1986. "Sandinismo y revolución: posibilidades de una experiencia pluralista de izquierda en la revolución." Mimeograph, presented to the Fifth Nicaraguan Congress of Social Sciences.

1991. *Nicaraguan Repatriation to Mosquita.* Washington, DC: Center for Immigration Policy and Refugee Assistance, Georgetown University.

Ortiz, Roxeanne Dunbar.
1986. *La Cuestión Miskita en la Revolución Nicaragüense.* Mexico: Editorial Línea.
1987. "Indigenous Rights and Regional Autonomy in Revolutionary Nicaragua." *Latin American Perspectives* 14 (Winter): 43–66.

Palmer, Steven.
1988. "Carlos Fonseca and the Construction of Sandinismo in Nicaragua." *Latin American Research Review* 23, no. 1: 91–109.

Pardo-Maurer, R.
1990. *The Contras, 1980-1989: A Special Kind of Politics.* Washington, DC: Center for Strategic and International Studies.

Petras, James, and Frank T. Fitzgerald.
1988. "Authoritarianism and Democracy in the Transition to Socialism" and "Confusion about the Transition to Socialism: A Rejoinder to Haynes." *Latin American Perspectives* 15 (Winter): 93–111.

Petras, James, and Morris Morley.
1992. *Latin America in the Time of Cholera: Electoral Politics, Market Economics, and Permanent Crisis.* New York: Routledge.

Portes, Alejandro.
1985. "Latin American Class Structures: Their Composition and Change During the Last Decades." *Latin American Research Review* 20, no. 3: 7–37.

Poulantzas, Nicos.
 1975. *Classes in Contemporary Capitalism*. London: Verso Editions.
 1978. *Political Power and Social Classes*. London: Verso Editions.

Prevost, Gary.
 1990. "Cuba and Nicaragua: A Special Relationship?" *Latin American Perspectives* 17 (Summer): 120–37.
 1991. "The FSLN as Ruling Party." In Walker, 1991: 101–16.

Quijano, Carlos.
 1987. *Nicaragua: ensayo sobre el imperialismo de los Estados Unidos*. Managua: Vanguardia.

Ramírez Mercado, Sergio.
 1983. *El alba de oro*. Mexico: Sigo Vientiuno.
 1986. *Estás en Nicaragua*. Managua: Nueva Nicaragua.
 1987. *Las armas del futuro*. Managua: Nueva Nicaragua.
 1988. *El muchacho de Niquinhomo*. Havana: Editoral Política.

Reimann, Elizabeth.
 1987. *Yo fui un contra: historia de un "paldín de la libertad"*. Managua: Vanguardia.

Ricciardi, Joseph.
 1991. "Economic Policy." In Walker, 1991: 247–74.

Robinson, William I., and Kent Norworthy.
 1985. "Elections and U.S. Intervention in Nicaragua." *Latin American Perspectives* 12 (Spring): 83–110.
 1988. "A Critique of the 'Antidemocratic Tendency' Argument: The Case of Mass Organizations and Popular Participation in Nicaragua." *Latin American Perspectives* 15 (Winter): 134–41.

Rosset, Peter, and John Vandermeer, eds.
 1983. *The Nicaragua Reader: Documents of a Revolution Under Fire*. Revised Edition. New York: Grove Press.

1985 *Nicaragua: Unfinished Revolution: The New Nicaragua Reader*. New York: Grove Press.

Ruben, Raul, and Jan P. de Groot.
1989. *El debate sobre la reforma agraria en Nicaragua: Transformación agraria y atención al campesinado en nueve años de Reforma Agraria (1979–1988)*. Managua: Editorial Ciencias Sociales.

Ruccio, David F.
1988. "State, Class and Transition in Nicaragua." *Latin American Perspectives* 15 (Spring): 50–71.

Ruchwarger, Gary.
1987. *People in Power: Forging a Grassroots Democracy in Nicaragua*. South Hadley, MA: Bergin and Garvey.
1989. *Struggling for Survival: Workers, Women and Class on a Nicaraguan State Farm*. Boulder: Westview.

Ruiz, Henry.
1980. "La Montaña era como un Crisol donde se forjaban los mejores Cuadros." *Nicaráuac* 1 (May and June): 8–25.

Sabalos, Angela.
nd. *Mis preguntas: eleciones 90*. Managua: CIRA.

Salazar, Robinson.
1988. "Estado, hegemonia y pueblo en la sociologia contemporanea." *Cuadernos de Sociologia* 6 (January-April): 34–40.

Samillán, César.
1988. "Dinamica de la economía nicaragüense." In INIES, 1988: 45–66.

Sandino, Augusto César.
1984. *El pensamiento vivo*. Intro. and notes by Sergio Ramírez. Vol 1. Managua: Nueva Nicaragua.
1984a. *El pensamiento vivo*. Intro. and notes by Sergio Ramírez. Vol 2. Managua: Nueva Nicaragua.

Schulz, Donald E., and Douglas H. Graham.
1984. *Revolution and Counterrevolution in Central America and the Caribbean*. Boulder: Westview.

Selser, Gregorio.
1981. *Sandino: General of the Free*. New York: Monthly Review.
1984. *Sandino, general de hombres libres*. Buenos Aires: Editorial Abril.

Serra, Luis Hector.
1985. "The Grass-roots Organizations." In Walker, 1985: 64–90.
1991. "The Grass-Roots Organizations." In Walker, 1991: 49–76.

Snarr, Neil, and Associates.
1989. *Sandinista Nicaragua: Part 1: Revolution, Religion and Social Policy. An Annotated Bibliography with Analytical Introductions*. Ann Arbor: Pierian.
1990. *Sandinista Nicaragua: Part 2: Economy, Politics and Foreign Policy: An Annotated Bibliography with Analytical Introductions*. Ann Arbor: Pierian.

Sollis, Peter.
1989. "The Atlantic Coast of Nicaragua: Development and Autonomy." *Journal of Latin American Studies* (21): 481–520.

Somoza, Anastasio, as told to Jack Cox.
1980. *Nicaragua Betrayed*. Boston and Los Angeles: Western Islands, 1980.

Spalding, Rose J., ed.
1987. *The Political Economy of Revolutionary Nicaragua*. Boston: Allen and Unwin.

Stahler Sholk, Richard.
1990. "Stabilization, Destabilization, and the Popular Classes in Nicaragua, 1979–1988." *Latin American Research Review* 25: 58–59.

Thrupp, Lori Ann.
1988. "Pesticides and Policies: Approaches to Nicaragua and Costa Rica." *Latin American Perspectives* 15 (Fall): 37–70.

Tirado, Victor.
1986. *Nicaragua: una nueva democracia el tercer mundo.* Managua: Vanguardia.
1989. *Sandino y la doctrina de liberación nacional.* Managua: Vanguardia.

Torres, Rosa Maria, and José Luis Coragio.
1987. *Transición y crisis en Nicaragua.* San Jose: Editorial Departamento Ecuménico de Investigaciones.

Torres-Rivas, Edelberto.
1985. "Estado, democracia, crisis: notas informales." *Documentos de trabaja*, ICADIS (August).

Towell, Larry.
1990. *Somoza's Last Stand (Testimonies from Nicaragua).* Trenton, NJ: Red Sea.

Trobo, Claudio.
1983. *Lo que pasa en Nicaragua.* Mexico: Siglo Vientiuno.

USOCA (U.S. Out of Central America).
1985. *Democracy in Nicaragua: An Eyewitness Report on the 1984 Election and Popular Democracy in Nicaragua.* San Francisco: USOCA.

Valenta, Jiri, and Esperanza Durán.
1987. *Conflict in Nicaragua: A Multidimensional Perspective.* Boston: Allen and Unwin.

Vanderlaan, Mary B.
1986. *Revolution and Foreign Policy in Nicaragua.* Boulder: Westview.

Vargas, Oscar-Rene.
  1990. *Partidos políticos y la búsqueda de un nuevo modelo.*
  Managua: Centro de Investigación y Desarrollo
  ECOTEXTURA.

Vargas Lozano, Gabriel.
  1988. "Gramsci y America Latina." *Caudernos de Sociologia*
  6 (January-April): 30–33.

Vickers, George R.
  1990. "A Spider's Web." *NACLA Report on the Americas* 24
  (June): 19–27.

Vilas, Carlos M.
  1984. *Perfiles de la revolución Sandinista.* Habana: Casa de las
  Americas.
  1986. *The Sandinista Revolution: National Liberation and Social
  Transformation in Central America.* New York: Monthly
  Review Press.
  1988. "Popular Insurgency and Social Revolution in Central
  America." *Latin American Perspectives* 15 (Winter): 55–77.
  1989. *State, Class and Ethnicity in Nicaragua: Capitalist
  Modernization on the Atlantic Coast.* Boulder: Lynne Rienner.
  1990. "La contribución de la política económica a la caída del
  gobierno sandinista." *Crítica* 1 (July): 34–47.
  1990a. "La contribución de la política económica a la caída
  del gobierno sandinista: segunda y última parte." *Crítica* 1
  (August): 34–36.
  1990b. "What Went Wrong." *NACLA Report on the Americas*
  25 (June): 10–18.
  1992. "Family Affairs: Class, Lineage and Politics in
  Contemporary Nicaragua." *Journal of Latin American Studies*
  24: 309–42.

Walker, Thomas, ed.
  1985. *Nicaragua: the First Five Years.* New York: Praeger.
  1987. *Reagan versus the Sandinistas.* Boulder: Westview.
  1991. *Revolution and Counterrevolution in Nicaragua.* Boulder:
  Westview.

1991a. *Nicaragua: The Land of Sandino*. 3d ed. Boulder: Westview.

Weber, Henri.
1983. *Nicaragua: the Sandinist Revolution*. London: Verso.

Wheelock, Jaime.
1980. "No Hay 2 Reformas Agrarias Iquales." *Nicaráuac* (May and June): 58–75.
1984. *El gran desafío*. Mexico: Katün.
1985. *Imperialismo y dictadura*. Managua: Nueva Nicaragua.
1985a. *Jaime Román Wheelock on The Nicaraguan Revolution*. San Francisco: Institute for the Study of Militarism and Economic Crisis.
1985b. *Raices indigenas de la lucha anticolonialista en Nicaragua*. Managua: Neuva Nicaragua.
1986. *Vanguardia y revolución en las sociedades periféricas*. Mexico: Siglo XXI.
1986a. *Entre la crisis y la agresión*. Managua: Nueva Nicaragua.
1986b. *El papel de la vanguardia*. Buenos Aires: Editorial Contrapunta.

Williams, Philip J.
1985. "The Catholic Heirarchy in the Nicaraguan Revolution." *Journal of Latin American Studies* 17: 341–69.

Wilson, Patricia.
1987. "Regionalization and Decentralization in Nicaragua." *Latin American Perspectives* 14 (Summer): 237–54.

Wright, Bruce E.
1988. "Class and Revolutionary Actors in Latin America." *Review of Latin American Studies* 1, no. 2: 65–80.
1990. "Pluralism and Vanguardism in the Nicaraguan Revolution." *Latin American Perspectives* 17, no. 3: 38–54.

Wright, Erik Olin.
1978. *Class, Crisis and the State*. London: Verso Editions.

Zelaya, José M.
    1985. *Ensayo: el estado sandinista.* Managua: Unión de
    Cardoza.

Zwerling, Phillip, and Connie Martin
    1985. *Nicaragua: A New Kind of Revolution.* Westport, CT:
    Lawrence Hill and Company.

INDEX

agrarian reform 22, 24, 30, 76, 94, 96, 108, 110, 123, 133-139, 143, 165-169, 173-174, 180, 182-199, 205, 208, 219, 223-227, 235-236, 239

Alemán, Arnaldo 23, 47, 176, 190

Alfredo César 31, 124

AMNLAE 96, 126, 156, 162, 164, 228, 231

ANDEN 147

Arce, Bayardo 75, 77, 90, 93, 95, 103

armed struggle 10, 14, 17, 19, 21, 49, 53-55, 65-74, 92, 102
    politics and the PSN 55

ATC 11, 40, 44, 97, 110, 114, 126, 131-134, 135, 138-145, 147, 153, 162, 164, 173-174, 188, 194, 198, 224, 225

Bayardo Arce 75, 77, 90, 93, 95, 103

Belli, Humberto 23, 31

Borge, Tomás 11, 19, 36, 50, 51, 52, 53, 60, 67, 75, 75

Cabezas, Omar 33, 98

Cardenal, Ernesto 66

CAS 133, 140, 141, 187

Caudra, Norma x

CAUS 144-148

CDS vi, 33, 97-100, 110, 126-131, 126, 138, 153, 154, 156, 162, 164

central planning 114, 118, 119, 170, 173, 202

CEPA 131

César, Alfredo 31, 124

CGT 144, 146

Chamorro, Pedro Joaquin 31, 50

Chamorro, Diego Manuel 62

Chamorro, Emiliano 62

Chamorro, Violetta 23, 24, 25, 31, 38, 39, 46, 94, 100, 104, 121, 124

class xi, 1-3, 7-9, 12, 28, 58-64, 67-72, 79-80, 81, 84, 85, 87, 88, 98, 111, 112, 114-118, 121, 137, 140-142, 145, 146, 159-161, 165, 173-175, 178, 179, 181, 186, 188-190, 194-196, 198, 207-244
    and understanding of 1990 campaign 208
    and Carlos Fonseca 59
    "third force" 212, 219
    worker-campesino alliance, changing conception of 188

co-government 25, 26

Communist International 8, 10, 19, 20
concertación 110, 190, 205
contras 26, 28, 31, 37-41, 45, 111, 143, 147, 154, 155, 166, 171, 177, 180, 192, 201, 209, 225, 227, 236
cooperatives 40, 133, 140-141, 162, 173, 188-190, 219, 227
COSEP 110, 122-125, 139-140, 143, 157, 166, 190, 192
Council of State 79, 93, 95-97, 121, 126, 146, 147, 154, 156
CPT 45
CSN 147
CST 44, 45, 110, 114, 126, 144-149, 162
CTN 45, 154
Cuba
July 26 Movement 8
CUS 146, 154

demobilization 38 127, 158, 164-166, 201
dictatorship of the proletariat 87

El Salvador 15, 18, 44, 66, 103, 105, 180
elections 7, 16, 92
1984 8
1990 8, 21, 27, 32, 82, 108, 171, 180, 207
ENABAS 128, 185, 186
Esquipulas 28, 38, 171, 201, 202

FETSALUD 146
FMLN 15, 18, 105

FNT 45-46
FO 144, 146-147
Fonseca, Carlos xii, 10, 11, 19, 20, 22, 47, 49-76, 78, 79, 105, 160, 161, 211, 242
and Cuba 20, 53
and PSN 51
and Soviet Union 51
and Marxism 51, 58, 74
FPN 154
FSLN 2, 8, 10-14, 16-24, 26-37, 40, 42-58, 60, 66-69, 71-82, 84-126, 131-194, 197-199, 202, 205, 207-244
"demobilization" as critique of FSLN 163
militants 10, 34, 130, 160

Garcia, Edgardo 132
Godoy, Virgilio 22, 23, 29, 31, 39, 45, 156
Governing Junta of National Reconstruction vi, 78, 93, 94, 121
GPP 75, 182
Gramsci, Antonio 11, 86, 87

Hegel, G. W. F. 11, 175, 178
hegemony 14, 30, 62, 66-69, 84-93, 97, 100-105, 107, 112-125, 143, 149, 151, 157, 170, 212, 220, 222, 232, 242
pluralism and the vanguard 86

informal sector 149, 163, 174, 188, 201, 208, 233, 237, 238

Juventud Sandinista 126, 162, 164

Kant, Immanuel 11

Lacayo, Antonio 22, 23, 25, 39
Lancaster, Roger xi, 4, 235
Lenin, Vladimir Ilich 2, 51, 66, 81, 87
liberation theology 13, 107, 161, 216

MAP 144, 146, 156
MAP-ML 156
Martínez Cuenca, Alejandro 111, 114, 119-122, 172, 190, 199, 200, 202, 203, 205, 206, 208, 237
Marx, Karl 51, 66, 81, 116, 196, 197, 206, 213, 214, 222, 228, 229, 236
Marxism 1, 2, 4, 5, 7-11, 13, 49, 50-58, 63, 74, 49, 53, 54, 80-85, 107, 161, 179, 211, 217, 222, 229
  and analysis of agriculture 196, 236
MDN 122, 123
Meister, Robert 1
mixed economy 18, 21, 73, 78, 80, 88, 95, 113, 117, 123, 128, 165, 166, 169, 170, 211
Moncada, José María 62, 63
Munck, Ronaldo 230

national bourgeoisie 20, 56, 57, 63, 67, 87-90, 113, 117, 120, 121, 124-126, 211-212, 218
National Congress, 1992 35
National Directorate 14, 24, 27, 28, 34-36, 55, 76-78, 93-95, 114, 154, 133, 161, 164, 199, 202, 203
Nicaraguan Institute for Economic and Social Research (INIES) x
Nuñez, Daniel 40, 141
Nuñez Soto, Orlando 133-134, 184, 185, 212-214, 217, 220, 221

Ortega, Daniel ix, 24, 26, 28, 35-37, 42, 43, 45, 47, 76, 156, 203, 205, 207, 209, 242
Ortega, Humberto 23, 39, 42, 43, 51, 75-77, 93, 100, 104, 115, 161

participatory democracy 1, 8, 12, 79, 84-86, 88, 93, 97, 98, 100, 105, 107, 108, 111-114, 118, 121, 124, 126, 130, 142, 154, 157, 159, 165-167, 170, 174-181, 193, 211, 213, 214, 217, 221, 242
Pastora, Eden 50, 124
patriotic producers 121, 124, 166, 169, 193, 195, 224
PCD 156
la piñata 24, 239
Pineda, Orlando xi
PLI 25, 154, 156
pluralism xii, 1, 2, 8, 18, 21, 73, 78, 80, 81-102, 105,

107, 108, 111-114, 117, 118,
124, 126, 135, 143, 150,
152-154, 159, 165, 167, 170,
173-176, 179, 183, 208, 211,
214, 218, 219
pluralist theory 86, 95, 97, 99,
107, 117, 130, 166, 167,
178, 181
Portes, Alejandro 230
proletarian tendency 74-76,
182
PSN 8, 10, 14, 16, 19-21, 51,
52, 54-56, 91, 144, 156

Ramirez, Sergio x, 11, 35-37,
156
recompas 40, 41
recontras 39-41
revueltos 38, 40, 41, 104
Rivas, Rafael Cordoba 94
Robelo, Alfonso 94, 97, 121,
122, 124
Ruiz, Henry 36, 71, 75
Rural Workers Committees
131

Sacasa, Juan B. 62
Sandino, Augusto C. xii, 8,
10, 11, 19, 20, 22, 30, 48,
49-60, 62-67, 70-74, 78, 79,
89, 90, 116, 133, 137, 160,
177, 179
and international
communism 8
and Marxism 66
and the Mexican
Revolution 62
and socialism 64
on the United States 58

social wage 109, 120, 127,
145, 146, 148-149, 170, 185
Somocismo 26, 37, 67, 69, 92,
113, 212
Somoza(s) 5, 7, 8, 10, 11, 23,
31, 38, 42, 46, 53, 67, 68,
71, 76, 85, 87-92, 94, 102,
107, 113, 119-121, 124,
133-138, 145, 169, 191,
197, 207, 215, 221, 238
Soviet Union 2-5, 8, 13-15,
21, 51, 65, 79, 82, 116,
171-173, 176, 177, 180, 197
aid to Nicaragua 8, 15,
109
state farms 44, 110, 112, 135-
144, 165-166, 169, 174,
180-184, 189-198, 219, 223-
227, 236-237

tercerista 74, 76, 78
Tirado López, Victor 66, 76,
189

UNAG 40, 41, 96, 110, 126,
131, 135, 140, 141, 143,
153, 157, 162, 173-174,
183, 188-198, 219, 224-
227, 236-237
UNO 16, 21-26, 29, 31, 32,
39-46, 99, 104, 105, 159,
174, 180, 218, 238, 241,
243
UPANIC 139
UPN 146

vanguard 11, 16, 30, 53,
68-72, 74, 79, 81, 82,
86-91, 93, 95, 99-101, 103,
105, 107, 108, 113, 122,

126, 130, 144-145, 149, 151,
153, 157, 162-163, 179, 181,
207, 211-216, 220-223, 226,
231, 232, 235, 237-243
vanguard party 82, 88, 90-91
105, 214, 222
verticalism 33-34, 165, 157,
210, 240
Vilas, Carlos 6, 140, 145, 147,
159, 178, 179, 203, 205-207,
209, 213, 216

Walker, Thomas ix
Wheelock Roman, Jaime 53,
57, 69, 72, 73, 75-77, 87,
90-93, 102, 114, 115-118,
134, 136-138, 191, 205, 223,
234
Williams, Harvey ix

Zamora, Carlos x
Zelaya, José Santos 21, 50,
61

Monographs in International Studies
Titles Available from Ohio University Press
1995

Southeast Asia Series

No. 56 **Duiker, William J.** Vietnam Since the Fall of Saigon. 1989.
Updated ed. 401 pp. Paper 0-89680-162-4 $20.00.

No. 64 **Dardjowidjojo, Soenjono.** Vocabulary Building in Indone–
sian: An Advanced Reader. 1984. 664 pp. Paper 0- 89680-
118-7 $26.00.

No. 65 **Errington, J. Joseph.** Language and Social Change in Java:
Linguistic Reflexes of Modernization in a Traditional Royal
Polity. 1985. 210 pp. Paper 0-89680-120-9 $25.00.

No. 66 **Tran, Tu Binh.** The Red Earth: A Vietnamese Memoir of Life
on a Colonial Rubber Plantation. Tr. by John Spragens. 1984.
102 pp. (SEAT*, V. 5) Paper 0-89680-119-5 $11.00.
No. 68 **Syukri, Ibrahim.** History of the Malay Kingdom of
Patani. 1985. 135 pp. Paper 0-89680-123-3 $12.00.

No. 69 **Keeler, Ward.** Javanese: A Cultural Approach. 1984. 559 pp.
Paper 0-89680-121-7 $25.00.

No. 70 **Wilson, Constance M. and Lucien M. Hanks.** Burma-Thai
land Frontier Over Sixteen Decades: Three Descriptive Docu
ments. 1985. 128 pp. Paper 0-89680-124-1 $11.00.

No. 71 **Thomas, Lynn L. and Franz von Benda-Beckmann,** eds.
Change and Continuity in Minangkabau: Local, Regional, and
Historical Perspectives on West Sumatra. 1985. 353 pp. Paper
0-89680-127-6 $16.00

No. 72 **Reid, Anthony and Oki Akira,** eds. The Japanese Experience
in Indonesia: Selected Memoirs of 1942-1945. 1986. 424 pp.,
20 illus. (SEAT, V. 6) Paper 0-89680-132-2 $20.00.

No. 74 **McArthur M. S. H.** Report on Brunei in 1904. Introduced and
Annotated by A.V.M. Horton. 1987. 297 pp. Paper 0-89680-
135-7 $15.00.

No. 75 Lockard, Craig A. From Kampung to City: A Social History of Kuching, Malaysia,1820-1970. 1987. 325 pp. Paper 0-89680-136-5 $20.00.

No. 76 McGinn, Richard, ed. Studies in Austronesian Linguistic 1986. 516 pp. Paper 0-89680-137-3 $20.00.

No. 77 Muego, Benjamin N. Spectator Society: The Philippines Under Martial Rule. 1986. 232 pp. Paper 0-89680-138-1 $17.00.**No. 79 Walton, Susan Pratt.** Mode in Javanese Music. 1987. 278 pp. Paper 0-89680-144-6 $15.00.

No. 80 Nguyen Anh Tuan. South Vietnam: Trial and Experience. 1987. 477 pp., tables. Paper 0-89680-141-1 $18.00.

No. 82 Spores, John C. Running Amok: An Historical Inquiry. 1988. 190 pp. Paper 0-89680-140-3 $13.00.

No. 83 Malaka, Tan. From Jail to Jail. Tr. by Helen Jarvis. 1991. 1209 pp., three volumes. (SEAT V. 8) Paper 0-89680-150-0 $55.00.

No. 84 Devas, Nick, with Brian Binder, Anne Booth, Kenneth Davey, and Roy Kelly. Financing Local Government in Indonesia. 1989. 360 pp.Paper 0-89680-153-5 $20.00.

No. 85 Suryadinata, Leo. Military Ascendancy and Political Culture: A Study of Indonesia's Golkar. 1989. 235 pp., illus., glossary, append., index, bibliog. Paper 0-89680-154-3 $18.00.

No. 86 Williams, Michael. Communism, Religion, and Revolt in Banten in the Early Twentieth Century. 1990. 390 pp. Paper 0-89680-155-1 $14.00.

No. 87 Hudak, Thomas. The Indigenization of Pali Meters in Thai Poetry. 1990. 247 pp. Paper 0-89680-159-4 $15.00.

No. 88 Lay, Ma Ma. Not Out of Hate: A Novel of Burma. Tr. by Margaret Aung-Thwin. Ed. by William Frederick. 1991. 260 pp. (SEAT V. 9) Paper 0-89680-167-5 $20.00.

No. 89 Anwar, Chairil. The Voice of the Night: Complete Poetry and Prose of Chairil Anwar . 1992. Revised Edition. Tr. by Burton Raffel. 196 pp. Paper 0-89680-170-5 $20.00.

No. 90 Hudak, Thomas John, tr., The Tale of Prince Samuttakote: A Buddhist Epic from Thailand. 1993. 230 pp. Paper 0-89680-174-8 $20.00.

No. 90 Hudak, Thomas John, tr., The Tale of Prince Samuttakote: A Buddhist Epic from Thailand. 1993. 230 pp. Paper 0-89680-174-8 $20.00.

No. 91 Roskies, D.M., ed. Text/Politics in Island Southeast Asia: Essays in Interpretation. 1993. 330 pp. Paper 0-89680-175-6 $25.00.

No. 92 Schenkhuizen, Marguérite, translated by Lizelot Stout van Balgooy. Memoirs of an Indo Woman: Twentieth-Century Life in the East Indies and Abroad. 1993. 312pp. Paper 0-89680-178-0 $23.00

No. 93 Salleh, Muhammad Haji. Beyond the Archipelago: Selected Poems. 1995. 247pp. Paper 0-89680-181-0 $20.00.

No. 94 Federspiel, Howard M. A Dictionary of Indonesian Islam. 1995. 327 pp. Bibliog. Paper 0-89680-182-9 $25.00.

No. 95 Leary, John. Violence and the Dream People: The Orang Asli in the Malayan Emergency 1948-1960. 1995. 275pp. Maps, illus. tables, appendices, bibliog., index. Paper 0-89680-186-1 $22.00

No. 96 Lewis, Dianne. *Jan Compagnie* in the Straits of Malacca 1641-1795. 1995. 176pp. Map, appendices, bibliog., index. Paper 0-89680-187-X. $18.00.

Africa Series

No. 43 Harik, Elsa M. and Donald G. Schilling. The Politics of Educa tion in Colonial Algeria and Kenya. 1984. 102 pp. Paper 0-89680-117-9 $12.50.

No. 45 Keto, C. Tsehloane. American-South African Relations 1784-1980: Review and Select Bibliography. 1985. 169 pp. Paper 0-89680-128-4 $11.00.

No. 46 Burness, Don, ed. Wanasema: Conversations with African Writers. 1985. 103 pp. Paper 0-89680-129-2 $11.00.

No. 47 Switzer, Les. Media and Dependency in South Africa: A Case Study of the Press and the Ciskei "Homeland". 1985. 97 pp. Paper 0-89680-130-6 $10.00.

No. 49 Hart, Ursula Kingsmill. Two Ladies of Colonial Algeria: The Lives and Times of Aurelie Picard and Isabelle Eberhardt. 1987. 153 pp. Paper 0-89680-143-8 $11.00.

No. 51 Clayton, Anthony and David Killingray. Khaki and Blue: Military and Police in British Colonial Africa. 1989. 347 pp. Paper 0-89680-147-0 $20.00.

No. 52 Northrup, David. Beyond the Bend in the River: African Labor in Eastern Zaire, 1864-1940. 1988. 282 pp. Paper 0-89680-151-9 $15.00.

No. 53 Makinde, M. Akin. African Philosophy, Culture, and Traditional Medicine. 1988. 172 pp. Paper 0-89680-152-7 $16.00.

No. 54 Parson, Jack, ed. Succession to High Office in Botswana: Three Case Studies. 1990. 455 pp. Paper 0-89680-157-8 $20.00.

No. 56 Staudinger, Paul. In the Heart of the Hausa States. Tr. by Johanna E. Moody. Foreword by Paul Lovejoy. 1990. In two volumes. 469 + 224 pp., maps, apps. Paper 0-89680-160-8 (2 vols.) $35.00.

No. 57 Sikainga, Ahmad Alawad. The Western Bahr Al-Ghazal under British Rule, 1898-1956. 1991. 195 pp. Paper 0-89680-161-6 $15.00

No. 58 Wilson, Louis E. The Krobo People of Ghana to 1892: A Political and Social History. 1991. 285 pp. Paper 0-89680-164-0 $20.00.

No. 59 du Toit, Brian M. Cannabis, Alcohol, and the South African Student: Adolescent Drug Use, 1974-1985. 1991. 176 pp., notes, tables. Paper 0-89680-166-7 $17.00.

No. 60 Falola, Toyin and Dennis Itavyar, eds. The Political Economy of Health in Africa. 1992. 258 pp., notes. Paper 0-89680-168-3 $17.00.

No. 61 Kiros, Tedros. Moral Philosophy and Development: The Human Condition in Africa.1992. 199 pp., notes. Paper. 0-89680-171-3 $20.00.

No. 62 Burness, Don. Echoes of the Sunbird: An Anthology of Contem–porary African Poetry. 1993. 198pp. Paper 0-89680-173-X $17.00.

No. 63 Glew, Robert S. and Chaibou Babalé. Hausa Folktales from Niger. 1993. 100pp. Paper 0-89680-176-4 $15.00.

No. 64 Nelson, Samuel H. Colonialism in the Congo Basin 1880-1940. 1993. 248 pp. Index. Paper 089680-180-2 $23.00.

Latin America Series

No. 9 **Tata, Robert J.** Structural Changes in Puerto Rico's Economy: 1947-1976. 1981. 118 pp. Paper 0-89680-107-1 $12.00.

No. 12 **Wallace, Brian F.** Ownership and Development: A Comparison of Domestic and Foreign Firms in Colombian Manufacturing. 1987. 185 pp. Paper 0-89680-145-4 $10.00.

No. 13 **Henderson, James D.** Conservative Thought in Latin America The Ideas of Laureo Gomez. 1988. 229 pp. Paper 0-89680-148-9 $16.00.

No. 16 **Alexander, Robert J.** Juscelino Kubitschek and the Develop–ment of Brazil. 1991. 500 pp., notes, bibliog. Paper 0-89680-163-2 $25.00.

No. 17 **Mijeski, Kenneth J.,** ed. The Nicaraguan Constitution of 1987: English Translation and Commentary. 1991. 355 pp. Paper 0-89680-165-9 $25.00.

No. 18 **Finnegan, Pamela.** The Tension of Paradox: Jose Donoso's *The Obscene Bird of Night* as Spiritual Exercises. 1992. 204 pp. Paper 0-89680-169-1 $15.00.

No. 19 **Kim, Sung Ho and Thomas W. Walker,** eds. Perspectives on War and Peace in Central America. 1992. 155 pp., notes, bibliog. Paper 0-89680-172-1 $17.00.

No. 20 **Becker, Marc.** Mariategui and Latin American Marxist Theory. 1993. 239 pp. Paper 0-89680-177-2 $20.00.

No. 21 **Boschetto-Sandoval, Sandra M. and Marcia Phillips McGowan,** eds. Claribel Alegría and Central American Litera–ture. 1994. 263 pp., illus. Paper 0-89680-179-9 $20.00.

No. 22 **Zimmerman, Marc.** Literature and Resistance in Guatemala: Textual Modes and Cultural Politics from El Señor Presidente to Rigoberta Menchú. 1995. 2 volume set 320 + 370 pp., notes, bibliog. Paper 0-89680-183-7 $45.00.

No 23 **Hey, Jeanne A. K.** Theories of Dependent Foreign Policy: The Case of Ecuador in the 1980s. 1995 280pp. map, tables, notes, bibliog.,index. Paper 0-89680-184-5 $22.00.

ORDERING INFORMATION

Individuals are encouraged to patronize local bookstores wherever possible. Orders for titles in the Monographs in International Studies may be placed directly through the Ohio University Press, Scott Quadrangle, Athens, Ohio 45701-2979. Individuals should remit payment by check, VISA, or MasterCard. * Those ordering from the United Kingdom, Continental Europe, the Middle East, and Africa should order through Academic and University Publishers Group, 1 Gower Street, London WC1E, England. Orders from the Pacific Region, Asia, Australia, and New Zealand should be sent to East-West Export Books, c/o the University of Hawaii Press, 2840 Kolowalu Street, Honolulu, Hawaii 96822, USA.

Individuals ordering from ouside of the U.S. should remit in U.S. funds to Ohio University Press either by International Money Order or by a check drawn on a U.S. bank.** Most out-of-print titles may be ordered from University Microfilms, Inc., 300 North Zeeb Road, Ann Arbor, Michigan 48106, USA.

Prices are subject to change without notice.

* Please add $3.50 for the first book and $.75 for each additional book for shipping and handling.

** Outside the U.S please add $4.50 for the first book and $.75 for each additional book.

Hill HLC 6698 8-4-95

MFM